Ideology, Absolutism and the English Revolution

Ideology, Absolutism and the English Revolution

Debates of the British Communist Historians 1940–1956

Edited and introduced by

David Parker

IDEOLOGY, ABSOLUTISM AND THE ENGLISH REVOLUTION
Edited and introduced by David Parker

First Published in India 2014

ISBN 978-93-5002-254-2

Published in agreement with Lawrence and Wishart Limited,
London for publication and sale only in the
Indian Subcontinent (India, Pakistan,
Bangladesh, Nepal, Maldives, Bhutan and Sri Lanka)

Published by
AAKAR BOOKS
28 E Pocket IV, Mayur Vihar Phase I, Delhi 110 091
Phone : 011 2279 5505 Telefax : 011 2279 5641
info@aakarbooks.com; www.aakarbooks.com

Printed at
Mudrak, 30 A Patparganj, Delhi 110 091

Contents

Documents 17-26: Ideology

Acknowledgements

Sadly Bill Moore, for decades a stalwart of the History Group and the present Socialist History Society, died as this book went to press. Without his dedication in assembling and cataloguing the papers of the History Group, now held by the Labour History Archive and Study Centre at Manchester, this study would have been infinitely more difficult if not impossible.

Its completion has also depended on a considerable number of people who received and responded to my enquiries about members of the History group. I am grateful to them all, in particular Anthony Howe and Brian Pearce. The first has been generous way beyond the call of professional obligation with both his time and his willingness to share material acquired during the course of his doctoral research into Dona Torr and the History Group. Without this generosity my own efforts would have been seriously weakened by major gaps and errors. Brian Pearce not only made available his personal papers but sustained me with his thoughtful and informative recollections of the post war discussions, not to mention the erudition so characteristic of his generation of Marxists. Thanks too go to Joanna Bornat for her hospitality and help whilst I rummaged around in Allan Merson's papers and to Penelope Bulloch, Balliol College Librarian, for her willingness to facilitate perusal of Christopher Hill's papers and almost before the cataloguing was complete.

I am also grateful to the following for permission to publish the papers included in this volume: Victor Kiernan; Stephen Mason; Brian Pearce; the Estates of Maurice Dobb, Rodney Hilton and Melvyn James respectively; the Archive Trust of the Communist Party of Great Britain (1920-1991); the Socialist History Society.

David Parker

Note on The Documents

Whilst it was necessary to render uniform the format and punctuation of the original documents, they are otherwise unchanged. Words that were originally underlined for emphasis have been italicised. Square brackets indicate my own editorial insertions; round brackets indicate original parentheses. Numbered footnotes are editorial additions but they have been kept to a minimum.

Introduction

Ideology, Absolutism and the English Revolution Debates of the British Communist Historians 1940-1956

The immense contribution to historical studies made by the members of the History Group of the Communist Party of Great Britain is now almost universally recognised. For a decade, after the end of the second world war, until its membership and – perhaps more importantly – its cohesion was sapped by the crises which shook the Communist movement in 1956, the Group provided an extraordinary forum for intense debate, opening up lines of thought and enquiry which laid the basis for a number of exceptionally productive and distinguished careers. None was more so than that of Christopher Hill, who, thirty-five years after resigning his party membership, went out of his way to acknowledge his debt to the 'most stimulating intellectual experience I have ever had', from which 'anything I have written since derives…'.[1]

Until 1957 the Group sheltered a number of period sections, of which the 16th/17th century section was the most dynamic and productive.[2] Its members produced over forty discussion papers, varying from a few hundred words to nine and half thousand; the extant papers, minutes of discussions and other relevant statements total over 110,000 words. Originally it was intended to publish them all in this book, and thus enable readers to draw on them and make judgments, assured that all available material had been included. As more and more came into view, however, this idea had to be abandoned; but rather than engage in the risky procedure of selecting passages across the complete range of papers, I decided it was preferable, given the practical constraints, to present as many as possible of the contributions to the two major debates, on 'Absolutism' and 'Ideology'. Appendix 2 provides a complete list of all the extant and accessible papers forming the basis of my own observations. These are not intended to be comprehensive but contextual and reflective.

Apart from the historical reflections of Marx and Engels – mostly Engels – the concerns of the section took a large part of their inspiration from the hugely influential works of two elder comrades. The first was Leslie Morton's *A People's History of England* (1938), the proposed revision of which prompted the formation of the group in 1946; the second was Maurice Dobb's *Studies in the Development of Capitalism*, the appearance of which in the same year led Hill to declare that 'nine-tenths of the discussion on Morton can now be scrapped by simply telling him to read it [Dobb] and rewrite accordingly'.[3] However, although Morton and Dobb furnished the group as a whole with a challenging long overall perspective, it was Hill who drove the agenda of the early modern section, generating debates of remarkable intensity. His later rather laconic comment that 'Kiernan kept us on our toes' belies the passionate character of their persistent disagreements: over the Tudor state, the English Revolution and the connections between Protestantism and Capitalism and much else.[4] Hill and Kiernan therefore loom larger in what follows than I had imagined at the outset.

This should not obscure the fact that no fewer than 27 people made contributions of varying weight to the discussions at one moment or another in the course of ten years.[5] These included both Rodney Hilton and to a lesser extent Eric Hobsbawm, nominally members of other sections, but whose interest in the long transition from feudalism to capitalism drew them to the discussion of the critical early modern period. Others, less well known in later years outside academic circles, made a significant intellectual and organisational input. Kenneth Andrews and Eric Kerridge both acted as section secretary and both were to have highly distinguished careers as early modern specialists; Stephen Mason had a glittering one as both medical chemist and historian of science. Amongst those who did not follow university careers, Brian Pearce was perhaps the most influential, at least in the early post-war years; he shared with Hill and the History Group's doyenne Dona Torr a passionate desire to establish a definitive view of the English Civil War of the 1640s as a bourgeois revolution that conformed to their reading of the Marxist classics. Outside the nucleus of members who made up the section's driving force, there were a number of talented individuals whose energies later went in other directions but whose historical capacities were far from negligible. One thinks of Edmund Dell, future minister of state, Iris Morley, best known as a successful historical novelist and ballet critic, and Louis Marks, one of Britain's most accomplished producers of TV drama.

Not all the former members of the section share Hill's unalloyed appreciation of its contribution to their intellectual development. Yet, in almost every case the substantial number of surviving papers and discussions reveals affinities with their authors' published work. Of the 27 identified contributors to the discussions, nine had already published books before the war, or were to do so by 1956. Of these it was perhaps Stephen Mason's *A History of the Sciences*, published in 1953, which first achieved truly international stature.[6] In the 1950s Mason also published a series of articles on science and religion, a subject to which the section devoted some time and to which he returned in his eightieth year. It would indeed be tedious to resume the number of significant articles produced by members of the section in the early 1950s. Eric Kerrridge, for example, published ten articles on English agrarian history between 1951 and 1956, laying the foundation for major and controversial works to come. Amongst those who either published nothing during this period, or were writing on other historical matters but later returned to issues raised in the group, Kiernan stands out. His 1980 work *State and Society in Europe 1550-1650* must have taken his mind back to his disagreements with Hill.[7] Still more recently, his works on Shakespeare are more than an echo of the challenge he flung at him during the course of their exchanges to explain the vibrancy of Elizabethan culture.[8] Mervyn James, whose much cited contributions to Tudor history appeared only from the mid 1960s, lived and worked throughout his academic career in the north of England – the subject of his contribution to the discussions in 1948 and of most of his later publications.[9] The later work of Ken Andrews on English privateering, though declared to be free of ideological baggage by one reviewer, nevertheless contains much material which is pertinent to any consideration of the nature and role of merchant capital – one of the controversial currents which flowed through the section meetings.[10]

Not only were there clear continuities in the work of the members of the section, lasting well beyond its demise, but none of them have gone in for strenuous and public renunciation of earlier views in the manner of former communist historians in France. If the political crisis of 1956 finally precipitated the demise of the section, the consequences were complex. Some, like Hobsbawm, Dobb and Morton, stuck with the Communist Party; others, like Brian Pearce, found different left-wing homes, and a few quietly distanced themselves from their Communist affiliations. Hill, Hilton and Kiernan left the Party but never moved far in spirit from their former comrades. Friendships and professional relationships were largely unbroken. The most eminent continued to assert their Marxism.

It is also remarkable, given the constraints on the time and knowledge of the section, how many of the issues it dealt with worked their way into the academic mainstream. The most signal success was perhaps in confronting Whiggish and religious interpretations of the English civil war with the idea of a bourgeois revolution. Hill itemised the areas where greater clarity was required in a paper on 'Problems of the Bourgeois Revolution' in 1954.[11] The list was long enough to require at least one lifetime's work, ranging from the gentry's role in capitalist development, through the question of elections to the Commons and the franchise, to the central administration, the role of popular forces and the part played by women. In the half century following the paper, all of these matters were explored, sometimes by Hill's own students, and sometimes by those taking issue with him or with a general eye on Marxist interpretations. The transformation of the agenda was immeasurably facilitated by the extraordinary impact of *Past & Present*, which was launched by the Group in 1952 in the midst of the Cold War, but which, within a matter of years, acquired a reputation as the pre-eminent historical journal in the English language. It was as much through its pages as through his early books that Hill provoked the public controversy over the connections between science, Puritanism and capitalism that had engaged the members of the section.[12] *Past & Present* was also the means by which Hobsbawm projected on to a larger stage his views about the unevenness of European economic development. His seminal two-part article on the 'general crisis' of the seventeenth century appeared in 1954, generating the first of the collective debates for which the journal has since become known.[13]

POINTS OF DEPARTURE

E.P. Thompson once described English Marxism as 'quaintly empirical'.[14] His comment, made in kindly fashion, was certainly an accurate comment on the approach developed from the outset by the Communist Party historians, who were mostly very reluctant to devote their time or energies to abstract theory. In 1953 the group did decide to hold a meeting on historical materialism, apparently referring the proposal to the professional historians, who agreed to hold one for students in Oxford.[15] If it took place it left no trace. Two years later the group felt that it was not a priority to write a book on 'Marxist Approaches to History', as requested by Emile Burns. Rodney Hilton insisted on the need for 'concrete historical writing as against theoretical polemics of the recent King Street kind'.[16] It was left to *Daily Worker* journalist Peter Fryer, in October 1955, to give a series of six lectures on Materialism as part of the Party's education programme, including one on 'Historical Materialism' and another on 'Base and Superstructure'. The historians meanwhile put their efforts into a School on British Labour History, 1832 to the present.[17] Only two papers written by members of the section ever directly confronted theoretical questions in abstract fashion with no historical context. Neither formed part of its own programme.[18] Nor did the early modernists ever prepare for a meeting in the manner of the Ancient Historians, who on one occasion circulated six large sheets of extracts from Marx and Engels 'relating to the history of Classical Antiquity'.[19]

Of course, this did not mean that the early modernists had not done their homework. Amongst Hill's private papers there is a folder of assiduously copied extracts from Marx and Engels, many of which were used in an early article on their interpretations of the Civil War.[20] However, the article is striking for the way in which, with a little apology, the question of 'historical materialism' is rapidly dispensed with, in order to plunge into their substantive historical observations: on the emergence of a new nobility of bourgeois derivation, the expropriation of the peasantry, the role of the yeomanry in pushing through the Revolution, the Levellers as the forerunners of the proletariat, the rise of science with the middle class and so on.[21] From the outset, members of the section were clearly of the view articulated many years later by Hobsbawm in his observation that Marx's statements about history were of more value to historians than his statements about society in general, and that Marxist history in its most fruitful versions uses Marx's methods rather than commenting on its texts.[22]

Over the decades that followed, as the historical output of the historians rose, theoretical reflections on the methodology that guided formed only the tiniest part of their output. The exception is obviously provided by Thompson, whose celebrated attack on 'The Poverty of Theory' paradoxically required a considerable amount of it. Thompson, it should be noted in passing, played no part in the proceedings of the 16th/17th century section, and probably not much in the group as a whole. Of the section members Kiernan was perhaps the most willing to integrate history and theory; but, comfortable though he was in his ruminations on Marxist methodology, his probing, discursive style is as likely to raise questions as answers.[23] George Rudé's essay 'Marxism and History' (1983) was essentially an historiographical tour through modern Marxist history, emphasising in particular his own concern with the formation of popular ideology, and how ideas 'come (in Marx's phrase) to "grip the masses"'.[24] Of 21 pieces 'On History' written by Hobsbawm between 1970 and 1996, only two deal systematically with Marxism. The first, written in 1973, offered a careful appraisal of the influence, merits and limitations of 'vulgar' Marxism, with only limited allusions to creative alternatives.[25] For this one had to wait till 1983, when Hobsbawm directly addressed the problems embedded in historical materialism, the concept of modes of production and base and superstructure. Even then he felt it appropriate to conclude his remarks not in theoretical vein but by stressing the success of Marxism in transforming mainstream history, so that 'it is often impossible to tell whether a particular work has been written by a Marxist or non-Marxist'. This was not, he felt, a cause for regret.[26]

Nonetheless, he might have been startled by the reader of his four books on the history of capitalism who wanted to know whether these would be considered socialist history, and expressed curiosity about the sense in which 'if any... 'Hobsbawm's Marxism appears in these works'.[27] In similar fashion it is entirely possible that a student today reading Hill's seminal work, *The Century of Revolution*, without any sense of the ideological battles of the pre-Thatcher era, might well not discern what is specifically Marxist about it. Although it would be silly to regret the impact of such works, the determination to write in empirical and accessible style does have a downside. One consequence has been that much of the space for Marxist disquisitions on 'History' has been occupied by those who have not been engaged in the historical discipline itself.[28] More unfortunate is the opportunity which has been given to others, hostile or sympathetic, to put their own gloss on the assumed assumptions, aims and methodology of 'The British Marxist Historians'.

The best known commentator is Harvey Kaye, who attributes its quality to their efforts to 'overcome the base-superstructure model with its tendency to economic determinism'.[29] This, he claimed, gave way to a much more fruitful concern with class struggle and history from the bottom up. The Marxist historians derived 'their central working hypothesis from the celebrated declaration of the Communist Manifesto that "the history of all hitherto existing society is the history of class struggle"'.[30] Other critics have not shared this perception. In 1988 Mary Fulbrook noted that in Hill's earliest work the model is somewhat crude – one of ruling, rising and oppressed classes, old feudal aristocracy, historically progressive bourgeoisie and exploited direct producers, a model which, 'apart from vestiges', subsequently disappeared. 'Hill now emphasises that the English revolution originated as a split within the "ruling class" (never very precisely defined) and can be characterised as a bourgeois revolution only because of its consequences for subsequent economic and political development ...'[31] Even less sympathetically, Alaistair Machlachlan took 400 pages to claim that the model of revolution employed by Hill was originally 'not so much Marxist, as Leninist or Stalinist'.[32] As early as 1948, he suggests, 'the model which the group had self-consciously applied and the empirical idiom in which they conducted their work were beginning to fall apart'.[33] Hill thus had abandoned the claim that the bourgeoisie consciously desired or willed a revolution and increasingly resorted to discussions of religion and ideas, which was a way of filling the void left by the absent bourgeoisie.[34] By the 1980s, Marxist history 'had long ceased to be primarily about the social underpinning of high political events, but had become the history of ideological and cultural determinations in their own right'.[35] David Underdown concluded that Hill 'moved away from a rigid Marxist framework which sees economics *and class struggle* [my italics] as driving history toward a more flexible approach that gave greater force to ideas'.[36] He also claimed that when Hill revisited the bourgeois revolution in 1980 he offered a significantly changed view of it, as a 'total' experience embracing 'all aspects of social life and activity'.[37] For Keith Tribe, Hill's developing concern since the 1950s 'with religion and politics' was 'a steady departure from principles of orthodox Marxism expressed in the earlier writings'.[38] Tribe's entire discussion is predicated on the assumption that all that interested the Marxist historians was the transition from feudalism to capitalism understood as economics. Kaye, more willing than most of these critics to recognise continuities in their work, nonetheless reinforces this assumption when he pays tribute to their help in clearing away 'the (supposedly) Marxist presentation of history in which historical development is conceived of in unilinear, mechanical, and techno-economistic terms'. This', he continues, 'may not have been their intention back in the early days of the Historians Group, but surely their persistent stress on the historical in historical materialism led them to it'.[39]

If these varied perceptions are not entirely in accord, to a greater or lesser extent they assume that Hill's point of departure was a highly economistic one, which he subsequently abandoned. The critics are indeed right, as will be seen, in thinking that the concept of base and superstructure was an initial organising concept. However, the fact that our historians did not dwell on the base-superstructure model in later years does not mean (with the obvious and important exception of Thompson) that they discarded it. As Hobsbawm has quite rightly insisted, 'Marxist history takes Marx as its starting point and not as its point of arrival'.[40] The assumption that this particular starting point was jettisoned or displaced is not sustained by a close examination either of the historical writings or the passing theoretical observations of the section's members. For Kiernan, writing in 1968, 'base and superstructure' becomes a misleadingly mechanistic image only at those times of upheaval and crisis that Marxism has oftenest been concerned with, 'when inert elements come to life and enter into chemical reactions with each other'.[41] But the problem is not with the image, but rather with Marxism's preoccupation with periods of rapid transition, 'which is like picturing a river from a few waterfalls along its course', in preference to the torpid or decadent epochs that make up the bulk of human history.[42] Twenty years later Kiernan, not having been included in Kaye's first work on the British Marxist historians, had an opportunity to review it. Observing that the latter showed little desire to join Thompson's anti-structuralist crusade, Kiernan merely noted that Kaye 'is satisfied' that Hill has 'managed' to break away from the base-superstructure model.[43] At the same time Kiernan distanced himself from Kaye's gloss. Although he welcomed 'this loosening up of a muscle-bound orthodoxy', he argued that there could be 'more hazards in it than Kaye takes account of':

> The priority of economic life, even if warnings against one-sided statements of it go all the way back to Engels, was the sheet-anchor of historical Marxism ... Recomposition may do much to revitalize, but it might end in revising out of recognition ... If the 'base', or the 'mode of production', is enlarged so as to make room for the totality of social life, Marxists may find themselves pronouncing that everything is caused by everything else, which is true but not helpful ... The proper safeguard may be to judge every human activity as having some of its roots in the soil of social production, but experiencing its influences directly or indirectly, at one or more remove, each of these imparting to it a quality peculiarly its own.[44]

Kiernan might also have pointed out that Kaye's view about the position of both Hill and Hilton depends on some highly questionable inferences.[45]

Hilton explicitly deployed the base-superstructure image in his discussion of the crisis of feudalism that was first published in 1978 and reprinted in 1985.[46] That this was no accidental hang-over from earlier years is confirmed by the fact that in the latter year he also wrote an article on feudalism addressing problems for historical materialists. In this essay the concept itself was deployed unproblematically.[47] As far as Hill is concerned, the only possible indication of a change of approach is in a paper given to the School on Capitalism in 1954. In this he suggested that a survey of recent work 'shows that we must no longer be content with attacking the purely religious or constitutional interpretation of the English revolution but must counter the economic determinist views of Tawney, Trevor-Roper, Stone and others by emphasising the importance of religious and ideological factors'.[48] It does not however follow that for Hill this involved a major theoretical or conceptual leap, as he immediately went on to criticise Trevor-Roper for ignoring 'the urban basis of revolutionary Calvinism'. Despite the disparagement of attempts to explain the English revolution simply by reference to either a rising or declining gentry, much of Hill's paper and the ensuing discussion was preoccupied with the need for greater clarity about the way in which agrarian relations were being transformed by emergent capitalism. If, as Corfield says, capitalism later became a '"given" in the background', Hill never abandoned his view that 'the Revolution was caused ultimately by economic developments which could not be absorbed within the old regime'.[49] In theoretical terms, the bourgeois revolution was about a revolutionary transformation of a state apparatus (superstructure) that impeded capitalist development (base) into one that that did not.

Hilton's article on the Crisis of Feudalism also serves nicely to make the point, pace Kaye, that the development of a class struggle analysis did not amount to an alternative conceptual framework developed in lieu of the base-superstructure model; for in this piece Hilton has much to say about the comparative success of peasant struggles in England and France whilst retaining the conventional imagery. Likewise Hobsbawm's supposedly more orthodox stance did not prevent him writing *Primitive Rebels* (1959) and later cooperating with George Rudé, a pioneer of history from below, in publishing *Captain Swing* (1969). As Hobsbawm has pointed out, a distinguishing virtue of Marxist structural-functionalism is that it both insists on a hierarchy of social phenomena that help systems cohere, whilst simultaneously positing the presence of internal tensions which promote change. For this reason, as well as personal inclination, it was entirely to be expected that Communist historians would give prominence to class struggle, as they did from the very beginning; but they did not need to detach it from its structural moorings in order to do so. In the ensuing years the techniques of studying history 'from the bottom up' undoubtedly made great advances. Through their published work at least five members of the section played a part in rescuing the history of the common people.[50] There is however no justification for Kaye's assertion that '*their central* [my italics] working hypothesis was "the history of all hitherto existing society is the history of class struggle"'. The misconceived desire to give this primacy is reflected in Kaye's transformation of George Rudé into a 'most active member' of the group.[51] In fact Rudé spent much time in France; his first and possibly his only appearance at a meeting of the section was in April 1954. On this occasion he asked it to consider a suggestion from George Lefebvre that historians of the English revolution might consider some topics which lent themselves to the sort of methodology which Lefebvre had employed in his study of the 'Great Fear' of 1789.[52] Lefebvre has some claim to be the originator of history from the bottom up as a methodology and not just a preferred perspective. Moreover it was Brian Manning – a student of Hill's but politically to the left of the Communist Party – who must take the credit for bringing home the significant impact of the populace on the course of the English revolution.[53]

If Kaye has been over-enthusiastic in deploying his impressive familiarity with the work of Marxist historians for a particular but far from hostile perspective, Machlachlan's shallow preconceptions are of a very different character. The most charitable thing that might be said is that he was unlucky in publishing his indictment of Hill's 'fabrication' of the English Revolution just before Hill published a revised and extended *Intellectual Origins* (1997). No-one reading the new introduction and additional essays, which include one on 'Religion, Politics and Economics', and another on 'Literature and Revolution', could possible conclude that Hill had ceased to connect ideas to either their material base or with major political battles. Less charitably, Machlachlan should have known this from Hill's earlier work on Milton (1978) and Bunyan (1988), let alone *Some Intellectual Consequences of the English Revolution* (1980), in which Hill apologised for his inability to separate these out from 'the society which the

Revolution produced'.[54] Also pertinent are the shorter pieces spread over twenty years which gave him an opportunity to repeat his message that the value of Marxism lay in its 'determination to see society as a whole, to relate philosophy, literature and science to the society from which they sprang ...[55]

For David Underdown, it was precisely this insistence on 'total' history which in fact marked a departure from earlier rigidities, a view which merits some further consideration. However, any suggestion that Hill only belatedly turned to intellectual history in order to rescue an otherwise unsustainable interpretation of the bourgeois revolution is the product either of sloppy scholarship or unrefined preconceptions. Back in 1940 Hill had already expressed the view that the social history of ideas was 'the most interesting [aspect] of the seventeenth-century revolution for our generation of historians because most neglected by the preceding generation'.[56] Although his original essay on the English Revolution written in the same year did not deal with ideas discretely, it contained detectable anticipations of later work on Puritanism; moreover the essay is rounded off with a discussion of the Levellers and a citing of Winstanley's vision of freedom.[57] Hill's early articles gathered together in *Puritanism and Revolution* (1958) included his influential essay on 'The Norman Yoke' (1954), an article on Andrew Marvell (1946), and the wonderfully perceptive piece on Clarissa Harlowe (1955), the ideas for which had been resumed by him at the School on British Capitalism.[58] His challenging *tour d'horizon* of the religious, philosophical and scientific dimensions of the bourgeois revolution that he presented to the section in July 1949 set off a wide ranging debate that was prolonged into the autumn of the following year in an effort, as the Chairman noted, to clarify the 'difficulties' which had arisen.[59] The intensity and depth of the discussions makes them still worth perusal. It was no accident that the special number of *Modern Quarterly* devoted in 1949 to celebrating the tercentenary of the English Revolution included, in addition to Hill's contribution on the state, essays on education, science and Milton, by Joan Simon, Stephen Mason and Mary Visick.[60] It was with considerable justification that Hill asked readers of his 1950 historiographical article on 'Historians and the Rise of British Capitalism' to note that Marxist historians 'discuss Shakespeare, Milton, Hobbes, Bunyan, Purcell as well as Charles

I and Oliver Cromwell: education, science and philosophy as well as industry, agriculture, trade; changes in the ideological as well as the political superstructure can be related to economic changes'.[61]

Although, in response to Hill's critics, and in recognition of his instrumental role in shaping the programme of discussions, it is necessary to pay particular attention to him, it should also be made clear that his preoccupations met up with and indeed reflected the cultural interests of his fellow historians and the wider Communist milieu in which they moved. It is worth recalling that A.L. Morton's second book, written in 1945, was *The Language of Men*, and the third, which appeared in 1952, was *The English Utopia*. By 1956 Kiernan, having already completed his manuscript on Shakespeare, had published an essay on Wordsworth as well as the first of his three volumes of translated Urdu and Hindi poetry.[62] Two other contributors to the section's discussions – Jack Lindsay and Roy Pascal – were primarily literary and cultural scholars.[63] It is also remarkable that, although E.P. Thompson was little engaged with the group, his *William Morris* (1955) contained a generous tribute to the support and 'guiding ideas' of Donna Torr.[64] This does not appear to make sense until one realises that her quasi-official role as group mentor and party liaison agent, buttressed by her scholarly editing of Marx and Engels, belied an extremely rounded literary and cultural education. She was, recalled John Saville, 'a woman of great erudition', and Hill described her as 'a cultural historian, very learned in English literature'.[65] Her unpublished private papers, notes Dave Renton, 'return us to a world of emotion and feeling', distant from the formal requirements of party life. 'Perhaps the single fact to take from these books is the dazzling range of sources which spoke to this veteran Communist, not just Rosa Luxemburg, but Sigmund Freud, Calvin, Ellis, William Wordsworth, Joseph Conrad, Aristotle and William Blake as well.'[66] As an editor and board member of Lawrence and Wishart she was close to her colleague Douglas Garman, and she collaborated with poet and critic Edgell Rickword as well as the eminent Alick West, with whom Garman himself conducted a twenty year personal and very philosophical private correspondence.[67] West's *Mountain in the Sunlight*, published in 1958, included essays on Defoe and Bunyan. Hill's essay on the English Revolution was originally published in a single volume, edited by himself, along with two other essays; one of these was Rickword's 'Milton: the revolutionary intellectual'. Hill's most extended and powerful literary-historical works were to be on Bunyan and Milton. There is every reason for taking seriously his assertion that what drew him to Marxism was its help in understanding the metaphysical poets![68]

Hill clearly breathed the same literary air as those around him. Yet it is unlikely that any one individual influenced him more than the scientist Stephen Mason, with whom Hill enjoyed conversations while Mason was teaching in Oxford, in addition to their encounters in the Section. Hill acknowledges Mason's part in arousing his interest in science in the preface to his *Intellectual Origins of the English Revolution*.[69] The text shows Mason's direct influence: Hill's comments about Bacon's association with craftsmen, on the manner in which Copernicus 'democratised the universe', and on the effect of the Restoration and science, all owe much to Mason's published work and to the two papers included in this volume.[70] Hill's highly controversial attempt to explain the changing political imagery employed by William Harvey in his work on the circulation of the blood also took up and extended Mason's much earlier observations on the same theme.[71]

The assertion that in the early years an interest in ideas was absent or overwhelmed by vulgar economism is thus profoundly mistaken. Indeed this interest was central to the political as well to the cultural identity of those involved. Morton's *The English Utopia*, tracing the aspirations of the poor and oppressed across seven centuries, was both a political and a historical statement; it opens with the poem 'Land of Cockayne' (c.1330) and closes with the conviction that the Soviet Union might at last make utopian aspirations real. For these historians the Russian Revolution was indeed proof of the power of ideas. Hill's article on 'Stalin and the Science of History' (far more revealing about Hill than Stalin or his view of history) concluded that 'Stalin had showed how an insistence on the importance of individuals is part and parcel of the general historical outlook of Marxism'; and that 'In the Soviet Union man the maker of history is coming to consciousness of his powers'.[72] This was a far cry from Thompson's later onslaught on Stalinism for its belittling of human agency. Even in the aftermath of 1989 Hill continued to argue that, although 'dictatorship of the Soviet type has failed, the ideas of collectivism, of full employment and a right to work for all citizens and other similar ideas will survive.[73] It is strange that critics should overlook the possibility that committed Communists or Marxists, driven by their own ideals, might be the last people to reduce ideas to a simple matter of economics. To which one might add that Hill's nonconformist background (shared with Kiernan, Hilton and Thompson) was a formative component of his egalitarianism and of his affection for the dissenters and rebels, the seventeenth century 'losers'. One can sense his reluctance when he felt partially constrained to agree with his colleague and comrade Mildred Gibb that the suppression of the Levellers was 'necessary': necessary in order that capitalism should fulfil its progressive role in laying the economic foundations of a real democracy. 'But', he went on, 'necessity is not blind: it can be understood so we can be free'. Winstanley, he pointed out, believed that sin owed its origin to private property and wanted to know why we could not have our heaven on earth, a sentiment entirely embraced by Hill and never lost.[74] The often noted linkages between Protestant dissent and the Marxist historians may require careful handling though, for a number of the Comrades came from Anglican backgrounds, notably Dona Torr, whose father was a vicar and honorary Canon of Chester Cathedral. In Hill's case, however, his empathy for his Protestant subjects, famous or otherwise, is unmistakable. In his paper on Calvinism, written with Clark, it can be seen that he even likens – though with a certain professional detachment – Calvin's church organisation to the modern international revolutionary movement, possessing as it did a vanguard of the Elect, the organisational characteristics of party and 'a kind of democratic centralism' led by trained cadres.[75]

The argument that it was the partial or complete abandonment of an economistic model which liberated Marxist historiography thus rests on misconceptions both about its early and also its later development. These misconceptions are rooted in a failure to grasp (as Hobsbawm noted many years later but perhaps too quietly) that the base-superstructure model, far from being an impediment to the discussion of ideas, actually ensured that they were explored, and explored in some depth.[76] The syllabus for the 1954 school on capitalism, for example, was structured around eleven sessions, each proceeding from a discussion of the economic base to an exploration of the state of political developments and ideology. When Brian Pearce received the outline syllabus, with it came a reassurance about its unfortunate 'economic' appearance: this had been recognised and 'we are making certain that every topic and period is treated in all its aspects'.[77] Ironically, it might not have been unreasonable to expect the contrary problem. For in 1949 the first paper on the 'Ideology' agenda, clearly intended to set the context, was a fine contribution by Dobb on the mode of production. Totally neglected in the ensuing discussion, it was later acknowledged that the economic base had not been given the requisite attention – possibly one reason for the decision to prolong the discussions by a session on 'The Reformation and Class Struggles in Europe'.[78]

The section's conception of the base-superstructure model was itself drawn from that extraordinary condensation of the historical process contained in the *Preface to the Critique of Political Economy*. If there was a fundamental theoretical text, it was this rather than the Communist Manifesto. Donna Torr, on whose editions of Marx and Engels 'all of us', in Hill's words, 'had been brought up', set out the basics in the *Communist Review* of 1946.[79] 'In applying the method of historical materialism', she wrote, 'the chief clue is the degree of correspondence or conflict between productive forces and social relations', a statement amplified by reference to the *Preface*, which explains what happens when developing forces of production 'come in conflict with the existing relations of production':

> there begins an 'epoch of social revolution'. With the change of the economic foundation the entire immense superstructure is more or less rapidly transformed. In considering such transformations a distinction should always be made between the material transformation of the economic conditions of production ... and the legal, political, religious, aesthetic or philosophic ... in short, ideological forms in which men become conscious of this conflict and fight it out.

Hence the importance for Torr and the others of the ideas through which men 'become conscious of this conflict', and which meet the needs of development. Stalin, she said, stresses 'the tremendous organising, mobilising and transforming value of new ideas, new theories, new political views and new political institutions'. This view of Stalin was repeated by Hill seven years later, when he cited the use made by him of the same passage from the *Preface*.[80] In similar style Andrews felt it appropriate to extract from the *History of the Communist Party of the Soviet Union (Short Course)* its description of the *Preface* as 'a brilliant formulation of the essence of historical materialism'.[81] These genuflections in Stalin's direction, though of political interest, were without much consequence, as he merely led them back to the *Preface*; more importantly, if surprisingly, he appears to have been regarded as a proponent of the autonomy of the superstructure and not an economic determinist.[82] The *Preface* once read there remained the problems posed by its condensation and ambiguities. For this purpose nothing was more important than Torr's edition of the Marx-Engels correspondence, which was 'absolutely central' and 'everybody read'.[83] It included what Kiernan has described as 'a wonderful set of letters written very late, between 1890 and 1894'; in these, Engels famously made clear that 'historical materialism' was not economic determinism.[84] Hill drew from them in his 1948 article, citing Engels's lengthy insistence that 'economic development of society only ultimately determines the political superstructure and its ideology':

> If therefore somebody twists this into the statement that the economic element is the only determining one, he transforms it into a meaningless, abstract and absurd phrase. The economic situation is the basis, but the various elements of the superstructure – political forms of the class struggle and its consequences, constitutions established by the victorious class after a successful battle, etc. – forms of law – and then even the reflexes of all these actual struggles in the brains of the combatants: political, legal, philosophical theories, religious ideas and their further development into systems of dogma – also exercise their influence upon the course of the historical struggles and in many cases preponderate in determining their form. There is an interaction of all these elements, in which, amid all the endless host of accidents … the economic movement finally asserts itself as necessary. Otherwise the application of the theory to any period of history one chose would be easier than the solution of a simple equation of the first degree.[85]

So, Hill observed, there were two errors to avoid: one is to deny the ultimate economic origin of ideas and the other is to imagine that they drop out of the sky like Newton's apple.[86] Somewhat more elegantly, he went on to conclude that 'Marxists believe neither that history is made by great men nor that economic changes automatically produce results. Ideas are borne in on people by their environment ...'.[87] This is very close to Marx's famous contention in the *Preface* that it is not consciousness that determines being but being which determines consciousness. At the same time it is not a huge stride away from Thompson's later view that class consciousness arises not directly from class position but from the way in which that class experience 'is handled in cultural terms'.[88] It is also quite clearly from the *Preface* that Hill got his concept of 'total' revolution – a period of social revolution in which the mental universe as well as its economic foundations were transformed. His statement in 1949 that 'this vast economic and political revolution naturally had its ideological counterpart' no doubt lacked the sophistication that came with greater maturity, but it is virtually straight out of the *Preface*, and heralded the beginnings of his immense contribution to our understanding of the dialectical interplay between ideas and the material world.[89] His view of social totality was not, as Underdown thinks, a later development. From its early years the section endeavoured to deploy the base-superstructure model in a non-mechanistic non-reductive fashion

IDEOLOGY

Aptly enough, this aspiration was probably better fulfilled in the series of discussions on Ideology than in the prior discussion of the state, to which I shall return. The participants – not always the same – were extremely alert to the danger of reductionism. They were particularly sharp in their criticism of the theses brought forward by William Joseph, the Chairman dismissing them as 'an attempt to establish a direct relation between the forces of production and ideological trends without reference to classes and human beings'. Hill declared them to be 'too abstract and schematised, depending too much upon undefined categories, such as "feudal merchant-capital"'.[90] If Joseph's approach was particularly schematic and unconvincing, other members of the section also had to work their way towards formulations and interpretations which could survive comradely criticism. For example Mason's preliminary association of the emergence of experimental methods with petty bourgeois craftsmen, representing revolutionary capital, and of the mathematical tradition with the bigger merchants, did not go without challenge. By 1953 Mason seems to have had discarded this view, whilst retaining the emphasis on the essential contribution of craftsmen.[91]

More significant was the prolonged debate arising from Hill's view of the connections between Protestantism and Capitalism. Hill recognised at the outset the limitations of his statement that 'the ideology of the revolutionary bourgeoisie was Puritanism' – because 'it does not get us very far'.[92] Yet his subsequent elaboration ran into such 'difficulties' that the two sessions on ideology overflowed into a third specifically devoted to the Reformation and Class Struggle.[93] Hill's starting point was Engels's view that that 'the long fight of the bourgeoisie against feudalism culminated in three great, decisive battles', the first being the German Reformation, and the second the 'great bourgeois upheaval' in England that found in Calvinism 'its doctrine dried and cut'.[94] According to Engels, the Calvinist Reformation provided 'the ideological costume for the second act of the bourgeois revolution' – a passage cited with approval by Hill in his paper on 'Bourgeois Ideology after 1660', and given a substantial gloss in that which he produced with Clark on 'Calvinism and the Bourgeoisie'.[95] This was designed to show firstly how Calvinism adapted to the needs of bourgeois society, and secondly how 'it served the specific needs of the bourgeoisie as a revolutionary class'. Calvinism, in contrast to Lutheranism, Hill suggested in discussion, enabled the bourgeoisie to lead the peasantry in an organized way. He had in mind English developments in the period 1570-1640 and the earlier national revolt of the Netherlands against Spain.[96] Hill and Clark were careful to qualify their claim that 'Calvinism represented the ideology of the sixteenth and seventeenth century bourgeoisie organized for revolutionary struggle' by acknowledging some differences in national patterns. This was insufficient to prevent a string of critical observations from those who were evidently more familiar with European social and political developments.[97] Andrews and James thought that Hill oversimplified the relationship of social movements to the Reformation in the Netherlands and Germany, whilst Kiernan cast doubt on whether Lutheranism and Calvinism were purely bourgeois in character, stressing the appeal in many countries of Calvinism to the feudal gentry and nobility.

Kiernan developed his argument – whether before or after the meeting in March 1950 is not clear – in a provocative and stimulating 9,500 word synthesis of European political, social and economic developments; in this he explained why it was only in England that Calvinism joined forces with capitalism and only there that it conquered state power for a brief period. Elsewhere Calvinism remained true to its medieval, particularist and defensive character. It was, for Kiernan, first and foremost the religion of the middling strata both urban and rural: strata which naturally displayed virtues of thrift, honesty and sobriety, and without whose energy a bourgeois revolution could not have been accomplished – and even then only in the most exceptional circumstances. Indeed had the Calvinists' original petty bourgeois ethos with its attachment to guild democracy taken practical shape, it would have prevented rather than fostered capitalist development.[98]

The section returned to the ideological fray in September 1950. Although the eminent German Marxist scholar Roy Pascal defended Engels's view of the German Reformation as the first of three decisive battles of the bourgeoisie against feudalism, the tone of the meeting was perhaps set by the Chairman, who drew attention to Engels's comments about the indecision of the burghers. He also suggested that it was worth considering the view that 'in later phases the role of Protestantism as the ideology of a developed bourgeois revolutionary movement was exceptional'. Despite Hobsbawm's suggestion that the Reformation movements were failed revolutionary movements, much of the discussion, reinforced by papers on specific countries, showed a reluctance to bestow a revolutionary capacity on either the bourgeoisie or, in most circumstances, on Calvinism. James's view of French Calvinism as 'moderating and disciplinary, not revolutionary', weakened by its association with the great nobility and the opportunistic and unstable support of urban oligarchies, is a remarkable piece; it anticipated conclusions which I was to reach some fifteen years later, unfortunately unaware of its existence or of the discussion to which it had contributed.[99]

Over a year later the section Committee noted that the discussion had not succeeded in resolving the disagreements between Kiernan and James on the one hand and Hill and Pascal on the other. 'Bearing in mind', it said, 'the flexibility of Protestant and Puritan ideas, and the fact that Engels's statement is a dogmatic framework into which the ideological development of the bourgeoisie movements in all countries can be fitted, the discussion did not produce any acceptable refutation of that statement'. It was not thought profitable to pursue the question any further without looking more closely at the roots of the crisis of feudalism and the role of bourgeois elements.[100] This ponderous and opaque conclusion was clearly insufficient to settle matters, which shortly spilled over into the pages of the newly launched *Past & Present*; here Kiernan took issue with Hill's use of the writings of the Calvinist theologian William Perkins (1558-1602) as an exemplar of a burgeoning capitalist ethic diametrically opposed to 'a traditional medieval economic morality'.[101] Nonetheless it is difficult not to detect the impact of the arguments with which he was confronted in the position at which Hill had arrived by 1961; then he observed that whilst Protestantism did not make men capitalists, nor vice versa, the bourgeois values of thrift, accumulation, and hard work were the 'natural consequence of the religion of the heart' in a society where capitalism was already developing.[102] Two years later, in his pioneering examination of the sociology of Puritanism, Hill brought the 'middling sort', rather than the bourgeoisie as such, centre stage.[103]

The section's discussions must also have brought home the inadvisability of constant references to the 'revolutionary bourgeoisie'. In later years Hill acknowledged that he had thrown the terms 'bourgeois' and 'feudal' around in ways that he came to regard as inappropriate. However, whilst the undoubtedly loose terminology almost certainly reflected a need for much greater clarity and precision, it is difficult to conclude that Hill thought the bourgeoisie were consciously willing a revolution. In the paper on Calvinism that he wrote with Clark, the argument is developed by reference to 'necessity' rather than to a conscious voluntarism, by alluding to the principal 'requirements' for a bourgeois society and to what the bourgeoisie needed for a revolutionary struggle. Moreover, although Calvinism might be the 'disguise' or costume of the English bourgeoisie, discarded once the revolution was accomplished, Hill was certainly nowhere near suggesting that this was a conscious deception. Morton many years earlier had stated without ambiguity that

> The practical men who led the opposition to the Stuarts were content to defend their earthly possessions and, at first, to see no more than one step ahead at a time. Their profound religious convictions were important here because they helped to give them confidence in the divine justice of their cause and the courage necessary to take each step as it appeared. In their own desires they saw the hand of the Lord of Battles, leading them as certainly as He led the Israelites through the wilderness. It was perhaps largely the absence of theory and of clear objectives which cast the political movement and thought of the Seventeenth Century so often into religious forms.[104]

Hill, who read Morton line by line and suggested a number of amendments, seemingly had no problems with this passage. He certainly recognised that Calvinism did not bring with it an inherently revolutionary perspective, its political thought being 'vague' and readily adaptable to different purposes.[105] Kiernan nonetheless felt that it was necessary to remind the section that 'no-one in this age was fighting for capitalism'.[106]

That Hill concurred with this view, even if he had not fully worked out its analytical and historical implications, is suggested by the fact that, when he directly addressed the question of economic change, that too was framed in terms of necessity. Thus he referred to the 'tasks of the bourgeois revolution in the countryside', and 'the need to feed London', which '*demanded* [my italics] that agriculture should be put on a capitalist basis' as did the maximalisation of national wealth. 'Economic motives', he observed, were not necessarily conscious ones – an unhappy choice of words but the intention is clear.[107] Hill's approach was almost certainly derived from the letter to Bloch already cited, in which Engels concluded that 'amid all the endless host of accidents ... the economic movement finally asserts itself as necessary'. Thirty years later Hill drafted a major restatement of his view of England's bourgeois revolution, apparently intending to refer to this letter to refute the charge that he had said that the bourgeoisie had willed the Revolution. Thom· ·on, to whom Hill had sent his draft, advised that use of this letter might leave him vulnerable to criticism. Hill substituted a passage from Engels's *Ludwig Feuerbach*, in which he had much to say about the relationship between accident, intentions, will and history. It just happens to be the same work from which Hill had drawn Engels's comments on Calvinism as the disguise of the bourgeoisie.[108]

Amidst the disagreements and the search for analytical clarity, one important feature of the section's approach requires emphasis. It was very little concerned by the notion of false consciousnesses or the 'illusion of the epoch'. Ideology was treated as an expression or emanation of real interests, sets of ideas through which people made sense of the world and engaged with it. This assumption permeates all the discussions and was articulated by Pascal.[109] When Hill opened the first session he did so with a passing reference to Caudwell's *Crisis in Physics*, with which he assumed the members were familiar; but they seem fairly quickly to have rejected the appropriateness – at least for the seventeenth century – of Caudwell's view that the ideology of a ruling class reflects the conditions of functioning of the working class as seen by the ruling class.[110] Exposition of the concept of the illusion of the epoch, which Caudwell had derived from the *German Ideology*, was left to the classical historian George Thomson, who, in 1952, published a highly abstract article emphasising the affinity between Greek and modern (bourgeois) thought, both resting on philosophical illusions made possible by the rise of commodity production and money fetishism.[111] The early modern section, as we have seen, worked at a much lower level of abstraction, beginning with Engels's views of the Reformation, or statements such as 'Modern science and modern political thought reflect the needs and interests of the bourgeoisie'.

ABSOLUTISM AND THE TUDOR STATE

The discussions on ideology make it easy to understand why Hill felt he owed so much to his years in the group. They also show that the members of the section were well on the way to a non-reductionist understanding of 'ideology' well before 1956. By comparison, the earlier discussions on Tudor Absolutism were less productive. In part this was because the participants were sometimes less well prepared and less knowledgeable, but the debates also had more political overtones. This left them with a rather reified view of the monarchy, and a misconception about its absolute character, which would later be discarded.

As with the discussions of ideology, much of the agenda and the problems that arose flowed from Hill's initiatives. Indeed the real point of departure was the controversy that had erupted prior to the Second World War with the publication of his pioneering extended essay on *The English Revolution*. In retrospect it seems amazing that this Marxist sketch of the origins and character of the English revolution should have been at all controversial, for the underlying conception of the revolutionary process came straight out of the pages of Marx and Engels: developing productive forces reached a point at which they came up against the feudal legal and political superstructure; resolution of this problem required a revolutionary transfer of class power and the creation of 'a new political structure within which capitalism could freely develop'.[112] This revolutionary moment came in the 1640s. In an aggressive review in *Labour Monthly*, a certain P.F. (in reality Jurgen Kuczynski[113]) latched on to a rather loose formulation in which Hill said that the structure of Tudor society, as well as its political superstructure, were 'still essentially feudal'.[114] Hill, according to Kuczynski, was un-marxist, as, contrary to the teachings of Marx and Engels, he had totally underestimated the extent to which feudalism had already been undermined by capitalism in Tudor England. Queen Elizabeth herself was 'the most prominent capitalist in capitalist bourgeois society' and the civil war was precipitated by a subsequent counter-revolutionary movement as Charles I endeavoured to recover the monarchy's authority. Hill's supporters in turn attacked Kuczynski's Marxist credentials, accusing him of being a reformist gradualist who belittled the role of class struggle.[115]

In a subsequent comment Kuczynski withdrew the term 'counter-revolutionary' and substituted 'reactionary' to describe the policies of the early Stuarts.[116] This was a significant concession, which in a calmer atmosphere might easily have been used to find some common ground about English developments prior to 1640, as there was little doubt that Hill's interpretation did postulate a substantial growth of capitalism prior to the revolutionary transfer of power. For reasons which remain obscure, Palme Dutt, the ultra-orthodox editor of *Labour Monthly*, was either unable or unwilling to recognise the validity of Hill's position. Had he realised that the highest Soviet authorities had earlier come down firmly against Pokrovsky's (d. 1932) conception of a gradual transition from feudalism to capitalism, he would, no doubt, have been less resistant to Hill's interpretation. Be that as it may, it was only after considerable pressure from Torr, Garman and Hill that Dutt produced a draft statement (unfortunately never published) which, although still unacceptable to Hill, escaped sufficiently from political correctness and Marxist exegesis to set out the opposing historical views.[117] These turned on the allied questions of whether the Tudor state was still controlled by a feudal ruling class, and the extent to which agrarian capitalism had already modified class relations, changed the nature of the landowning class and therefore the balance of class forces in which to situate the state.

Six years later Hill returned to the defence of his position. Curiously enough his opening set of propositions to the section in 1947 contained what might be construed as a major concession to Kuczynski, when he noted that 'after about 1588' the Crown was 'driven back to increasingly conscious "refeudalisation" in the state and "recatholicisation" in the church'.[118] His basic position, however, was that the Tudor state was not merely 'a feudal landowners' state'; it was an absolute monarchy. As a gloss on this proposition he called up a couple of quotations from Engels to the effect that absolute monarchies arise en route to capitalism when the state was able to achieve a certain independence from the evenly balanced feudal nobility and emergent bourgeoisie. However, because English capitalism was largely rural the Tudor Absolutism had some distinctive characteristics, contributing to the survival of Parliament and the Common Law, the importance of Justices of the Peace, and the failure of the Crown 'to develop a powerful centralised bureaucracy'. The progress of agrarian capitalism also meant that 'the split between feudalists and bourgeoisie is not merely one of country v town; it also takes place in the heart of the ruling class, the gentry'. In addition to which, by virtue of England's maritime character, the Crown did not have a standing army at its disposal, merely a 'private-enterprise' navy. Hill was not only clear that in its early years royal policy 'helped the bourgeoisie'; he also recognised that its capacity to execute policies designed to limit capitalist development was itself limited.

In the ensuing discussion Hill further acknowledged that 'the gentry played a big role in the absolutist state', and 'that there was a significant and growing capitalist sector in this class in the later sixteenth century'. Yet, all that said, the bourgeoisie were not the basis of state power and for that to happen a revolution was necessary.[119] Indeed, the primary contradiction which determined the character of the state remained that between a dependent peasantry and feudal landowners. Conceding that serfdom had almost entirely disappeared, Hill confronted this problem by arguing that this was essentially a legal change, without significance for the nexus of exploitation and relations of production: 'Both the new (Capitalist) landowners and the old (feudal) landowners had an interest in holding down the peasantry'.[120] Both, Dona Torr summarised as the discussion reached its final stages, needed the state, and it was the state which enabled the landowners to 'maintain the conditions of exploitation', forcing the peasantry 'to cede surplus value to the ruling class as a whole'.[121]

Hill's theses were riddled with inconsistencies and could easily have been re-arranged to suggest that agrarian capitalism had developed sufficiently and had so transformed the class structure as to preclude the development of continental style absolutism. Kiernan, who had not participated in the pre-war debate, was not slow to point out that theses five and six amounted to admitting that there was no real absolutism in England.[122] There was, he said emphatically, 'no stage of Absolutism in English history, which is in many respects unique'.[123] In a subsequent note Kiernan identified some characteristics of the Tudor regime and its policies which meant that it could not simply be described as revised feudal state: its base in the economically advanced south east, the use of its coercive machinery against the remnants of feudalism in the North and West, its reformation of the church, and its progressive international alignments. The ending of serfdom and the widespread use of money rents contributed to the further stratification of the peasantry, and thereby to economic development. Personal serfdom having effectively disappeared, the manor, largely superseded by other administrative mechanisms, 'survives only as the framework of land-tenures'.[124] Merchant capital entered increasingly into productive processes and modified the mode of production; it could not be treated simply as parasitic. The 1640s were 'not a decisive turning point', as the bourgeois revolution in England was spread over several centuries – a formulation which he then modified, suggesting that if the main phase of the bourgeois revolution occurred in 1642 this should not prevent us from seeing 1485 as 'a necessary preliminary phase'. His view did not exclude the possibility of 'a situation emerging later in which capitalism, further matured, would have to seize direct control of the state and remould it more thoroughly'.[125] In discussion he explained that he did not maintain that the Tudor state was a bourgeois state, but a mixed one, 'in which elements of the old feudal classes still existed, but in which the bourgeoisie was important'.[126]

According to one observer, who wrote what were virtually a second set of minutes, at this point Kiernan also clearly *said* that his thesis was not incompatible with a revolution in 1642.[127] Given the general agreement about the significant progress of capitalism in the sixteenth century, it is not at first sight obvious why the discussion should not have moved towards a generally acceptable synthesis of the developments which first subverted and then overthrew the foundations of monarchical rule. Indeed this was available in Morton's superbly modulated discussion of the Tudor regime in his *People's History*. For Morton the Tudor absolutism was 'of a most peculiar kind, absolutism by consent'. If its destruction of the independent power of the Church and nobility had created the preconditions for capitalism:

> the monarchy was itself too much the product of feudalism and contained within itself too many feudal survivals to be able to carry the revolution to its completion. Once a certain point had been reached, and with a startling suddenness, its objective character underwent a complete transformation, and it appeared as the main obstacle to the bourgeois revolution and the centre around which the forces of reaction gathered for the decisive struggle.

There then follow a few pages of the most elegant and lucid prose, in which Morton explains how England's comparative lack of involvement in land warfare and its consequent lack of a standing army precluded a 'true absolutism'. The inadequate feudal revenues of the Crown were not improved by the fact that, although the middle classes and the Crown participated in a mutually necessary alliance, 'the middle classes had been prepared to do almost anything for the Tudors except pay heavy taxes'. Moreover: 'Parliament, which had begun as a check on the theoretically absolute power of the feudal king to dispose of the property of his subjects, had become in time the guardian of the absolute right of the individual to the enjoyment of his private property'; and this belief in the sanctity of property had grown 'as the bourgeoisie grew tall'. Only by a direct attack on it could the Stuarts create the state apparatus for a thoroughgoing absolutism after the continental style. The ensuing Civil War was nonetheless 'a class struggle', and was 'revolutionary' and progressive'.[128] Though these pages were written over seventy years ago, the level of perception and the carefully nuanced argument means that more recent scholarship may certainly improve on it but cannot dismiss it. They could be given as a starting point to any new student today, and could well have guided the section to more enduring conclusions than Hill's theses.

As it was, to the apparent surprise of the participants, Morton announced his general concurrence with Hill's 'theses', 'merely' pleading, in the words of the anonymous scribe:

> for more emphasis on the fact that the Tudor Monarchy was not *purely* a feudal landowners' state ... It was true that the king was the greatest feudal land-owner; but it was also true that the very existence of a state on a national scale was a stage in the disintegration of feudalism. Therefore, although the king was a feudal monarch, he developed something contrary to feudalism. 1640 was the culmination of a long process.[129]

Notwithstanding his support for Hill's view of the Revolution, the gist of Morton's remarks brought him very close to Kiernan's view of the Tudor state. Kiernan also received emphatic support from John Morris for his view of the transforming effect of money rents. Andrews, despite almost unqualified support for Hill's view of the state, reminded the section that merchant capital did play 'a progressive role in disintegrating feudalism', a conclusion evidently emerging from his investigation of Elizabethan privateering.[130] Hobsbawm observed that the character of absolute monarchy on the continent was much clearer where, however hostile it might be to bourgeois aspirations, it was obliged to assume bourgeois forms of organisation, which then lead to an impasse.[131]

In the end, however, only one of those present appears to have defended Kiernan's overall perspective.[132] Part of the reason for Kiernan's isolation was that he pushed his own argument to the limits, disputing virtually every element of the contrary case. His suggestion that merchant capital, for instance, did not merely have a disintegrating effect but played a revolutionary role in Western Europe had little chance of meeting with approval, given that Dobb's *Studies* strongly suggested otherwise.[133] Although Dobb's conclusions were later challenged by Paul Sweezy, setting off a much wider debate (not yet exhausted) about the economic dynamics of the transition to capitalism, the generally held view of the conservative nature of the London merchant oligarchy has been well sustained by later scholarship, Marxist and otherwise.[134] Kiernan's attempt to push back the onset of capitalism into the fifteenth century, transforming the victorious Yorkists into a 'progressive' party, simply invited criticism. It came in the form of a paper from Hilton, who, whilst carefully refraining from commenting on the question of Tudor absolutism, had little difficulty in demolishing Kiernan's interpretation of its origins.[135] At the second session, Hilton, speaking at length, gave a fully worked out critique of Kiernan's views, concluding that, far from bringing the bourgeoisie into power, the Tudor state 'was based on a progressive concentration of feudal property and jurisdictions in the hands of the Crown'.[136] A few months later Hilton underlined his differences with Kiernan by insisting that 'the polarisation of the English peasantry did not attain sufficient proportions, even after the sixteenth-century enclosures for pasture, to alter the legal and institutional framework of the feudal regime ... the manor was still the dominant rural institution ... the primary machines for extracting feudal rent'.[137]

By the time of the meeting in January 1648 at which Kiernan formally withdrew his general thesis, he was clearly on the back foot in relation to a number of historical issues. However the minutes of this meeting make it absolutely clear that the reasons why the argument was pursued to this point were as much political as historical. What was at stake was a certain conception of the nature of revolutions; the controversy, said Hill, was 'of great political importance because the bourgeois revolution is still a real political issue in Asia, South East Europe, Spain and other parts of the world'. Pokrovsky's error of antedating the bourgeois revolution led to reformism and the assumption that a transfer of power is possible without a revolution. This diminished the role to be played by human agency, specifically the Party. Furthermore, it was not possible to have a revolution by stages; whilst it was true that '1688 and 1832 carried forward the Bourgeois Revolution in England', 'there is always a nodal point when power is really transferred'. Kiernan's view was particularly 'dangerous', because it is 'in fact identical with the old bourgeois heresy that English development is in some sense peculiar, peaceful, non revolutionary'. Marx and Engels noted the 'peculiarities and difficulties' of England but did not for all that abandon the Marxist categories of analysis, and 'nor should we': it would mean abandoning 'all the revolutionary traditions of 1640 and our own party'.[138]

Hill's political and historical considerations were so interwoven that it is not easy to say how much the former weighed with Kiernan as he deferred to them. He agreed that he had been unable to support his view of 1485, and that 'in the light of the definition of feudalism which had been brought forward there was nothing illogical in the thesis that Tudor state remained feudal whilst there was a rapid accumulation of bourgeois elements in the economic system'; but otherwise he merely noted without much apparent conviction that 'there were objections to any theory of bourgeois revolution appearing by stages', and that 'it was *necessary* [my italics] to stress the character of 1642 as the English bourgeois revolution'.[139] Furthermore, in a lengthy last word Kiernan took the opportunity, under the somewhat disingenuous guise of 'questions of detail', to spell out, some significant caveats to his acceptance of the majority view. Greater clarity and precision was needed about the way in which existing institutions impeded the development of the new forces. In showing how they broke through, 'it is necessary to be on guard against falsifying the details of an extremely complex process'. Account should be particularly taken of 'the degree to which the bourgeois groups were forced into a revolutionary programme by the pressure of mass discontent'. He also persisted with his view that 'the often-repeated idea of Merchant Capital being essentially parasitical is liable to be misleading', and continued to insist that there was 'no sharp absolute breach between feudal and capitalist rent'. In conclusion he reminded the section that Dobb himself had raised the 'extremely important' question of 'what is the mode of production in an agrarian system worked by peasant proprietors and/or tenant farmers paying money rents, not visibly burdened by "non economic compulsion", and not employing hired labour'. Such a system appeared to be neither feudal or capitalist. Given that Hill's position depended on the characterisation of sixteenth century agrarian relations as predominantly feudal, this was surely more than a question of detail.

Nonetheless Dona Torr regarded the outcome of the final discussion as 'a good victory'; writing to Brian Pearce the same day she said, 'we have certainly achieved something since the almost incredibly difficult struggles of 1940 ... and the refusal to publish anything on the tercentenary of the English Revolution or to accept it in the category of bourgeois revolutions'.[140] The most tangible sign of this 'victory' was the publication in *Communist Review* in July 1948 of a substantial ex-cathedra statement from the History Group (almost certainly drafted by Hill, Pearce and Torr) in which was enshrined the view that the revolution of the 1640s swept away the barriers to capitalist development constituted by the Tudor and early Stuart state. This view has certainly continued to command considerable support even from those who were at times most critical of other aspects of Hill's interpretation.[141] Yet in other respects the group's statement suggests that much remained to be resolved, particularly about the state. Hill, as we have seen, had always recognised that the bourgeoisie were able to use both parliament and the law, and that if the 'royal bureaucracy was destroyed' ... 'the Old State system was not wholly but partially destroyed and modified'.[142] The statement asserts that royal absolutism was 'smashed', but immediately elaborates with the observation that 'only after the revolution of 1640-49 does the state in England begin to be subordinated to the capitalists'. Push this latter emphasis too far and the differences with Kiernan's seemingly abandoned view of revolution by stages might appear to fade away. Furthermore it is striking that whilst the statement describes the Tudor state as 'an executive institution of the feudal class more highly organised than ever before', it nevertheless concludes that the bourgeoisie represented in Parliament was able to smash the absolute monarchy '*before* [my italics] the latter could build a great apparatus of bureaucracy and militarism like that in France, an apparatus which Laud and Strafford consciously strove to reproduce in England'.[143] This sentence is not only indicative of the difficulty of categorising the Tudor monarchy as a continental type absolutism, but might also be considered to be a major concession to Kuczynski's view of the reactionary orientation of Stuart policies.

All this makes it difficult to understand why Kiernan apparently abandoned his well founded objections to the idea of a Tudor absolutism at a relatively early stage in the discussions. He may well have thought better of it, opportunistically using the discussions on Calvinism as a vehicle for some further thoughts on absolute monarchy. In his extraordinary and stimulating 9,500 word disquisition on 'Calvinism and the Transition from Medieval to Modern' he moved decisively towards the view which he was to enunciate in 1965: absolute monarchy was a mechanism for saving the feudal ruling class from itself.[144] It may have come into being with the support of the middle strata, the lesser nobility and gentry, for whom it offered a 'breathing space', but it rested on no radical transformation of the mode of production. The result therefore was only a re-shuffling of power within the same group of interests, and the beginning of a 'new feudal cycle'. His only and guarded comment about England was that it did not conform to the generally 'firm principle' of absolutist regimes 'that nobles should pay no direct taxation'.[145] Yet Kiernan had sufficiently recovered from Hill's admonitions about the bourgeois heresy of English exceptionalism to reassert his conviction that the path to modernity in England was 'a very exceptional and unique development': a specifically 'British Road', he suggested, in a barbed allusion to the view developing in the party that Socialism in Britain might come by a distinctive route.[146] Unfortunately he did not really pursue these insights when he returned to the subject in 1980. His *State and Society In Europe 1550-1650* is a curiously descriptive work offering few analytical touches – amongst which is a disappointing reversion to Engels's equilibrium theory to explain Louis XIV.[147] The authority of the Tudors, however, was so dependent on the gentry and so exiguous 'in terms of an apparatus of government', that 'to call them "absolute" may seem more a misnomer than in any other case'.[148]

At some point Hill must have accepted that Kiernan was right, and that it was not necessary to transform the Tudor regime into a continental absolutism in order to preserve the revolution. He rarely revisited Tudor England in later years, and when he did so in 1967 absolutism was no longer mentioned. England, he says, following Professor Macaggrey, 'became a hybrid political society, in which centralized monarchy existed side by side with a kind of confederation of political interests' which were represented through Parliament; the monarchy was also dependent on the gentry, who occupied key administrative positions.[149] This view is much closer to Morton, whose view of the importance of consent to the Tudor regime has been well sustained by modern scholarship, with only the rarest dissenting voice.[150] It has even been suggested that England was a 'monarchical republic', resting on a multitude of self governing villages. This may be excessive, but there is no doubt that effective government did depend not only on the cooperation of the gentry as circuit judges and JPs but also on the 'middling sorts' who acted as Constables and Churchwardens, and sat on Juries.[151] In the course of discussion Andrews perceptively suggested that it was precisely the growing unreliability of these allies around the turn of the century that was one of the stimulants to the increasingly authoritarian policies of the Stuarts.[152] This is not to say that the Tudors had not engaged – as did most self-respecting monarchs – in measures to bolster the power of their office, particularly because their own claim to a throne won in battle was tenuous. Henry VII's establishment of the Councils of the North and of Wales certainly contributed to the inexorable attrition of magnate rule in distant parts of the realm. And at its centre the evolution of the Privy Council into a relatively small body under Elizabeth concentrated power in fewer hands, whilst the emergence of the Navy Board – a centralised ordnance office – and a permanent diplomatic service added some bureaucratic weight. However such developments should be seen in the perspective of a country which for centuries had been exceptionally homogenous by European standards, with a unified system of justice, a common law and a single representative institution. Paradoxically, this made absolutist solutions less necessary and less likely than in countries subject to powerful decentralising forces.[153] Even Geoffrey Elton, who is generally thought to have overdone the 'Tudor Revolution in Government', never associated it with absolute monarchy.[154] On the contrary, central to his interpretation was the undoubted growth in legislation by parliamentary statute, which meant, as Williams has noted, that 'especially after 1529, Parliament became a more dynamic and a still less dispensable part of English government than it had been before'.[155] Of course the Tudors could make use of royal proclamations, but 'it cannot be said that … they ever came near to replacing statute', whilst the status of laws approved by both houses was such that even the Crown's ability to amend them was constrained.[156]

The question inevitably arises as to how the section managed to get so confused about the Tudor state. It is true that most of what we know about Tudor government has come in the wake of the controversies aroused by the publication of Elton's seminal work published in 1953. By comparison with the discussion on ideology, that on absolutism lacked empirical depth. It also took place at a time when the notion that the Tudor monarchy was amongst a number of 'new' monarchies that were renewing themselves from the crises of the late middle ages was very much in the air. Yet Hill realised that in some very crucial ways England was different; following Marx's view of the peculiarly rural nature of English capitalism, he stressed the consequent divisions within the ruling class and their significance for the survival of Parliament and the Common Law. It is truly remarkable that none of this was sufficient to override either his distaste for the idea of English exceptionalism or the conviction, again derived from the classics, that the English revolution was analogous to the French Revolution, both of which were preceded by a period of monarchical absolutism – the last phase of feudalism. Even Louis XIV, Hill argued, 'staffed his court and administration with many bourgeois', but this did not make the bourgeoisie the ruling class. He evidently had less difficulty in swallowing this myth about the French monarchy, largely promoted by liberal historians, than in accepting 'the bourgeois "special English" legend'. For him 'the absolutism of the Tudors and Stuarts must be seen as essentially comparable to other absolutisms'. Those who used Engel's equilibrium statements to deny the feudal character of the absolute state had failed to take account of Engels's qualifications. However, Hill never convincingly explained what these were, and by the end of the discussion seemed to have realised that his own use of Engels's statements had only muddied the waters. The only period of English history, he now argued, when such a 'balance' might be said to have existed was 1654/58, when it was based on Cromwell's army.[157] In 1955 with one of the very few amendments to the second edition of his 1940 essay he altered the opening sentences of the chapter on the Tudor Monarchy to make clear that it was 'rooted in feudal society' and that it could balance only 'to a certain extent' between the contending classes.[158]

One of the consequences of Kiernan's premature and temporary abandonment of his opposition to Hill's view of English absolutism was that no attempt was made to explain the distinctiveness of the English polity. Yet Morton's observations about England's lack of continuous involvement in foreign wars and its attendant lack of a standing army already offered the beginnings of an explanation. Moreover, Hilton, perhaps conscious of a tendency by Marxists to treat warfare as external to the fundamental processes of social change, stated without ambiguity that 'the military aspect of feudalism' was an '*essential* characteristic'.[159] This was a statement full of implications for the section's view of the English state, but Geoffrey Lee's attempt to explore them in discussion fell on unresponsive ears.[160] If, as was originally intended, the section had returned in 1950 to the question of the European state, this might have brought into focus the significance of large-scale and costly warfare in the formation of absolutist regimes, and England's insular good fortune.[161]

As it was, all the participants in the discussion of the Tudor state, including Kiernan, sought to deduce its nature from that of the ruling class itself, constructed in unmediated fashion by reference to the mode of production. Dobb exemplified the problem when he concluded that the only possible choices were between a Pokrovsky-like view of an intermediate phase of merchant capitalism with the bourgeoisie already in power or one which said that the state was still in the hands of a feudal ruling class.[162] For Andrews, who vigorously pursued the lead offered by Hill and set the parameters for the second set of discussions, the state was the 'instrument of the feudal ruling class as a whole in its struggle with the peasantry'.[163] Mounting popular unrest from the late 1530s culminated in the major crisis of 1549, which, as later scholarship has shown, affected twenty-five counties throughout lowland England.[164] This was followed, according to Andrews, by a decade in which the state 'smashes the peasantry', and 'the notable extension of the coercive machine'.[165] The first half of the sixteenth century certainly saw a dramatic increase in the fiscal burden. Henry VIII was granted over twice as much in parliamentary taxes between 1541 and 1547 as his father had received for the entirety of his reign. Yet his dependence on parliament, wherein sat representatives of the tax-paying classes, had been forcibly brought home to him by the way in which he had been forced to abandon the so called 'amicable grant' or forced loan of 1625. After the Pilgrimage of Grace (1636), the government withdrew its threat of major tax reforms, and from mid-century it 'gave wide birth to taxes on livestock and excises', which had aroused the West Country. Elizabeth was much less demanding and, unlike Henry, repaid her forced loans. Whether or not continued fear of revolt played its part, the English in the second half of the century were, by European standards, a very lightly burdened people.[166] The Tudor state certainly did not appropriate the surplus product of the peasantry in the manner of the French monarchy, where from the 1620s ever-mounting burdens were siphoned off, to the huge benefit of a multitude of venal, frequently ennobled, officeholders and financiers.

Nor can the relative calm of the Elizabethan years be explained by more effective coercion. True, in the wake of the 1548-9 rebellions, Parliament had made it a treasonable offence for forty or more persons to assemble together for two hours or more for the purpose of destroying by force enclosures, parks or fishponds, or for killing game. And in the 1590s rioters who went from village to village advocating the general destruction of enclosures were charged with treason and some ringleaders were tortured.[167] However the overall response of those in authority to popular discontent was more flexible than this suggests. Most obvious were the measures to assuage the fears and anger aroused by enclosing and engrossing, notably the 1552 act for the maintenance of tillage. When its restrictions were loosened in 1593 this was perceived to have contributed to grain shortages and a renewed discontent. Although the government responded by hanging the leaders of the Oxford rebellion of 1596, the following year saw a rather 'hasty re-enactment' of the law.[168] However it did retain some significant exemptions, which reflected perfectly the ambivalence of England's legislators to the progress of commercial farming, in which some of them undoubtedly had an interest.

If the full weight of the state was directed against any one group it was against the increasing number of 'masterless men'. Elizabethan poor law legislation pushed the country towards a national system of outdoor relief for the 'deserving' poor but those who were not so considered could be savagely treated. The Vagrancy and Poor Relief Act of 1572 was, it has been said, the 'most repressive vagrancy law of the Elizabethan period'.[169] First offenders were to be imprisoned until the next quarter sessions or gaol delivery and upon conviction were to be whipped and burnt in the ear unless some worthy householder accepted them into service for one year. Second offenders were to be adjudged felons unless a householder took them into service for two years. A second offender who ran away was to be hanged. After 1588 the problem was compounded by the presence of mutinous or discharged soldiers. This led to the appointment of provost marshals, who became part of local government and poor law administration until the end of the reign. Martial law, seemingly applied only against the propertyless but vigorously contested by common lawyers, was an indication of what might have been had England been really put to the test of prolonged bouts of warfare.[170]

The view of the Tudor state offered by Hill and Andrews, elaborated with only the barest mention of its actual operation, must surely have been vulnerable to criticism, even though the section did not have the benefit of the explosion in knowledge which began with the publication of Elton's *Tudor Revolution in Government* in 1953. It is difficult to believe that Morton, who found the English peasantry 'freer and less exploited' than their French counterparts, would not have demurred from Andrews picture.[171] Unfortunately, without a surviving record of the discussion on the 'Peasantry and Absolutism', we do not know what the reaction was, or even whether Hill was present to support the argument presented by Andrews. However, the empirically weightier papers given by Mervyn James and Allan Merson, on the 'backward' North of England and the 'economically advanced' East Anglia, provided the section with more nuanced and effective explanations for the decline in rebellion from mid-century: in the former case the explanation was the slow attrition of magnate power as it lost its base in both the middle-ranking gentry and the peasantry; and in the latter case it was a widening gulf between the substantial yeomanry and the mass of the peasantry under the impact of commercial farming and rural cloth manufacture.[172] Merson's suggestion that the absence of significant popular rebellion after 1549 flowed from the increasing closeness of yeomen and gentry has been well sustained by later work.[173] 'It was', says the most recent major study of Norfolk, 'the last occasion when tenants of all levels of wealth united in their hostility to landlords'.[174] Such a view has become part of the standard explanation for the decline of large scale revolt in the Elizabethan years.[175]

One of the objections levelled against the Povroksky-Kiernan view of the transformation of the monarchical state under the impact of commercial capitalism was its economistic character: the state in unmediated fashion simply responding to changes in the economic base.[176] Yet Kiernan's critics themselves had only partially absorbed Engels's comments about the relative autonomy of the superstructure, allowing room for the impact of conscious revolutionary action, but not much else. Remarkably, of the leading members of the section, only Morton, in a few brief untheoretical words, suggested that, although the Tudor state had its roots in feudalism which may have set limits to its development, it was itself subject to change. It was, however, a paper produced by a certain Olwen Stocker that pointed up the possibilities of a non-reductive solution to some of the problems which the section had created for themselves. Stocker took Hill and Dell to task for their failure to appreciate that the 'law is generally and was in England an important ideological field in which the class struggle is fought', remarking not only that 'the law courts in the sixteenth-century came gradually under the influence of the bourgeoisie', but also that Lord Chief Justice Coke proclaimed as law rules that were favourable to bourgeois economic needs'.[177] With these few words Stocker anticipated the benefits of a non-reified concept of the state, itself subject to contradiction and contestation. In future decades such perceptions would enable Marxists to overcome the limitations of simply seeing the state as an instrument or simple reflection of class interest. Unfortunately the section never found time to discuss her paper and consider its implication. This left it without the analytical tools to confront the 'problem' enunciated by Dobb and seized on by Kiernan, of how to relate the Tudor state to a mode of production which, resting on an agrarian system worked by peasant proprietors or tenant farmers, appeared to be neither feudal nor capitalist.

AGRARIAN RELATIONS

Kiernan's own inclination, entirely consistent with the reductionist tendencies in the section's approach, was to postulate an intermediate stage between feudalism and capitalism. In early 1951 he wrote to Dobb pointing out that Lenin, basing himself on Marx, insisted that there was not a direct transition from feudalism to capitalism; Marx had also noted that 'the specific economic form in which surplus labour is pumped out of the direct producers determines the relation of rulers and ruled'.[178] Dobb reacted cautiously to Kiernan's apparent attempt to renew discussion about the nature of the English state. Whilst 'unconvinced' about an 'intermediate stage' between feudalism and capitalism, he recognised that there was 'a long drawn out transition in which a petty mode of production dominated, independent of some or even to a large degree of feudal exploitation which may have had some significance for superstructure and it was developing capitalist relations by differentiation within its ranks'.[179]

The section was certainly aware of the significance of the steady stratification of the peasantry. Hilton's emphasis on the freedom of the peasant land market in the late middle ages, which had already produced 'a far-reaching class differentiation within the peasantry', offered an excellent platform on which to build a picture of Tudor agrarian relations.[180] Although reluctant to stray beyond his own area of expertise, he drew attention to the fact that many of the sixteenth-century enclosers were mere Kulaks or lesser gentry. Dobb, in his *Studies*, had also stressed the truly revolutionary route to capitalism taken by the petty producers both rural and urban. In July 1948 he raised the question of whether the Kulak class was not a 'fully fledged rural bourgeoisie' by the 1640s.[181] The following year he offered the section a sophisticated and carefully constructed elaboration suggesting that:

> the petty mode of production (production by small commodity producers) had to a large extent but still incompletely (and far from completely in the more backward agricultural districts of

> the W. & N.) emancipated itself from feudal exploitation (compulsory exaction of the surplus product of the petty production for the benefit of feudal overlords). This petty mode of production was in process of being penetrated by capital and subjected to capital. At the same time it was being itself disintegrated by this subjection to capital and by the burgeoning of capitalist relations of production.

On the other hand, the money-rent payments of tenants 'still bore many of the characteristics of feudal rent', and 'had not completed the transition into capitalist rent (implying a free-market in land and unfettered right of movement on the part of the tenant farmer)'. Nevertheless, a profound shift in agrarian relations was taking place:

> The fact that the dividing line between yeomen, or kulak-peasant, and the squirearchy became increasingly blurred (the latter investing in bourgeois forms of production, and the former buying manors and gentility) is a crucial feature of Tudor England.

It was these 'petty capitalists', Dobb concluded, who, together with the 'smaller capitalists associated with the farmer (e.g. the clothiers of the provincial towns and the country clothiers)', provided 'the principal driving force of the bourgeois revolution'.[182] This view was seemingly shared by Andrews, who had earlier observed that the process of differentiation was to provide the revolutionaries of the 1640s with a left wing.[183]

Unfortunately, as has already been remarked, Dobb's paper 'disappeared' in the discussion on ideology, and in subsequent private communications he was very reluctant to go any further. Pressed by Brian Pearce, who wanted to know whether he stood by his position in 1940, when he had been much nearer Kuczynski's view of the development of capitalism, all he would say was that 'the mode of production was a very complex admixture of elements in agriculture', predominantly feudal in form 'but with strong emerging elements of capitalist relations'.[184] Anything he could add would be 'woolly'. It might be thought that this fully justified the unpublished views of one contributor to the pre-war debate, who had written that 'a long and polarised discussion into pro-feudal, pro-bourgeois views of the sixteenth century will not get anywhere. All we can say is the capitalist sector was making rapid progress ... economically the sixteenth and seventeenth centuries were an age of transition between feudalism and capitalism'.[185] Morton did indeed summarise that this was 'a clearly transitional age ... when feudal and capitalist traits jostle one another to form a total world which is neither feudal nor capitalist'.[186] Perhaps it is only fair to add that in terms of theory or historical sociology the issue has never been resolved. In her recent penetrating investigation of agrarian change in Norfolk, Jane Whittle suggests that the only way to resolve it is by treating feudalism as a particular type of peasant society, the latter concept offering 'a more useful and flexible theorization of the type of economy preceding capitalism in England and other parts of the world than feudalism can provide'.[187]

The member of the section who knew far more than the rest about peasant farming in the sixteenth and seventeenth centuries was Eric Kerridge. His approach, despite passing comments derived from Marx about money rents, was resolutely empirical. In his paper 'Agrarian Development 1500-1600' he focused on 'the generation of capitalist tenant farmers', rising investment in technical improvements and production for the market.[188] Six years later, in his paper to the School on Capitalism, he drew a sharp contrast between family farmers and their landlords – predominant in grassland and grass dairy regions – and the capital farmers and their landlords characteristic of the south and east. By the early seventeenth century, agrarian capitalists farmed the greater part of land in value and output.[189]

This paper received a stunningly cool reception, the scribe merely and laconically noting that in the ensuing discussion 'some doubt was thrown on the extent of capitalist farming'.[190] Yet what Kerridge offered, albeit in descriptive mode, was a picture of developing productive forces – one with which a room full of Marxists, much concerned with the revolutionary transformation of English society, should have been well content. It is possible that the inadequate summary of the discussion does not convey the sympathetic reception that he could have expected from both Dobb and Hobsbawm. Dobb certainly shared Kerridge's view that capitalist farming was associated with 'improved farming', bringing with it 'important changes in productive methods in agriculture, and ... increase of productivity (both of labour and per acre of land)'.[191] Hobsbawm, in opening the 1954 School, stated that, together with the rise of wage labour, production for the markets and the use of technically progressive agricultural methods were the 'three essentials of capitalist farming'.[192]

It is also clear, however, that Kerridge's relationships with some other members of the section were not entirely 'comradely', and in Hilton's case were compounded by fundamental differences about the key to understanding English economic development in the early modern period. On receiving a draft of Kerridge's 1948 paper, Hilton wrote a sharply worded letter stating that Kerridge was no help in understanding rural capitalism and insisting that the first requirement was to deal with the question of wage labour:

> someone ought to show how and to what extent the exploitation in the countryside ceases to be by the extraction of feudal rent and becomes instead the extraction of surplus value. And if this is not the determining factor in rural capitalism I would like to know what is.[193]

Kerridge, evidently appraised of this criticism, pointed out in his paper that it was not possible to measure agrarian capitalism by the size of the proletariat, given the difficulties in identifying agricultural labourers from the available sources. Five years later, no doubt having received a copy of Kerridge's forthcoming paper for the School on Capitalism, Hilton wrote again to Merson, insisting that the main area requiring investigation was the management of their Estates by nobility and gentry, 'not the big peasants'. 'The big question' was still: 'to what extent were the gentry and nobility using wage labour and selling on the market and to what extent a forward policy on leases and rents'.[194] This was a direct attack on Kerridge's view that 'farmers rather than landlords were the key people and it is confusing to talk of the gentry... a generic term applied to those who did no manual work and whether they were forward or backward depended on the region and the farmers'. It was all the more surprising given that Hilton himself saw the stratification of the peasantry as the 'essential precondition for the growth of the rural bourgeoisie'.[195]

Ironically, it was Kerridge who went on to furnish the material necessary for an effective synthesis which could assimilate

Hilton's view of the stratification of the peasantry in the later middle ages into subsequent developments. Within fifteen years he published two works which shook the conventional wisdom about English agrarian history. The first, in 1967, argued that an early 'agricultural revolution' occurred in the century from 1560. This was certainly controversial and has remained so until this day.[196] Yet despite the over-estimation of the part played by costly technical innovations (enclosing, convertible husbandry and the floating of water meadows), Kerridge's picture of agricultural progress helps to explain England's increasing prosperity in the seventeenth century. The undoubted growth in agricultural yields and regional specialisation was critical to the sustenance of a buoyant and increasingly urbanised population, and thus to the development of a self sustaining home market, without which capitalism had no future.[197]

Kerridge's next book, published in 1969, was even more iconoclastic, amounting to a long contemplated frontal attack on the assumption bequeathed by Tawney that the English peasantry were by and large helpless victims of 'a relentless and remorseless agrarian capitalism'.[198] In this work Kerridge argued that copyholders (technically those whose title was recorded in the manorial rolls) and not just freeholders benefited from substantial security of tenure by virtue of the common law. A considerable body of work has since confirmed the capacity of tenants, frequently with the support of the royal courts, to resist efforts by their lords to increase rents or adversely change the nature of their leases. Whilst the most advanced agricultural regions did experience two waves of depopulating enclosure (1450-1524 and 1575-1674), this was not the prime route to capitalism. Even in such regions as Norfolk, where Merson's perception of the widening gulf between yeomen and smallholders has been well sustained, the emergence of a totally landless force of wage labourers was a protracted business, not complete until the eighteenth century. Despite Robert Brenner's persistent rejection of the argument that the transition to agrarian capitalism in England came through the differentiation of the peasantry and his insistence that the market economy was forced on peasants by their Lords, modern scholarship has largely disagreed.[199] On the contrary, the precocious development of English capitalism may in large part be attributed to the presence of a class of lightly taxed and secure prosperous small capitalist farmers, farming 50-70 acres, who with their families constituted 12 to 15 per cent of the population.[200] Many of the yeomen who emerged from the ranks of the peasantry joined the expanding ranks of resident gentry, precisely as Dobb suggested.

Although Kerridge's attack on Tawney was in some ways overdone, it did mean that he freed himself from the idea that agrarian capitalism flowed primarily from the activities of the larger landlords. As we have seen even Hilton thought the prime focus should be the gentry. This was also largely true of Hill, whose treatment of the economic role of the yeomanry was inconsistent, drawing attention to it in 1940 but belittling it seven years later in his review of Dobb's *Studies*. His sole reservation about Dobb's work was that he 'underestimated the importance of the gentry in the development of English capitalism', a remark juxtaposed with a reference to the limited numbers of 'lucky' yeomen, 'independent small producers about whom bourgeois historians make such a song and dance'.[201] In later years Hill, despite according a large place to the 'middling sort' in his discussion of religion, culture and politics, did not pay much attention to their contribution to economic development. Kiernan, reviewing the *Century of Revolution* in 1953, thought that Hill, 'through keeping his eye too closely on his landlords, has not taken sufficient notice of the new-style *farmer*, as the humble but really "progressive" and transforming agent in English agriculture'. This was connected with a tendency to treat the commoners prior to 1640 as 'more or less passive victims of oppression' who then 'start to life abruptly, angry and clamorous'.[202]

Running through the whole of Hill's work is the idea that there were two revolutions: that of the bourgeois gentry which succeeded, and a popular revolution which aimed at turning the world upside down and which failed. It is undeniable that this insight has led to some of Hill's most impressive writing. Yet the application of the same idea to economic development has resulted in some significant and persistent oversimplifications. In one of his last essays he restated his long held view that the key moment in the establishment of absolute property rights came in 1646 with the abolition of Wardship and the transformation of feudal tenures into freehold, thus ending the situation in which the patrimony of the great landowners could revert to the Crown for up to twenty-one years in the event of a minor heir.[203] On the other hand, despite pressure from the Levellers, the copyholders failed to secure the same status for what Hill describes as their 'servile tenure', thus opening the way for their eviction as and when required. The abolition of feudal tenures was the basis for the agricultural revolution of the later seventeenth and eighteenth centuries. This argument not only fails to recognise the degree of security achieved by copyholders and their contribution to the agricultural progress already in train; it also vastly oversimplifies the processes which led to their ultimate expropriation. Indeed, as Thompson had privately but pointedly reminded Hill twenty years earlier, 'it was a hundred years before massive enclosure was the order of the day', notwithstanding the difficulties suffered by the small landowner in an era of low prices and the attendant shift towards larger landed estates.[204] Whether the heyday of the yeomanry could have been prolonged had the Levellers' demands been implemented is a moot point.[205] Be that as it may, Hill's preoccupation with the losers reduced his grasp of the contribution made by the upper echelons of the English peasantry to an increasingly prosperous commercialised society – a society over which the Stuarts had less and less control. There is thus a striking disjunction between his recognition of the political weight of the middling groups during the revolutionary years and his underestimation of their economic importance. It is all the more surprising given his insistence on seeing society as a whole, on establishing 'connections', and his undeviating wish to demonstrate that in the final analysis the Revolution was caused by economic developments which could not be absorbed within the old regime.

IN RETROSPECT

The criticisms which may be properly levelled at Hill's work are thus not those which have generally been made. It is not true that his interest in ideas came late, still less to replace an earlier model of revolution. Nor is there any justification for the argument that he significantly changed his view of the class basis of the revolution. From the outset he emphasised the peculiarly rural nature of British capitalism, which led to a division within the ruling class. Mary Fulbrook is quite mistaken in her contention that this was an idea to which he turned later. As early as 1940 he had noted the divisions between 'progressive' and 'unprogressive' gentry, particularly in face of popular unrest, and by 1955 his early formulations were tidied up into the unambiguous statement that 'the landed class was divided'.[206] The gentry were not belatedly summoned up as a surrogate bourgeoisie; they were there from the beginning. Arguably, Hill later conceded too much by modifying his vocabulary to accommodate the inability of some critics to describe anything other than a town dweller as bourgeois, or to see that a bourgeois landed class had indeed come into being. Whether or not the transfer of power to this class was accomplished in a single movement during the 1640s is another matter. But this was the guts of Hill's conception and it was with justice that he claimed he had stuck to it throughout his career.

Machlachlan's accusation that Hill began with a specifically Leninist, indeed Stalinist, conception of Revolution is unsustainable. Most of the references made by the section to Stalin were superfluous, as he only pointed them back to Marx. The reading list for the sessions on ideology found a place for Stalin's *Dialectical and Historical Materialism*, but there is no evidence that anyone had digested it. The rest of the reading matter was a conventional collection of secondary works, whilst Hill and Clark threw in the works of Luther and Calvin for good measure.[207] If Lenin's influence can be detected anywhere it was in the discussion on the peasantry. Here the term 'kulak' was mostly preferred to that of 'yeoman', testimony to the use of Lenin's *Development of Capitalism in Russia* as a paradigm for sixteenth century England. As far as the related questions of the state and the English Revolution were concerned, the view defended by both Hill and Dona Torr came straight from the pages of Marx and Engels, with virtually no reference to the Soviet gurus.[208] The key texts for everybody were *The Preface to the Critique of Political Economy*, together with the glosses contained in Engels's later correspondence, which reminded them of the need to use the base-superstructure model in a non-reductive way. From the *Preface* Hill also drew his general conception of 'total revolution', in which all the inter-connected parts of society were transformed. If he unwisely quoted Stalin's view that 'the history of society, because of the interdependence of its parts, can become a science as say biology…', this assimilation of history to the natural sciences, which was not in any event confined to Marxists, was without consequence.[209] It was Engels who provided the point of departure for the debates on the Tudor state and the Reformation. Hill appealed to Lenin on only one occasion and this was precisely to emphasise that whereas a bourgeois revolution has 'ready at hand the forms of capitalist relationships', a socialist one 'does not inherit ready-made relationships'.[210] It is true that others, completely missing Lenin's point, did endeavour to transfer his insistence on the need to smash the twentieth century state to the seventeenth century. But it required more than a little historical ingenuity to maintain that this was what occurred. Hyme Fagan was only able to do so by excluding parliament from his definition of the state.[211] The section's view of the transformation of the monarchical state was never so crude. Ironically, had Lenin been a critical point of reference, Kiernan rather than Hill could have found succour in his rather obscure analogy of bourgeois revolution with successive 'waves', each of which may batter the old regime without entirely destroying it.[212]

What was striking about the 'victory' proclaimed by Torr was that it was not the result of any line imposed by higher authority. On the contrary she, Garman and Hill had to battle for their view that the English Civil War amounted to a bourgeois revolution against Palme Dutt, chief guardian of orthodoxy. He probably never forgave them, provoking more irritation some years later when he used a review in *Labour Monthly* to express the wish that 'some of our Marxist historians' might have been 'lured from the recesses of the seventeenth-century, [and] the peasants' revolt...'[213] One wonders what he thought of those distinguished Soviet historians who lurked in these same recesses and did have an influence on members of the section. Foremost perhaps was the medievalist Kosminsky, whose work on England influenced both Dobb and Hilton, particularly in relation to the differentiation of the peasantry and on the nature of feudal rent.[214] Hill's view of the revolutionary significance of the agrarian legislation of the interregnum similarly owed much to the inspiration of Arkhangelsky.[215]

If there was a moment at which Soviet 'authority' was deployed in an ideological fashion, it was when Hill and Pearce provided the group with a resumé of the Pokrovsky controversy, which led to the formal rejection in the Soviet Union of his view of the transformation of feudalism and the feudal state by merchant capital.[216] Although the resumé was itself written in fairly detached academic style, Hill used it to berate Kiernan about the dangers of gradualism and reformism. It is however also worth remarking that the accompanying background piece summarising the discussions of absolutism amongst leading Soviet historians in 1940 reveals much less agreement. They certainly did not lend unqualified support to the view presented by Hill and Andrews that absolute monarchy was a response to the pressure of the peasantry. 'The historical facts', they noted, 'do not confirm the view that the prerequisites for the rise of Absolutism must be sought exclusively in the strengthening of the popular anti-Feudal movement for the suppression of which a new form of the Feudal state was necessary'. Moreover English Absolutism was 'a very serious and interesting problem', with some Soviet historians denying its existence. 'Class differentiation proceeded at the social basis of English absolutism itself. This, of course, could not but be reflected in the fate of English absolutism'.[217]

The failure of the section to produce an enduring conceptual framework for the Tudor state, passing far too readily over the insights provided by Morton, may in part be attributed to Hill's political assumptions and his antipathy to any suggestion that English developments were in some way exceptional. No doubt, he was not in the business of replacing a Whig version of English precociousness with a Marxist one. Limited knowledge of European state formation did not help; despite Pearce's exhortation about the 'the importance of first understanding continental absolutism', the proposed discussion was pre-empted by that on the Reformation.[218] In addition, the section was undoubtedly confused, as others have been, by the uneasy, not entirely consistent, formulations of Marx and Engels that placed absolute monarchy somewhere on the road to capitalism. These have impeded recognition of the fact that absolutism was essentially a product of the combined pressures of warfare conducted on an unprecedented scale and the internal contradictions of unstable feudal regimes. It was, as Kiernan – the only participant to return to the issue – came to realise, a device for saving the feudal nobility from themselves. Where capitalism was most advanced and precluded this possibility there was no absolutism.[219]

Hill's opening theses on the Tudor state themselves pointed to this conclusion. What prevented him seeing it was not simply the conviction that the bourgeois revolution was yet to come or even the idea, absorbed from Engels, that absolute monarchy was the typical final phase of feudalism. It was perfectly possible, as Hill learnt, to dispense with a Tudor absolutism whilst retaining the bourgeois revolution. What really underlay the inability to resolve these issues more speedily was a failure to apply Engels's observations about the relative autonomy of the superstructure to the question of the state. It was certainly understood that the consciousness of human beings could not be reduced to economics. This made both for fruitful discussions of ideology and of the part ideas played in political change; but the section as a whole was a long way from analysing the functions, mechanisms and policies of the existing state with a sense of their relative autonomy in mind. The preconception that the state was simply an instrument in the hands of the dominant class helps to explain why these were explored in fairly superficial fashion. Olwen Stocker's short paper on the law was the only one devoted to a specific aspect of state activity, but her observation that the head of the judiciary might take decisions favourable to the bourgeoisie immediately opens up a more subtle perspective. It has been amply confirmed by the later work of Kerridge and others, which showed that royal law courts regularly upheld the proprietory rights of copyholding tenants against the claims of their lords. In later years Hilton also came round to Kiernan's view of manorial jurisdiction and abandoned his insistence on their continuing importance for the subordination of the peasantry and the extraction of feudal rent. Indeed it could, he concluded, have been the relative weakness of the English manor, when compared with the resilience of the French *seigneurie*, which hastened the end of feudalism in England and helped the aspiring yeomen to transform his relationship with his lord.[220] All of which must have steadily reinforced the belief in the sanctity of private property, to which Morton had alluded, thus contributing to the hollowing out of the feudal regime and further accentuating the distinctiveness of English developments. In other words, the institutions of the English state were in some ways conducive to capitalist development, which was in considerable part driven by a lightly burdened and relatively secure stratum of 'kulaks'.

Hill may have taken Stocker's observations about the law and Chief Justice Coke to heart, as her paper, despite the fact that it was never discussed, was one of the few which he retained in his personal archives. In any event in the mid 1960s Coke assumed a central role in his wide-ranging analysis of the intellectual origins of the Revolution. What is surprising (although characteristic of his empirical style) is that at this point Hill did not summon up some analytical assistance from Gramsci, whose ideas were in the air and whom he had acclaimed in 1957 as possibly 'the greatest Marxist thinker since Lenin'.[221] They would certainly have helped to conceptualise the process whereby eminent members of the governing class became the 'organic intellectuals' of the bourgeoisie. In the same breath this would have also sharpened up his views of the division in the ruling class, and considerably eased the problem of defining the bourgeoisie. Hill was to claim, many years later, that members of the history group arrived independently at some of the ideas presented by Gramsci, whilst Hobsbawm asserted that had Gramsci not invented the term hegemony 'we would have called it something else'. Nevertheless, when Harvey Kaye overdid the Gramscian affinities of the British Marxists, Hill felt it necessary to recall, quite correctly, that the section had never considered them.[222]

It is of course easy in hindsight, with the benefit of a further half-century of historical and Marxist scholarship, to point out how the deliberations of the section might have been enriched. Yet its great achievement was not simply to reshape much of the historical agenda but precisely to provide an enduring platform for Marxist history, which made possible its continued development and refinement. The British Marxists were not imprisoned in a straitjacket – either economistic or Stalinist – from which they later escaped. If, like most historians, their work became better and more rounded as they grew older, this had nothing to do with abandoning the concept of base and superstructure, which was in any case a starting point and not a worked out view of history. Their persistent disagreements make this clear if nothing else. The one area in which early views really fell apart and rapidly disappeared was the characterisation of the Tudor monarchy as absolute. But not everyone had really gone along with that; Kiernan's scepticism was more than justified and Morton had offered a more enduring picture.

It was, however, Mervyn James who, from the 1970s, showed the way to a more complete picture of the processes at work within the Tudor polity, with his depiction of slow but steady transformation of the culture and values of the still conservative Tudor ruling class; the great household bounded by particularist values rooted in lordship, fidelity and service slowly gave way to a world in which domesticity, privacy, education, civic humanism counted for more. Whilst notions of gentility endured, the commercialisation of rural life brought in its wake a new possessive individualism. The politics of honour which characterised upper class dissidence also gave way by the 1640s to a politics of principle and ideological commitment, creating the conditions for the Civil War. In all of this there is not a whiff of Marx or Engels, let alone Gramsci. James discarded the term 'ideology', preferring a very occasional use of the Annaliste 'mentalité', but writing largely in the 'quaintly empirical style' alluded to by Thompson.[223]

It is nonetheless tempting to see in James's concern with social totality and the stress on ideas, as both social cement and solvent, the influence of former comradely discussions, and an approach of which Thompson would surely have approved. For all that Thompson was never an active member of the group and most distanced himself from the Communist Party, he went out of his way, in the midst of his pugnacious onslaught on Stalinism, Perry Anderson, the Althusserians and 'the incomprehensible philosophers of the Left Bank of the Seine, the Cartesian Well', to say this:

> Marxist historiography was never, in Britain, deformed beyond recovery, even when failing to make a clear intellectual dissent from Stalinism. We had, after all, the living line of Marx's analysis of British history – in Capital, in Marx and Engels's correspondence, continually present to us. To work as a Marxist historian in Britain means to work within a tradition founded by Marx, enriched by independent and complementary insights by William Morris, enlarged in recent times in specialist ways by such men and women as V. Gordon Childe, Maurice Dobb, Dona Torr and

George Thomson, and to have as colleagues such scholars as Christopher Hill, Rodney Hilton, Eric Hobsbawm, V. G. Kiernan ... I think it even possible that the English tradition of Marxist historiography may be able to stand comparison with that of any other.[224]

NOTES

1. Christopher Hill, 'Foreword' to Harvey J. Kaye, *The Education of Desire*, London 1992, pix.
2. In what follows 'Group' refers to the overall organisation and 'section' to its 16th/17th century component. See appendix 1 for a summary of the group's organisation.
3. Hill to Dobb, 8 October 1946, Dobb Papers CA 79(3). The group made numerous suggestions for the revision of Morton's text but only those from Hill survive. LHASC, CP/Cent/Cult//08/02.
4. Cited by Kaye, *Education of Desire*, p71.
5. For a full list with biographical and professional details and principal publications see appendix 4.
6. Revised in 1962, reprinted twenty five times by 1994, translated into several foreign languages.
7. See below pp00-00.
8. Doc 13, p00. Kiernan apparently wrote a 200,000 word MS on Shakespeare whilst a fellow of Trinity College Cambridge 1946-9; Kaye, *Education of Desire*, p69.
9. 'Notes on the Peasantry and State in the North during the 16th Century', LHASC, CP/Cent/Cult//08/03.
10. William Wallace, Review of *English Privateering Voyages to the West Indies, 1588-95*, in *The William and Mary Quarterly*, 3rd Ser., Vol. 17, No. 2 (Apr., 1960), pp269-270; cf. K. Andrews, 'Overseas Trade and Colonial Exploitation' (The Rise and Decline of Capitalism in Britain. Abstract of Papers 1954, hereafter 'School on Capitalism'), LHASC, CP/Cent/Cult/10/01.
11. C. Hill, 'Problems of the Bourgeois Revolution', 'School on Capitalism'.
12. See C. Hill, 'William Harvey and the Idea of Monarchy', *Past & Present* 27, 1964, pp27-54 and the ensuing debate in nos. 28-31.
13. The resulting articles were published in book form: T.H. Aston (ed), *Crisis in Europe, 1560-1660: essays from 'Past and present'*, London 1965; for anticipations of Hobsbawm's article: 'Minutes of

the 16th-17th century section 22-3 March 1952', Brian Pearce Papers; 'The general law of Capitalist Development in Britain', 'School on Capitalism'.

14. E.P. Thompson, 'An Open Letter to Leszek Kolakowski', 1973, in idem, *The Poverty of Theory*, London 1978, p124.
15. Group Minutes 17 May 1953 (ref. from Anthony Howe); Meeting of Professional Historians, 25 September 1953, LAHSC CP/Cent/Cult/7/ 9.
16. D. Parker, 'The Communist Party and its Historians 1946-89', *Socialist History*, 12, p48; Burns was a member of the Political Committee, propaganda chief and theoretician.
17. LASC CP Cent/Cult/09/07.
18. See appendix 2, Supplementary Documents.
19. 'Notes for Discussion on Classical Antiquity and the Emergence of Feudalism', University College London, Special Collections, Morris Papers 6.
20. Balliol College Library, Hill Papers Box VI.
21. C. Hill, 'The English Civil War Interpreted by Marx and Engels', *Science and Society*, 12, 1948, pp130-56.
22. E. Hobsbawm, 'Karl Marx's Contribution to Historiography', in R. Blackburn (ed.), *Ideology in Social Science*, London 1973, p273; 'Marx and History' (1983) in *On History*, New York 1997, p163.
23. 'Notes on Marxism in 1968', *The Socialist Register*, 1968; 'Revolution' in *History Classes and Nation-States: Selected writings of V.G. Kiernan*, Oxford 1988, pp199-231 (first published in 1979 and 'postscript' added in 1988); see also 'Problems of Marxist History', *New Left Review* 161, 1987, pp105-118
24. G. Rude, 'Marxism and History', in *The face of the crowd: studies in revolution, ideology and popular protest*, ed Harvey J. Kaye, New York & London 1988, p54.
25. Hobsbawm, 'Karl Marx's Contribution to Historiography'.
26. 'Marx and History', pp169 & 170.
27. www.londonsocialisthistorians.org/messageboard/archive/index.php?t-3.html 10/09/2005.
28. Parker, 'The Communist Party and its Historians 1946-89', pp48-9.
29. H.J. Kaye, *The British Marxist Historians*, Cambridge 1984, p129.
30. Kaye, *The Education of Desire*, p100.
31. M. Fulbrook, 'Christopher Hill and Historical Sociology', in G. Eley and W. Hunt, *Reviving the English revolution: reflections and elaborations on the work of Christopher Hill*, London 1988, p36.

32. A. Machlachlan, *The Rise and Fall of Revolutionary England. An essay in the Fabrication of Revolutionary England*, London 1996, p59.
33. *Ibid*, p121.
34. *Ibid*, p127.
35. *Ibid*, p252.
36. *New York Times*, obituary, 23.2.02.
37. David Underdown, 'Puritanism, Revolution and Christopher Hill', in Eley & Hunt, *Reviving the English revolution*, p336; C. Hill, 'A bourgeois Revolution', in J.C.A. Pocock, *Three British Revolutions*, London 1980, p132.
38. K. Tribe, *Genealogies of Capitalism*, London 1981, p5.
39. Kaye, *Education of Desire*, pp103-4.
40. Hobsbawm, 'Marx and History', p169.
41. V.G. J. Kiernan, 'Notes on Marxism', *Socialist Register* 1968, p169.
42. *Ibid*, p189.
43. V.G.J. Kiernan, 'Problems of Marxist History', pp108, 110.
44. *Ibid*, p107.
45. Kiernan, 'Problems of Marxist History', p110; David Parker, 'French Absolutism, the English state and the Utility of the Base-Superstructure Model', *Social History*, 15 1990, pp293-4.
46. Rodney Hilton, 'A Crisis of Feudalism', *Past and Present*, No. 80 1978, pp4-5, 13.
47. Rodney Hilton, 'Feudalism in Europe: Problems for Historical Materialists', *New Left Review*, 147 1985, pp86, 93.
48. C. Hill. 'Problems of the Bourgeois Revolution', 'School on Capitalism'.
49. C. Hill, *Change and Continuity in 17th Century England*, Newhaven & London 1991 (revised ed), p281. Hill deliberately left the concluding chapter from which this statement is drawn as it was when written in 1974, Preface p ix; P. Corfield, '"We are All One in the Eyes of the Lord": Christopher Hill and the Historical Meanings of Radical Religion', *History Workshop Journal* 58 2004, p121.
50. Hill, Hilton, Hobsbawm, Morton and Rudé.
51. Kaye, *Education of Desire*, p33.
52. Appendix 2 History From Below.
53. Brian Manning, *The English People and the English Revolution*, London 1976; for a complete list of Manning's publications and summary of their significance see Paul Blackledge, 'Historian of

the People and the English Revolution', *Historical Materialism*, volume 13:3 2005, pp219–228.

54. C. Hill, *Some Intellectual Consequences of the English Revolution*, Princeton 1980, p6.
55. *The Listener*, 10.8.67, p172; 'Partial historians and total history', *Times Literary Supplement*, 24.11.72, pp1431-2; 'Premature Obsequies', *History Today*, April 1991, pp44-7.
56. C. Hill, Review of Schlatter, The Social Ideas of Religious Leaders 1660-1688, Oxford 1940, in *Economic History Review*, Feb 1940, p165.
57. C. Hill, *The English Revolution*, London 1940, pp81-2.
58. C. Hill, *Ideas and the State 1660-1760*, 'School on Capitalism'.
59. Doc 18, Minutes of 23-24 September 1950; see below p27.
60. *Modern Quarterly*, 4, ii 1949.
61. C. Hill, 'Historians and the Rise of Capitalism', *Science and Society*, 14 1950, p317.
62. Appendix 4, Kiernan; Kaye, *Education of Desire*, p186 n 6.
63. Appendix 4, Lindsay, Pascal.
64. E.P. Thompson, *William Morris: Romantic to Revolutionary*, London 1955, p8.
65. Anthony Howe, 'Donna Torr', *Dictionary of Labour Biography* Vol. 12 2005, pp275-81.
66. David Renton, 'Opening the Books: the Personal Papers of Dona Torr', *History Workshop Journal* 52, 2001, p243.
67. For West's letters to Garman 1948-69 (though unfortunately not Garman's to West), University of Nottingham, special collections DG2/1-142.
68. C. Hill, 'Marx's Virtues', *The Listener*, 10.8.67, p172; P. Corfield, '"We are All One in the Eyes of the Lord"...', p116.
69. C. Hill, *Intellectual Origins of the English Revolution*, Oxford 1965, preface p x. Mason similarly acknowledged his own debt to Hill in *History of the Sciences*, 1962 ed., p8.
70. Hill, *Intellectual Origins*, pp66, 101, 114; cf. App XX and also Mason, 'The Scientific Revolution and the Protestant Reformation', *Annals of Science* 9 1953, pp 77-8; 'Some roots of the Scientific Revolution', *Science and Society* 1950, p242; 'The influence of the English Revolution on the development of modern science', *Modern Quarterly* 4, 1949.
71. Hill, 'William Harvey', p55, n5; cf Mason, 'Science and Religion in Seventeenth-Century England', *Past & Present* 1953, 3 pp28-34.

72. C. Hill, 'Stalin and the Science of History', *Modern Quarterly* 8, 1952-3, pp198-212, p211.
73. C. Hill, *England's Turning Point. Essays on Seventeenth-Century English History*, London & Chicago 1998, p9.
74. C. Hill, 'History and the Class Struggle', Review of W. Schenck, *The Concern for Social Justice in the Puritan Revolution*, London 1948, and M. A. Gibbs, *John Lilburne, the Leveller: a Christian democrat*, London 1947), in *Communist Review*, March 1949, p480.
75. Doc 22, p187; for Hill's nonconformist upbringing and outlook, Corfield '"We are All One in the Eyes of the Lord"...'.
76. E. J. Hobsbawm, 'British History and the *Annales*: A Note', in *On History*, p183.
77. Diane St John to Brian Pearce, 8 April 1954, Brian Pearce Papers.
78. Doc 17; Doc 24, pp220-1; Dobb was not present at the second session and the lack of minutes for the first session in September 1949 means that it is impossible to know whether he was there to introduce his paper.
79. D. Torr, 'Productive Forces: Social Relations', *Communist Review*, May 1946, p11; Hill interview with Anthony Howe.
80. Hill, 'Stalin and the Science of History', p199.
81. K.R.* Andrews, 'Marxism and the Role of Ideology' (from Anthony Howe).
82. For a most striking illustration of this perception see D. Glezerman, 'Base and Superstructure', *Communist Review*, January 1950. He appeals to Stalin against those like Bernstein who looked on 'social development as a fatalistic, automatic, pre-determined, spontaneous process' in which they 'underestimated the role of new ideas and new political institutions...', p27.
83. Anthony Howe interviews with John Saville and Eric Hobsbawm.
84. V.G. Kiernan, 'History' in Harvey J. Kaye (ed.) *History, Classes and Nation States. Selected Writings of V.G. Kiernan*, London 1989, p50, pp29-65; see also Hobsbawm, 'Marx and History', p162.
85. Engels to Bloch, 22 September 1890, cited in C. Hill, 'Marxism and History', *The Modern Quarterly* 3 ii, 1948, p54.
86. *Ibid*, pp54-5.
87. *Ibid*, p62.
88. E.P. Thompson, *The Making of the English Working Class*, London 1964, pp9-10.
89. Doc 18, p158.

90. Doc 24, p220; W. Joseph, 'Draft Theses: Capitalism, Science and Ideology', Brian Pearce Papers.
91. Doc 20, p171; cf. Mason *History of the Sciences*, chs. 13-1.
92. Doc 18, p158.
93. Appendix 3, n6; above p24.
94. Frederick Engels, *Socialism: Utopian and Scientific*, 1892 English Edition Introduction, Volume 27 *Collected Works Marx and Engels*, Lawrence & Wishart 1990, pp290-1.
95. Doc. 21, p176 & Doc. 22; cf. Frederick Engels, 'Ludwig Feuerbach and the End of Classical German Philosophy', Part 4, Volume 26 *Collected Works Marx and Engels*, Lawrence & Wishart 1990, p396.
96. Doc 24, p221.
97. Doc 22, p189; Doc 24, pp221-3.
98. Doc 23, pp212.
99. Doc 26; cf. David Parker, *La Rochelle and the French Monarchy*, London 1980; 'The Huguenots in Seventeenth Century France', *Minorities in History*, ed A.C. Hepburn, Edward Arnold 1978, pp2-30; 'The Social Foundation of French Absolutism 1610-30', *Past and Present* 53 1971, pp67-89.
100. Agenda/Note from Ken Andrews, 8 March 1952 (provided by Anthony Howe).
101. See C. Hill, 'Puritans and the Poor', *Past & Present* 2 (1952), pp32-50; communications from V. Kiernan & C. Hill, *Past and Present*, No. 3, 1953, pp45-54.
102. C. Hill, 'Protestantism and the Rise of Capitalism', in *Essays in the Economic and Social History of Tudor and Stuart England in Honour of R.H. Tawney*, ed. F.J. Fisher, Cambridge 1961, repr. in *Change and Continuity*, p99.
103. C. Hill, *Society and Puritanism in Pre-Revolutionary England*, London 1964.
104. A.L. Morton, *A People's History of England*, London 1938, p222.
105. Doc 22, p184.
106. Doc 23, p202.
107. C. Hill, 'Land in the English Revolution', *Science and Society* 1948-9, pp22-49, pp33, 30, 22.
108. C. Hill, 'A bourgeois Revolution', in *Three British revolutions: 1641, 1688, 1776*, ed J.G.A. Pocock, Princeton, c1980, p130; Thompson to Hill, 14 July 1977, Balliol College, Hill Papers Box 4. Amazingly, Thompson cautioned Hill against using Engels's letter on the grounds that it had been 'savaged by Althusser'.

109. Doc 25, p225.
110. Doc 18, p163; Doc 19, p165; Doc 24, p224.
111. G. Thomson, 'Basis and Ideology', *Communist Review*, June 1952, p246.
112. C. Hill, *The English Revolution*, p80.
113. German communist, labour and economic historian, who came to Britain in 1936. After the war he became Professor at Humboldt University.
114. 'England's Revolution', *Labour Monthly*, October 1940, pp558-9; cf. Hill, *English Revolution*, p25.
115. Notably contributions from D. Garman, *Labour Monthly* Dec 1940, pp651-653; D. Torr, *Labour Monthly* Feb 1941, pp90-3 and unsigned MS, 'Some Comments on the Present Controversy', LHASC CP/Ind/Dutt/08/08.
116. 'A Rejoinder', *Labour Monthly*, Dec 1940, p654.
117. 'Amended Draft Put in By R. Palme Dutt', LHASC CP/Ind/Dutt/08/08; see also Hill, 'Remarks on R.P.D.'s Draft' and the unattributed 'Proposed Amendments to L.M. Document'. The private exchanges were clearly very hard hitting with Dutt being criticised for his ex-cathedra use of quotations from Marx and Engels, his inadequate bibliography, as well as his inflexibility.
118. Doc 2, p78.
119. Doc13, p126.
120. Doc 2, p77.
121. Doc 14, p129.
122. Doc 13, p124.
123. Doc 5, p92.
124. Doc 5, p95.
125. Doc 10, p110.
126. Doc 13, p126.
127. Doc 12, p119.
128. Morton, A *People's History*, pp220-2.
129. Doc 12, p113.
130. Doc 12, p114; cf. 'Merchants' capital, like some parasitic growth, was gradually sapping away the power of the monarchy, thriving upon the rot it helped to spread.' *Elizabethan Privateering: English Privateering daring the Spanish War, 1585-1603*, Cambridge 1964, p238.
131. Doc 13, p122.
132. Doc 13, p125.

133. See Docs 8 & 9.
134. Paul Sweezy, 'A Critique', and M. Dobb, 'A Reply', *Science and Society*, Spring 1950; the first set of essays that this provoked were republished with supplementary material in R. Hilton (ed), *The Transition From Feudalism to Capitalism*, London 1978. By this time the debate had been renewed and extended in the pages of *Past & Present* with the publication of R. Brenner's article 'Agrarian Class Structure and Economic Development in Pre-Industrial Europe' (1976). The contributions were gathered together in T.H. Aston & C.H.E. Philpin, *The Brenner Debate*, Cambridge 1985. Allan Merson's brief but percipient comments on London Merchants in 'The Revolution and the British Empire', *The Modern Quarterly* 4 1949, have been fully born out by R. Brenner, *Merchants and Revolution*, Cambridge 1993; Andrews's later work, however, does show how the integrity of the Elizabethan regime was weakened by commercial interest.
135. Doc 7.
136. Doc 14, p130.
137. R. Hilton, 'Agrarian Discontent in the Later Middle Ages', LHASC, CP/Cent/Cult/08/03.
138. Doc 14, p136.
139. Doc 15, p138.
140. Torr to Brian Pearce, 14 January 1948.
141. See for instance L. Stone, 'The Bourgeois Revolution of Seventeenth-Century England Revisited', *Past and Present*, 109 1985, pp44-54.
142. *The English Revolution*, p63.
143. 'State and Revolution in Tudor and Stuart England', *Communist Review*, July 1948, pp212-3.
144. V.G. Kiernan 'State and Nation in Western Europe' *Past and Present*, 31 1965, p29.
145. Doc 23, p196.
146. The Communist Party formally adopted its new political programme, *The British Road to Socialism* in 1952 but it had been clearly prefigured in Harry Pollit's pamphlet *Looking Ahead* published in August 1947; see Willie Thompson, (2001) 'British Communists in the Cold War, 1947-52', *Contemporary British History*, 15:3, (2001) pp127-8.
147. V.G. Kiernan, *State and Society in Europe 1550-1650*, Oxford 1980, p105

148. *Ibid*, p107.
149. C. Hill, *Reformation to Industrial Revolution* London 1967, p18.
150. The literature is immense but two very thorough syntheses are P.H. Williams, *The Tudor Regime* (Oxford 1979) and Steve Hindle, *The State and Social Change in Early Modern England* (Basingstoke 2000)
151. P. Collinson, 'The monarchical republic of Queen Elizabeth I', *Bulletin of the John Rylands Library*, lxix (1987), pp394-424, reprinted in J.A. Guy, ed., *The Tudor Monarchy* (1997), pp110-34.
152. K.R. Andrews, Theses on the Relation of the Struggles of the Peasantry to the Development and Decay of Absolutism in England, LHASC, CP/Cent/Cult/08/03 4c.
153. Cf. D. Parker, *The Making of French Absolutism*, London 1983.
154. G.R. Elton, *The Tudor Revolution in Government* (1953). For a summary of his conclusions see his *England under the Tudors* (1955, 2nd ed 1974), ch. vii.
155. Williams, *The Tudor Regime*, p35.
156. *Ibid*, pp35, 37.
157. Doc12, p. 122 , Doc 14, p134; when Hill resumed this argument in print in 1953 he italicised parts of the key passage from Engels but even with this emphasis Hill's inferences remain unconvincing. C. Hill, 'A Comment' in Hilton, *The Transition from Feudalism to Capitalism*, p119.
158. C. Hill, *The English Revolution* (1955) p27; cf p38 (1940).
159. Doc 11, p111.
160. Doc 12, p113, Doc 13, p121.
161. The intended discussion was pre-empted by the extended debate on the Reformation. Minutes of discussion on the Reformation held at Garibaldi Restaurant, 23-24, Sept 1950, Provided by A. Howe; Notice of September Meeting, 9 June 1950, Allan Merson Papers.
162. M Dobb, 'A Reply' in R. Hilton (ed) *The Transition from Feudalism to Capitalism*, p63.
163. K.R. Andrews, 'Theses On the Relation of the Struggles of the Peasantry to the development and the decay of Absolutism in England' LHASC, CP/Cent/Cult/08/03.
164. A. Fletcher & D. MacCulloch, *Tudor Rebellions*, Harlow, 2004 (5th edn), p65.
165. K.R. Andrews, 'The Role of the State in England 1540-1588', 'Theses on the Struggles of the Peasantry, LHASC CP/Cent/Cult/08/03.

166. Fletcher, *Tudor Rebellions*, pp24, 135; Williams, *Tudor Regime*, p348.
167. R. B. Manning, *Village Revolts: Social Protest and Popular Disturbances in England 1509-1640*, Oxford 1988, pp55-6, Williams, *Tudor Regime*, p348.
168. Manning, *Village Revolts*, pp195, 246.
169. *Ibid*, p195.
170. *Ibid*, p178.
171. Morton, *A People's History* (1965 ed), p153.
172. M.E. James, 'Notes on the Peasantry and State in the North during the 16th Century'; Allan Merson, Untitled paper on Agrarian Relations in E. Anglia; 'A Note on the Peasant Revolts of 1548/49' all at LHASC, CP/Cent/Cult/08/03.
173. Merson, 'Agrarian Relations in E. Anglia', para 8.
174. Jane Whittle, *The development of agrarian capitalism: land and labour in Norfolk, 1440-1580*, Oxford & New York 2000, p312.
175. Fletcher, *Tudor Rebellions*, pp136-8; cf. Manning, *Village Revolts*, p65.
176. Doc 16; Doc 3, pp81-2.
177. O. Stocker, 'Law and the Revolution', Balliol College Library, Christopher Hill Papers, Box 4.
178. Kiernan to Dobb, n.d. Trinity College Library, Cambridge, Dobb papers CC4.
179. Dobb to Kiernan, 20 April 1951, Dobb papers CC4C1
180. R. Hilton, 'Agrarian Discontent in the Later Middle Ages', 2, LHASC, CP/Cent/Cult/08/03.
181. Doc 13, p123.
182. Doc 17, p155-6.
183. Andrews, 'Theses on ... the Struggles of the Peasantry'.
184. Dobb to Pearce, n.d. Dobb papers CA 172.
185. A.H. Hanson, Unpublished paper, Dobb papers CC4 (22).
186. Morton, *A People's History* (1965 ed), p165.
187. Whittle, *The development of agrarian capitalism*, p11.
188. E. Kerridge, 'Agrarian Development 1500-1640', LHASC, CP/Cent/Cult/08/03.
189. E. Kerridge, 'The Disappearance of the Peasantry', School on Capitalism (1954).
190. *Ibid*, 'The Disappearance of the Peasantry'. The brief two-sentence summary of the discussion on Kerridge's paper makes a striking contrast with the length of those arising from other papers.

191. Doc 17, p154.
192. Hobsbawm, 'The general law of Capitalist Development', School on Capitalism.
193. Hilton to Merson, May 3 1949, Merson papers.
194. Hilton to Merson, 16 June 1954, Merson papers.
195. Doc 7, p103.
196. E. Kerridge, *The Agricultural Revolution*, London 1967; for a recent critique see M. Overton, *Agricultural Revolution in England. The Transformation of the agrarian economy*, Cambridge, 1996
197. For an expansion of this argument and references see D. Parker, *State and Class in Ancien Regime France. The Road to Modernity?* London 1996, pp223-38.
198. E. Kerridge, *Agrarian Problems in the Sixteenth Century and After*, London 1969, p15; Kerridge wrote to Merson on 11 May 1954 indicating that he was planning a work which would supersede Tawney and others, Allan Merson papers.
199. R. Brenner, 'The Low Countries in the Transition to Capitalism'. *Journal of Agrarian Change*, 1 (2) (2001) pp169–242; T. J Byres, 'Differentiation of the Peasantry Under Feudalism and the Transition to Capitalism: In Defence of Rodney Hilton', *Journal of Agrarian Change*, 16 (1) (2006) pp17-78.
200. Parker, *State and Class in Ancien Regime France*, p236; to the references given there should be added Whittle, *The development of agrarian capitalism*, esp chapter 4 which deals with social differentiation; and R.C. Allen, *Enclosure and the Yeoman: The Agricultural Development of the South Midlands*, Oxford 1992
201. C Hill, Review of Studies in the Dev of Capitalism, *Modern Quarterly*, 2 no 3, (1947) pp 271-2.
202. Victor Kiernan, 'Review of *Century of Revolution*', *New Left Review* (September-October 1961), pp65, 62-66.
203. C. Hill, 'Feudal Tenures' in *idem*, *Intellectual Origins of the English Revolution Revisited,* Oxford 1997, pp318-326.
204. Thompson to Hill, 14 July 1977, Balliol College Library, Hill Papers Box 4.
205. Cf. Allen, *Enclosure and the Yeoman*, p77.
206. Hill, *The English Revolution*, London (1965 ed), p55.
207. Booklist for Conference on the Role of Ideology in the 17th Century', Brian Pearce Papers; Doc 122, p182.
208. For Torr's contribution to the 1940 debate see *Communist Review* (Feb 1941) pp90-3.

209. Hill, 'Stalin and the Science of History', p199.
210. Doc 14, p00.
211. H. Fagan, 'The English Revolution. Notes for Lectures & Classes', Educ. Dept LHASC CP/Cent/ Cult/ 8/03.
212. Lenin, 'The "Platform" of the Adherents and Defenders of Otzovism', (1910), www.marxists.org /archive/lenin/works. My thanks to Brian Pearce for this reference.
213. Secretary of the History Group to John Gollan, 13 October 1958, LASC CP\IND\Dutt\14\02.
214. For the influence of Kosminsky and a bibliography of his writing see Byres, 'Differentiation of the Peasantry Under Feudalism', pp17-68.
215. In 1947 Hill apparently revised and edited an English translation of Arkhangelsky's, *Agrarian Legislation of the English Revolution* (1935) and deposited the MS in the Bodleian library, presumably for want of a publisher. See also C. Hill, 'Soviet Interpretations of the English Interregnum', *Economic History Review* 8, (1938), pp165-6.
216. C. Hill & B Pearce, 'The Pokrovsky Controversy', LHASC, CP/Cent/Cult/08/03.
217. Doc 4, pp87, 90.
218. Doc 12, p117.
219. For an expansion of this view see Parker, *State and Class in Ancien Regime France*; and for a shorter but European wide development of the same argument, 'Absolutism', *Encyclopaedia of European Social History*, ed. Peter N. Stearns, New York, 2001, vol. 2, pp439-448.
220. 'Féodalité and Seigneurie', in R. Hilton, *Class Conflict and the Crisis of Feudalism*, London 1985, p238, first published in *Britain and France: ten centuries*, edited Douglas Johnson, François Crouzet and François Bédarida, Folkestone 1980, pp39-50.
221. C. Hill, 'Review of the *Modern Prince and Other writings* trans by Dr Louis Marks', *New Reasoner* 1 (4) (1958), p107.
222. Kaye, *The Education of Desire*, pp ix, 20.
223. For James's works see App 4.
224. 'Letter to Kowleski', pp113, 223.

Absolutism

DOCUMENT 1 (1940)

R. Palme Dutt
Amended Draft: The English Revolution 1640

(Note on the controversy which has appeared in preceding issues of the *Labour Monthly*)

Christopher Hill's 'The English Revolution 1640' is a lucid, vigorous and stimulating book, giving a birds eye view of the period in simple and popular language. It explains to the ordinary reader what the bourgeoisie tries to hide from him – that English history, like any other, is one in which the prime mover is the class struggle, and that the English bourgeoisie itself, now so eloquent on the virtues of gradualism, won political power in revolutionary and bloody battles. Today that reminder is exceptionally necessary. Christopher Hill and his associates, Margaret James and Edgell Rickword, are to be thanked for doing this valuable work in such a small compass.

This does not mean that further study of seventeenth century English society is not required, or that every formulation in the book is necessarily perfect. On one question in particular, controversy has arisen – Hill's characterisation of pre-1640 English society as 'essentially feudal' and the pre-1640 state as a feudal state.

The review of Hill's book by P.F. which appeared in the October 1940 Labour Monthly took up this point of controversy, but in doing so failed to do justice to the positive value of the book, and further brought in the new and untenable formulation, P.F. later withdrew, that the bourgeoisie had already won political power before 1640, and that the Civil War was 'a war against a counter-revolution' to 'keep the bourgeoisie in power'. The weakness of this review was largely responsible for the unsatisfactory character of the subsequent controversy, obscuring the main issue of controversy which required expert discussion, and bringing in a variety of issues of varying degrees of relevance.

A subsequent discussion organised by the Editorial Board among comrades interested showed that on the main point of controversy noted above two viewpoints exist, and that it would not be justifiable, at the present stage of Marxist research and discussion, to attempt to lay down a final judgment. We therefore content ourselves with indicating briefly the main outlines of the two viewpoints as a basis for further study.

The first viewpoint maintained

a) that during the greater part of the sixteenth century and up to 1640 English society had ceased to be 'essentially feudal', and was in a transitional condition, corresponding to the special character of English historical development, where the old feudal nobility had been in great part wiped out in the fifteenth century Wars of the Roses, and had been replaced by 'a new nobility of bourgeois derivation and bourgeois tendencies', 'the nobility had become plain bourgeois landowners with a bourgeois source of income – ground rent' (Engels, *Peasant War in Germany*; esp. Marx's essay on *The English Revolution*: 'This class of large landowners, which had originated under Henry VIII, unlike the French feudal landownership in 1789 did not find itself in conflict but rather in complete harmony with the conditions of life of the bourgeoisie; its landownership was in fact not feudal, but middle class.')

b) that the State during this period, the Tudor Monarchy or Absolutism, was different in character and in its basis of class support from the old feudal State, and corresponded to this transitional stage, maintaining its power on the basis of a balance between the newer rising class of bourgeois landowners and the town bourgeoisie, on the one hand, and the old feudal remnants, still strong, especially in the

> North and West on the other: In this sense the royal power of Tudor Monarchy was described by Marx as a 'product of bourgeois development'.

This balancing role became untenable, as the relative strength of the bourgeoisie increased, and the absolute monarchy, which in the early stages had especially built on the support of the bourgeoisie and promoted their interests, in the later stages, rccognising their potential challenge to its own power turned increasingly for support to the reactionary feudal survivals. In this way developed the political contradiction between the economic power of the rising bourgeoisie and the political forms in which it was developing, which in the seventeenth century exploded in the Civil War – in which the town and country bourgeoisie fought the Monarchy and the surviving feudal elements, for the purpose of seizing direct political power and bringing about the complete bourgeois transformation of society.

The other group considered that the State in England until 1640 was essentially feudal, since it was the instrument of the feudal landowning class. The absolute monarchy arose in the period when the stability of feudal society was being undermined by bourgeois developments and its primary function was to maintain the system of feudal exploitation against the direct producers, while using bourgeois developments to strengthen its own power. With the steady growth of the economic power of the rising bourgeoisie they came more and more into conflict with feudal barriers to bourgeois development and hence with the feudal-absolutist State which maintained these barriers.

The revolution of 1640 was, therefore, necessary as a bourgeois revolution to break the essentially feudal State power, and establish a bourgeois state power to smash the feudal fetters on production, thus opening the way for a more rapid bourgeois development.

Thus the point at issue on the question of the State is whether, as the first group maintained, the feudal landowning class had already lost State power before the bourgeois revolution without its passing directly to the bourgeoisie or whether, as the second group maintained, that the function of the bourgeois revolution was to take State power from the feudal landowning class.

Associated with the differences on the question of the State, there were also different views with reference to 'the specific economic form in which unpaid surplus labour is pumped out of the direct producers' at the period in question – since that form 'determines the relations of the rulers and ruled, and upon it is founded the entire formation of the Community' (*Capital*, Vol. III, Chap. 47, Section 2).

The first group considered that the vast majority of the English direct producers up to 1640 were free peasant proprietors or tenants, holding their land on capitalist terms, whatever the feudal titles which concealed those terms, and whatever the vexatious, impositions and obstacles which these surviving feudal titles maintained, also engaged in wage-labour for large Proprietors. There were even in the countryside a small number of wage workers pure and simple, both on the land and in the clothing industry (which existed in the villages, as well as in the towns), just as there were a small number of surviving serfs, in the classical sense of the word, in the more backward feudal areas. The old feudal nobility in the main had disappeared. The vast majority of the landowners had habits and tendencies more bourgeois than feudal, although the legal survivals of feudalism in many cases enabled them to extort additional surplus value from the peasants. The prevailing money economy and the growth of a large national market for corn centred in London, had hastened the development of this state of society, so far as agriculture is concerned. Thus society was largely non-feudal although not yet fully capitalist: and class relations were neither feudal nor capitalist, but transitional.

The other group taking part in the discussion considered that the specific form in which unpaid surplus labour was pumped out of the direct producers was essentially feudal. Within feudal society a vast sector of capitalist forms of exploitation had developed, gradually modifying feudal forms and creating the conditions for the growth of capitalism. But over the main field of production there was not wage labour, and the money rents generally paid were in substitution for labour service or payments in kind, thus being still feudal in essence, as was shown by the fact that they were below the economic rent. Thus in spite of the growth of capitalist agriculture and town industry, the main form of exploitation was feudal, and there was a considerable class of landowners living on the basis of their feudal rights, and continuing to wield State power through the absolute monarchy and the local political apparatus.

DOCUMENT 2 (1947)

Christopher Hill
Absolutism in England

(Theses for Discussion)

1. The Tudor and early Stuart monarchy was a feudal landowners' state in which much of the power of the big feudal lords was concentrated in the hands of the biggest landowner, the crown (see article by Mosina). Henry VII and his successors thus succeeded in doing what all medieval monarchs had tried to do. As cause and effect of their success they had the support of the lesser gentry and the estate of the burghers.
2. Nevertheless the basic antagonism in society continues to be that between feudal ruling class on the one hand and peasantry and lower classes in the towns on the other. (See Mosina article). The disappearance of serfdom in England was a legal change rather than an alteration in the mode of exploitation (See Maurice Dobb, *Studies in the Development of Capitalism*, chapters 1–5).
3. As Marx puts it, 'Absolute monarchy arises in transitional periods when the old feudal estates are decaying and the medieval estate of burghers is turning itself into the modern class of the of the bourgeoisie, but neither of the two classes has yet got the better of the other' (Marx-Engels Gesamtausgabe V1 p.313). The difference between absolutism and the 'estates monarchy' which preceded it consists mainly in the following:
   a) Change in personnel of ruling class. Elimination of some big feudal lords (debts and poverty and wars of Roses and dissolution of monasteries). The residuary legatees are the King and the rest of the gentry. But the funda-

mental form of exploitation still remains the landowner peasant relation.

b) Growing importance of bourgeoisie. At first this is exclusively the merchants and burgher oligarchies, still not anti-feudal (See Dobb, chapters 3-4). But gradually a new, capitalist bourgeoisie emerges to challenge the old order. (See 4. below).

c) The social changes accompanying the rise of absolutism increase the danger to the ruling class from the peasantry, enhance the need for a strong state machine (1549 etc.[1])

4. The national peculiarities of absolutism in England arise from the largely rural nature of English capitalism. The split between feudalists and bourgeoisie is not merely one of country v town; it also takes place in the heart of the ruling class, the gentry. But this split is slow in revealing itself because both the new (capitalist) landowners and the old (feudal) landowners are interested in holding down the peasantry. Both need the state. There is no change in the basic antagonism of feudal society (1607, e.g.[2]). It is only when (a) the new landed class is strong enough, and (b) the capital accumulated by trade and usury has spilled over to a significant degree into industry that the bourgeois challenge to the absolute monarchy comes. And then it comes from the new gentry (and the yeomen, a small section of the well-to-do peasantry pushing up to join the progressive gentry) and the unprivileged industrialists who are often the same people. The commercial bourgeoisie (Presbyterians) are never anxious to force things too far; they can get on in the absolute monarchy, and though of course they have no objection to the taking over of power by the bourgeoisie as a whole, they still find it easier than the more radical new bourgeoisie to compromise with the feudalists (1660[3]).

5. It is in consequence of the largely rural nature of English capitalism that we get:

a) The survival of Parliament as a functioning organ right down to the bourgeois revolution (contrast French States-General and Spanish Cortes)

b} The survival of the common law and no reception of Roman Law

c) Importance of local government (JPs) under absolutism; and concurrently

d) Failure to develop a powerful centralised bureaucracy, though the Stuarts were trying. This links up with:

6. The further national peculiarity that England is an island. The Tudors could never get a standing army put at their disposal in the interests of national defence. Instead there was the private enterprise development of the navy (sea-dogs etc.). Again the Stuarts tried and failed (Petition of Right[4]: 1641 v Ireland[5]).
7. Thus at the beginning of the Tudor monarchy a great deal of power was concentrated in the hands of the biggest feudal landowner, supported by the lesser gentry and the burghers. The gentry and burghers were still non-revolutionary feudal estates. The novelty by the seventeenth century was a change of quantity into quality, accumulation of capital leading to industrial and agricultural developments which produced a new challenge to the feudal-absolutist state from the progressive gentry and yeomanry and the new bourgeoisie.
8. Of course in its early days the Tudor monarchy objectively helped the new bourgeoisie. The monarchy's achievements – internal order, suppression of feudal armies, expropriation of church, internal peace, foreign defence – all worked to the advantage of the bourgeoisie as against feudal landowners other than the King. The crown for instance didn't like depopulating enclosures but could not effectively prevent them and had to put state power behind the repression of vagrants just because the basic social antagonism was still landlords v peasantry. Similarly the crown wanted to protect guilds against free suburban and rural industry; but it also wanted national prosperity. The Tudor bourgeoisie continually had to push the crown on in its foreign policy (See Morton, *People's History of England* chapter 7 section 1).
9. Perhaps detailed research would enable us to distinguish periods. Before about 1540 (?) the crown's main task is the elimination of its feudal rivals; it has few inhibitions or anticipations of future dangers. After about 1588 the crown is increasingly aware of the threat from the new bourgeoisie and gentry, is driven back to increasingly conscious 're-feudalisation' in state and 're-catholicisation' in the church. In between perhaps is a period of uneasy equilibrium of ups and downs, in which the Crown 'as apparent mediator acquires for the moment a certain independence' in

relation to its defeated feudal rivals and the nascent new bourgeoisie, and can play one off against the other (*Origin of the Family*, p196[6]).

NOTES

1. See above p. 43.
2. Presumably reference to Oxfordshire riots.
3. The restoration of the Stuart Monarchy.
4. Parliament's Petition of Right (1628) in opposition to forced loans and martial law.
5. Rebellion in Ireland provoked opposition to royal control of army raised for its suppression.
6. See above pp42-3.

DOCUMENT 3 1947/8

Christopher Hill and Brian Pearce
The Pokrovsky Controversy

1. During the 1920s the best-known historian in the USSR was M.N. Pokrovsky. Two of his works – *Brief History of Russia* and *History of Russia from the Earliest Times to the Rise of Commercial Capitalism* – were translated into English. In 1929-30, steps were taken by the CPSU(B) to expose and root out errors and weaknesses in ideology. The Academy of Science was thoroughly reorganised and a number of prominent philosophers, historians etc. were subjected to criticism. Pokrovsky came under heavy fire for certain historical conceptions contained in his works which were said to be (a) inconsistent with facts, (b) contrary to Marxism-Leninism and (c) linked with various undesirable political tendencies. Pokrovsky himself died in 1932, but keen discussion of his ideas continued until 1934, when it was summed up, adversely to Pokrovsky, in a joint resolution of the CC of the CPSU(B) and the Council of People's Commissars. This resolution is

held to have marked a major turning-point in the development of historical studies in the USSR.

2. Summaries of certain aspects of the Pokrovsky controversy will be found in Dobb, *Studies in the Development of Capitalism* p.34 and the article 'Soviet History', by B. H. Sumner, which appeared in the *Slavonic Review* in 1935 (volumes 16 and 17).
3. One of Pokrovsky's conceptions which was the subject of specially strong criticism and which is of particular interest to us was his conception of the transition from feudalism to capitalism, including the political changes which occur in this transition.
4. Pokrovsky saw as an essential and distinguishing feature of feudalism the predominance of 'natural', self-sufficing economy, production for direct consumption (*Brief History of Russia*, I, 289), with an insignificant development of exchange and money transactions. Capitalism he appears to have identified with factories and the factory proletariat. (Like bourgeois historians and unlike Marx and Lenin, he did not attempt to analyse either feudalism or capitalism as a *mode of production*, examining the relations of the different classes to the means of production and the process by which one class exploits the other.) Pokrovsky had to square his notions of feudalism and capitalism with the existence of a more or less prolonged period in the history of every European country between (a) the rise of extensive trade and market relationships and money transactions, with the appearance of a rich and influential merchant class and (b) the Industrial Revolution, inaugurating what he seems to have meant by Capitalism. This problem he overcame by characterising the awkward period as the reign of a distinct type of society, neither feudal nor 'industrial capitalist' – the epoch of 'Merchant Capitalism' or of the domination of Merchant Capital. Absolute Monarchy he saw as the State form corresponding to this type of society, a 'dictatorship of Merchant Capital' (*op. cit.*, I, 267).
5. Pokrovsky's critics pointed to a number of anomalies in his account of the transitional period which suggested that his conceptions were unsound – e.g., he called the chapter of his *Brief History* dealing with the sixteenth century 'Dissolution of Feudalism in Muscovy' because it was a period of growth of

commodity production; yet it was also the time when large sections of the Russian peasantry were subjected to labour-service obligations! His 'period of Merchant Capitalism' overlapped what Marx 'had seen as two distinct, though inter-penetrating, periods – (a) the last phase of feudalism, and (b) the first phase of capitalism, i.e. capitalist-controlled handicraft production. They claimed that Pokrovsky had felt obliged to invent a new historical conception, 'Merchant Capitalism', because he was *obsessed with changes in the sphere of exchange and finance,* while neglecting changes in the actual mode of production. He could not see the vital distinction between (a) a society in which merchants, operating with their trading 'capital' on the basis of a feudal economy, make their 'profit' out of the consumer and (b) a society in which merchants, who have become directors of production by an economically dependent (not necessarily *wholly* propertyless) class, extract surplus value from this class by means of their ownership of industrial capital. Un-Marxist conceptions both of feudalism and capitalism were at the root of his confusion, and these in turn arose from unclarity as to *what is meant by 'mode of production'*. Pokrovsky's error was seen by his critics, in fact, as a fundamental error of historical method, which led his disciples into mistaken notions of current political significance regarding the nature of social revolution, the role of the State in epochs of transition, etc.

6. In the last year of his life, Pokrovsky began to admit that he had made a big mistake. 'Merchant Capitalism' he acknowledged was 'an illiterate expression'. 'Capitalism is a system of production and merchant capital produces nothing ... It is production that always forms the foundation of the social structure...Merchant capital which produces nothing cannot determine the nature of superstructure of a given society ... However great the influence of merchant capital may have been at times the character of the political superstructure is always determined by relations of production and not by those of exchange.' (op. cit., I 283-3).
7. Pokrovsky also came to see how his views conflicted with the Marxist theory of the state. He wrote 'In the first edition of my scheme I did not sufficiently emphasize the relative independence of the political superstructure from the economic base, I had

forgotten Engels' words: 'Why do we make such a fuss about the dictatorship of the proletariat now, if political power is economically powerless?' Pokrovsky's mistakes in his conception of the roles of economics and politics, adds the Soviet historian Pankratova, 'arise from his acceptance of economics as a self-sufficient force acting without any intervening links. It is no accident that his methodology led Pokrovsky to real historical fatalism. "The past will have its way" he said, "Don't you worry; and without any assistance from our side ..."' Pokrovsky to the end of his life did not free himself from economic materialism, of which he himself correctly said: 'In itself the economic interpretation of the historical process is acceptable for any bourgeois, for it means Marxism minus dialectics, i.e. minus revolution.' (Article in [missing] 'Against the historical conceptions of M.N. Pokrovsky (in Russian) pp56-7). Bayevsky, writing in the same volume, concludes, 'In Pokrovsky's anti-Marxist scheme there is no room on the historical stage either for a revolutionary class or for the actions of the masses and their parties. In Pokrovsky's scheme the actors are "merchant capital", an impersonal "industrial capital" and all that together creates what Pokrovsky calls "the pitilessness of history inexorable as fate"'. (op. cit., p.429)

DOCUMENT 4 (1940)

(FROM ISTORIK MARKSIST, NO.6 1940, pp63-68)

Discussion on the Problem of Absolutism Sessions of the Academic Board of the Institute of History of the Academy of Sciences of the USSR, 16 and 20 March and 10 April 1940

Some differences of opinion among historians in the treatment of the problem of absolutism in the West and of autocracy in Russia disclosed themselves in the course of discussions on college textbooks published by the Institute of History and also during the preparation in the Institute of separate chapters of the many volume histories of the world and of the USSR. It was therefore decided to discuss the problem of absolutism at sessions of the Academic Board of the Institute of History and to draw into this discussion as many historians as possible.

At the session of the Academic Board on 16 March, Professor Skazkin gave his report, as also did Porshnev and Mosina. Skazkin's report was entitled 'Marx and Engels on West European absolutism'. In the first part Skazkin expounded the Marxist-Leninist theory of the state, emphasising the conception that the state always is and may be a political organisation of one class only. Further he tried to expound the views of the founders of Marxism on various subsidiary questions connected with the problem of absolutism: (i) the time and circumstances of the appearance of absolutism in the West; (ii) the relations of absolute monarchy to the various social classes and specially to the bourgeoisie; (iii) the various stages in the development of absolute monarchy in the West in connection with their 'various concrete forms'; and (iv) the objective historical meaning of absolute monarchy in the course of world historical development. Skazkin succeeded in thoroughly analysing only two questions: (i) the premises of absolute monarchy in the West, and (ii) the relation of absolute monarchy to the bourgeoisie. Following lines laid down by Marx, Skazkin established the fact that absolute monarchy was preceded by feudal monarchy. He quoted the words of the founders of Marxism that 'the unification of the most important regions in feudal kingdoms was a necessity both for the landed gentry and for the towns. Thus everywhere at the head of the organisation of the ruling class – the nobles – stood the king'. (Marx and Engels *Works*, IV, p.15).

The most important premise for the formation of absolute monarchy was the elimination of feudal aristocracy and of the towns. Skazkin considered that the elimination of the towns as specific corporations of feudal society was the most important moment for the establishment of the bourgeoisie as a class, since this helped them to emerge from their medieval burghers' shells.

Quoting many of the opinions of Marx and Engels on the question of the birth of absolutism, Skazkin drew attention to the fact that the classics of Marxism immutably put forward the moment of the formation of the bourgeoisie as a specific condition of the rise of absolute monarchy, 'as if purposely forgetting the fundamental contradiction of feudal society, the antagonism between feudal lord and serf or retainers'. How can this fact be explained? Skazkin offered the following explanation: 'Old feudal society goes to ruin ('the old feudal estates decay'- Marx and Engels, *Works*, V, p.212) and in the process of this destruction a new class arises – the bourgeoisie – as the bearer of new progressive means of production. At the same time as representing "free, private property", it becomes – consciously or unconsciously (at first of course unconsciously) – the cement consolidating all the forces directed against feudal society'.

Turning to Professor Porshnev's contribution, Udaltsov emphasised that Porshnev was right when he drew attention to the role of the workers in the period of the formation and functioning of absolute monarchy, but he was not quite right if he thinks that the working classes come forward on their own, quite independently of the new emerging class relationships. Porshnev evidently forgot Stalin's words that not only the October revolution but even the revolution of 1905 in Russia differ from preceding bourgeois revolutions in that in Russia already the peasantry was not a reserve of the bourgeoisie, whereas in the bourgeois revolutions of the West it was such a reserve. Udaltsov objected to the new conceptions put forward by Porshnev in his contribution, 'feudal bourgeoisie' and even 'feudal capital'. Further Udaltsov controverted Porshnev's point of view on the question of the times of the emergence of absolutism in the West and in the East. Porshnev's conception, according to which absolutism came into being contemporaneously in very different historical circumstances in the West and in the East, seemed to him quite incorrect.

The summing up of the discussion was made by Z. Mosina as follows:

The central point in the discussion on Absolutism was occupied by the question of the prerequisites for the rise of the Absolute Monarchy, a question which is most closely bound up with the question of the social roots, the class basis of absolutism. On this latter question Soviet historians have succeeded in getting beyond not only the traditions of the bourgeois historians, but also the influence of the Pokrovsky school, which distorted the Marxist-Leninist doctrine on the Absolute

Monarchy. According to M.N. Pokrovsky, the problem of Absolute Monarchy was linked with his theory of 'merchant capital'. In a special essay on Absolutism written for B.S.E. Pokrovsky asserted that 'the Absolute Monarchy as a form of state institution arose on the basis of merchant capital'. This conception was even more definitely formulated in the following thesis of Pokrovsky: 'the absolutism of an individual in fact covered up the absolutism of merchant capital'. This anti-Marxist conception of Pokrovsky was rejected when his theory of merchant capital was refuted.

At the present time the view of the Absolute Monarchy as a Feudal-landowners' state of the nobility, has, as it were, been assimilated by all Soviet historians. This basic thesis has also been laid down in the recently published text book on the history of the Middle Ages (Vol.2). This text book, however, raises the complaint that Soviet historians do not always draw correct conclusions from this basic thesis in working out particular problems connected with the history of the Absolute Monarchy. Such a problem is the rise of the Absolute Monarchy in the West and of the autocracy in Russia.

How is it to be explained that the feudal-landowning class at a certain stage of development of feudal society in most European countries passes from the Feudal-estates Monarchy to the Absolute Monarchy? What concrete causes bring about this change in the form of the feudal state? Soviet historians are not completely clear on this question. However, a whole number of important statements on this question are to be found in the classics of Marxism.

Marx concretely speaks about the prerequisites in his article 'Moralising Criticism and Critical Morals': 'contemporary historians have shown that the Absolute Monarchy arose in a transitional epoch, when the old feudal classes are disintegrating, and the medieval class of townsmen is being transformed into the contemporary class of bourgeois, and no one of the contending sides has yet achieved predominance over the other'. (Karl Marx & F. Engels *Collected Works*. (Russian) Vo1.5 Page 212)

From this thesis of Marx S.D. Skazkin draws the conclusion that the Absolute Monarchy is brought into being for the protection of the nobility from the increasing 'pressure' of the bourgeoisie. This is how it is put in the text book issued under

Skazkin's editorship, which literally states the following: 'The Absolute Monarchy fulfils the function of defending the nobility from the increasing pressure of the bourgeoisie'.

Skazkin's thesis so formulated is dangerous because it leads us away from the basic and decisive antagonisms of feudal society, the antagonisms between the feudal-lords and the peasantry exploited by them. The basic Marxist principle of the significance of the State retains its force for the Absolute Monarchy, as Comrade Stalin states this principle with classical clarity in the following words: 'Two essential functions characterise the activities of the state: internal (the main) to retain control over the exploited majority; and externally (not the main), to extend the territory of its own ruling class at the cost of the territory of other states, or to defend the territory of its own state from attack on the part of other states. This was so in the slave-owning order of society and also in feudalism. This is so under capitalism'. (Stalin 'Questions of Leninism', page 660).

Thus even though we may agree that the Absolute Monarchy arises as the dictatorship of the nobility, it is necessary to emphasise that the edge of the dictatorship of the nobility is directed against the peasantry and the lower orders of the towns. If we reject the description of Absolutism as a screen for the nobility from the pressure of the bourgeoisie, nevertheless the first question that remains unanswered, is in what condition the nobility is led to take refuge in the creation of the Absolute Monarchy. Comrade Porshnev tries to reply to this question, and his suggestion deserves serious consideration, on the basis of an analysis of the movements of the peasantry and plebians, which to his mind compelled the nobility to band together in order to safeguard their rule.

Amongst the Soviet historians who share Porshnev's view is V.V. Mavrodin who in his recently published popular work on the Russian national state, writes: 'The feudal princes and nobility came behind the great prince for the reason partly that they were interested in putting the fetters of serfdom on the peasantry. But to safeguard the serfdom of the peasants on an all-Russian scale required a strong all-Russian power'.

On the basis of independent research, Comrade Porshnev brings out the fact that the bourgeois historians have failed to appreciate or maybe have deliberately underestimated the significance on a wide scale of the popular movements in France in the 16th, 17th and 18th centuries. But this new material is not enough to prove that the peasant movement in France in the 16th century was stronger or more widespread than the movement for example of the *jacquerie*.[1] But it is well known that the French feudal lords were able to suppress the *jacquerie* without waiting for a victory of Absolutism or necessary strengthening of the King's power. In Germany in the 16th century, in spite of the political weakness of the feudal landlords, they were also able to cope with the great Peasant revolt of the 16th century, the Peasant war. Moreover in Poland where this serf exploitation in the 16th and 17th centuries was particularly heavy and the peasant movement really represented a menace to the continued existence of Poland of the Pans, the Absolute Monarchy all the same was not brought into existence.

The historical facts brought forward do not confirm the view that the prerequisites for the rise of Absolutism must be sought exclusively in the strengthening of the popular anti-Feudal movement for the suppression of which a new form of the Feudal state was necessary. It is evident that the danger of peasant revolts becomes particularly menacing only for the period when the bourgeoisie step on to the political stage.[2] In order to give a full discussion to the question we have raised it is necessary to go back to the basic theoretical principles and to analyse more carefully some of the statements of Marx, Engels, Lenin and Stalin. We must start with the statement of Marx already quoted. In this it is necessary to underline Marx's idea of the disintegration of the feudal classes as a prerequisite for the rise of Absolutism. In another context Marx formulates this idea more clearly as follows: 'The 16th century was the epoch of the formation of great Monarchies, which everywhere took place on the ruins of the contending feudal classes: the aristocrats and the burghers'. (Marx & Engels *Collected Works* Vo1.10. (Russian) page 721)

Engels in 'The Peasant War in Germany' showed how the gentry was falling into disintegration in Germany in the 16th century, on the eve of the Peasants' War. Simultaneously with this decline, growing poverty and ruin of the gentry, went its stratification. A top layer of big feudal princes was differentiated from a large group of ruined knights. The stratum of the middle gentry was reduced in numbers.

The French gentry experienced the same crisis in the 16th

century. Here too we can observe the same facts – poverty, growing indebtedness of the gentry, sale of family estates and castles. And here too, as in Germany, the cause of the crisis is the rise and development of capitalist relations in the framework of feudal France. Marx, in his controversy with Heinzen, depicted in a masterly way just this disintegrating influence of rising capital on the gentry.[3] He said: 'The burghers by means of trade and industry, on the one hand, extracted money from the pocket of the feudal lord, and mobilized landed property through debts; on the other hand they assisted the victory of the Absolute Monarchy over the weakened feudal magnates and purchased the privileges of the latter for themselves'.

Marx notes here, as the starting point of absolutism, shifts within the ruling class itself, occurring under the influence of the growth of trade, industry and money relations in Europe. The weakening and impoverishment of the feudalists established the necessary conditions for the strengthening of royal power. But the victory of Absolutism could only be attained in bloody struggle against the feudal aristocratic princelings, against the feudal landlords in England, against the grandees in France, the Pans in Poland or the boyars in Russia. In this war the monarchical power could rely not only on the lower ranks of the nobility but also on the towns. Compelled to choose between the strengthening of the monarchical power and the strengthening of the power of the separate princelings, the towns came down on the side of the King, supporting him against the princelings.

The struggle against the separatist tendencies of the big feudalists continued in the 16th and 17th centuries; it was historically progressive. In so far as absolutism led this struggle it could confidently lean on the support of all the advanced elements in society, including the new rising class – the bourgeoisie. In those countries where absolutism left significant privileges to the feudal magnates it soon lost its progressive character, as, for example, in Spain in the 16th century. In those European countries where for whatever reason the growth of the towns was checked and where the urban bourgeoisie could offer no counterweight to feudalism, there absolutism could not be established at all, as we see from the example of Poland.

In Russia absolutism differed neither in its character nor in its functions from west-European absolutism. (The reporter then went on to deal with the problem as it applied in Russia; this ended the first section of his report).

The second question which was also raised in the discussion and on which up to now full agreement has not been reached, is the question of the prerequisites for the fall of Absolutism. The question of which classes brought about the downfall of Absolutism. In its concrete form the question relates to how long the bourgeoisie puts up with the situation of the counter-weight of the feudal nobility in the Absolute Monarchy, when and under the influence of what causes it passes from supporting Absolutism to the war against it and finally what role the bourgeoisie plays in the preparations and carrying through of the bourgeois revolution which overthrows Absolutism.

There are two tendencies amongst Soviet historians on this question. One puts the full weight on the revolutionary role of the bourgeoisie in the period of the Absolute Monarchy, forgetting about the movement of the oppressed mass of the peasants; the second tendency altogether ignores the revolutionary role of the bourgeoisie.

Comrade Porshnev for example thinks that the French bourgeoisie did not play a revolutionary role either in the 16th or 17th centuries. He reaches the conclusion on the basis of his research into the popular revolts of this period, that it was precisely this uprising which spread everywhere which led to the overthrow of Absolutism, at the time when the bourgeoisie was hesitating and vacillating, not trying to come over to the peasant-plebeian camp or coming over to it only in order to betray them. Only at the last moment in the 18th century he suggests that it at last associated itself with the revolutionary war, but only in order to seize what were already the ripe fruits of victory. Porshnev associates himself in this view, with the view of E.V. Tarle, who in his book on the Fall of Absolutism says: 'Everywhere in Western Europe the bourgeoisie advanced to the political revolution as it were against their will, only because this Absolutism was in the position of defending all the bases of the old social juridical order'. But this was the basis for the completely wrong estimation by Tarle of the Russian Revolution of 1905. In general it has been shown that those bourgeois revolutions in which the oppressed masses, and in the first place the peasants, did not take part, were coups d'état.

It is absolutely clear that the bourgeoisie cannot be a consistent revolutionary force because the bourgeoisie is a class of owners, a class of exploiters. In the 16th and 17th centuries the revolutionary role of the bourgeoisie is seen primarily in the economic sphere.

The growth of production based on the new capitalist conditions must continuously undermine the feudal order. By the objective development of events the bourgeoisie advances to the role of leaders of all the revolutionary anti-feudal forces of society. The revolutionary role of the bourgeoisie disintegrating feudal society is clearly brought out by Engels in the following: 'When Europe emerged from the Middle Ages the town bourgeoisie, then in process of development, were the revolutionaries in it, the position which it won for themselves within the medieval feudal structure became too narrow for their urge to develop. The free development of the bourgeoisie becoming incompatible with the feudal order, the feudal system had to go'. (Marx & Engels. *Collected Works* Vo1.16 (Russian) page 295)

Marx says that 'for the English as also for the French revolutions, the question of property depended on the freedom of competition and the destruction of all feudal property relations'. (Marx & Engels Collected Works Vol.5 (Russian) page 208.

(The reporter then concluded with the following reference to Britain).

The problem of English Absolutism is a very serious and interesting problem. Some Soviet historians show a tendency to deny that there was real Absolutism in England. Others on the contrary regard the English Absolutism as being of the same classical type as the French.

The specific feature of 16th century England was the wild development of capitalist relations in agriculture, transforming a significant sector of the gentry into bourgeois. Class differentiation proceeded at the social basis of English absolutism itself. This, of course, could not but be reflected in the fate of English absolutism. Spanish absolutism also presents a very interesting problem. In considering the reasons for its rapid fall there is still much that is obscure. The problem of the formation and development of the bureaucratic machine of the absolute monarchy (civil servants, army, police) has also not been worked out.

NOTES

1. Presumably a reference to the peasant revolts of the early 14th century.
2. Despite these criticism Porshnev persisted with his analysis which appeared in his pioneering study of French popular revolts, *Narodnye vosstania vo Frantsii pered Frondoi*, (Moscow 1948). It was translated into German in 1954 and French in 1963 provoking further research and debate.
3. Heinzen was a German journalist. See Frederick Engels 'The Communists and Karl Heinzen', Mars and Engels Collected Works, Vol 6, pp291-306, Lawrence & Wishart 1976.

DOCUMENT 5 (1947/8)

Victor Kiernan
Theses for Discussion on Absolutism no 2: The Tudor State in English History

I. FEUDALISM

1. Feudalism is the exploitation over a wide area of an agrarian economy by a hierarchically organised military aristocracy.
2. Feudalism cannot exist without serfdom, though serfdom can exist without feudalism.
3. It combines two opposite tendencies; rigid discipline, and anarchism. On account of this contradiction, it must either (a) expand outwards, or (b) expand downwards (by intensifying exploitation), or (c) utilise its surplus energy in civil war.
4. In all these directions, limits are fixed by circumstances of geography, soil, technique, etc. In struggling to surpass these limits, feudalism tends to transform itself.
5. It at no time excludes the existence of towns, trade, and money; it even fosters them, on condition that it can dominate and exploit them.
6. Money economy however develops by profiting by the

internal contradictions of feudalism, and itself at every stage intensifies them.

2. ABSOLUTISM

1. Feudalism passes, in all feudal countries except England – and in parts of Eastern Europe, where it is largely derivative – into Absolutism.
2. The Absolutist State arises through a compromise between landlord and merchant-capital elements, on the basis of all State-burdens being transferred on to the peasantry.
3. It preserves a caste cleavage between noble and bourgeois (who are often racially separated also); it develops no free market in land; it keeps the mass of the peasantry at an undifferentiated level of semi-starvation; it provides no large home market, and capital concerns itself with long-distance trade, largely exchange of raw materials for luxuries.
4. For these reasons, capital does not enter freely into, and transform, the mode of production.
5. The Absolutist State is predatory, and directs its energies outwards in order to

   a) supply the Crown with more tax paying subjects;
   b) provide the surplus nobility with military employment;
   c) enlarge the monopoly area controlled by merchant capital.

6. It collapses finally as a result of military defeat.

3. PRE-TUDOR ENGLAND

1. There is no stage of Absolutism in English history, which is in many respects unique.
2. Feudalism in England underwent a sudden transformation in 1066 which left it with a series of very unusual features; their collective tendency was to predispose it in favour of an exceptionally rapid movement towards money economy, with early commutation of both military and servile obligations.
3. Its final attempt to save itself, the Hundred Years War, by its technical conditions had the opposite effect: this, and the Black Death, and the growth of trade, assisted the efforts of the peasantry to throw off manorial serfdom. This task was effectively

carried out before 1450 by the organised action of the peasantry, including a series of armed insurrections.

4. In the complex of factors at work in England, the change from servile to money payments is not a mere variant of the old form of exploitation, but radically affects the mode of production. Its essential effect on the agrarian system is to increase further and further the stratification of the peasantry.
5. This in turn favours industrial development, which in the 15th century receives a great impetus from the progress of cloth-weaving as an alternative to wool-export.
6. Capital enters increasingly into the productive process.
   a) through purchase of both arable and pastoral land by merchant capital;
   b) by the emergence of a class of farmers hiring labour and paying rent;
   c) by establishing the political and economic control of merchant bodies over craft gilds, whose work it subdivides and coordinates, and over individual craftsmen.
7. This intervention in agriculture and manufacture is in neither case merely parasitic. The economy as a whole gains in productive efficiency and standards of living rise.
8. The defeudalised nobility, left hanging in the air, hires the floating manpower cut adrift from the soil, and engages in futile faction-fighting in order to control the State and thereby plunder rivals and sponge on the new forms of wealth.

4. THE NATURE OF THE TUDOR STATE

1. The 'Tudor State' emerges under Edward IV as a result of the convergence of four interconnected processes –
   a) Financial exhaustion of the noble racketeers;
   b) Consolidation of a powerful group of rural middle classes, in the widening of the market;
   c) Emergence of London as far the most powerful section of merchant capital, desirous of breaking down the economic regionalism favoured by the weaker towns, and establishing a national market;
   d) Growth of a progressive and ambitious secular intelligentsia.

2. Its keynote is the administrative unification of the country, corresponding to the economic unity fast emerging, in the interest and with the support of all the 'economically progressive' classes. The bigger landlords share in its benefits, but are in no way essential to its operation, and in the long run fail to keep abreast of the economic developments which it liberates.
3. Its central coercive apparatus is trivial being in inverse proportion to the strength and solidarity of the classes interested in preserving it. It maintains order by means of the national militia (embodying the middle and lower-middle classes), and for foreign and colonial service conscripts the lumpen-proletariat.
4. Its central administrative staff is drawn from the educated upper middle class, both urban and rural.
5. Its local administration (now completely superseding the manorial local government) is carried on by an upper cadre of the middle gentry, and a lower cadre of the yeomen. Both are unpaid, and serve (as classes) voluntarily, because their work is in line with their class interests.
6. Its characteristic instrument, the Star Chamber, is directed to the liquidation of feudal remnants.
7. These are strongest in the N. and W. (the key region of the Tudor State being the more highly commercialised S. and E.), and here the anti-feudal struggle is carried on by special organs, the Councils of the North and of Wales.
8. The Reformation marks a further great step in (a) defeudalisation, (b) national centralisation, (c) growth of the speculative land-market and thereby of penetration of capital into agriculture. It provides an ideological basis for the struggle between the two economic regions.
9. In foreign policy the State

   a) Seeks the unification of the British Isles;
   b) Actively supports expansion of overseas commerce;
   c) After the Reformation, allies itself with governments and movements abroad whose class basis resembles its own, against the forces of counter-revolution.

10. As compared with the Absolutist States on the Continent, or with England before 1450 or after 1650, the Tudor State is not

organised for war, because its internal contradictions are still capable of internal solution.

11. A heavy price-rise stimulates the growth of capital, class-stratification in town and country, and control by capital over manufacture in town and country, largely through the medium of usury. There is a heavy decline in real wages and in the value of all fixed incomes.
12. The social policy of the State is not anti-capitalist. Legislation against enclosures and rural industry is not meant to be, and cannot be, seriously enforced. The real policy is to protect employers against demands for higher wages, and to prevent mass discontent from getting out of hand by, a, a system of poor relief, b, control of prices and the black market in times of scarcity.
13. The manor survives only as the framework of land-tenures. Personal serfdom has disappeared 99%. Labour services have lost importance and continue rapidly to disappear. Rents representing old commutations have become insignificant through price changes. Feudal tenurial categories however survive under altered forms.
14. The intricacy and variety of tenurial custom and of local circumstances involve a high degree of arbitrary risk. This is extremely favourable to the emergence of aggressively profit-seeking ownership. Those who benefit are: (a) up-to-date landlords unencumbered by protected tenants; (b) speculative land-dealers; (c) the yeomanry, i.e., freeholders, and copy-holders of inheritance with fines certain, having enough land to produce a market surplus, and tenant farmers able to pay competitive rents.
15. The financial basis of the Crown remains weak, because the classes which support it feel no need to tax themselves in order to supply it with strong means of coercion.
16. Part of the revenue remains quasi-feudal; but there is an increasing dependence on (a) taxes voted by Parliament; (b) loans; (c) revenue taxes on new articles.
17. This favours the growth in importance of the House of Commons – the central consultative organ of the classes supporting the Tudor State.

5. DECLINE OF THE TUDOR STATE

1. Between 1590 and 1640 there is a rapid and very complex reshuffling of forces, with the result that in 1642 the Crown is opposed by every class and region that supported the Tudor State, and vice versa.

   The split begins rather over access to office than over direction of policy –

   a) The Tudor State having fulfilled its historical mission, its governing cadres, especially the Privy Council, fall off in seriousness and enthusiasm;
   b) The classes now thoroughly trained in local government are mature enough to think of exercising central control directly instead of by delegation;
   c) There is a large overgrowth of the professional intelligentsia, involving competition for jobs and jealousy between lucky and unlucky politicians, officials, lawyers, clerics, etc. – the two being in each case largely drawn from the *same* class.

3. Dissatisfied classes range themselves behind the rival factions, which develop slogans – mainly religious – to enlist their support.
4. It is especially necessary for the bourgeois groups to put themselves at the head of an agitational movement, for fear of it being turned against *them*. Mass unrest from 1600 is directed above all against usury – i.e., against capitalism in general, since all the 'active' classes, including yeomen, engage in usury.
5. Unrest has two forms: Catholic (aristocratic and lumpen), nostalgic, mediaeval; Left-Puritan (petty-bourgeois), enlightened and progressive.
6. The Crown is able to develop no coherent policy, but it tends to drift, under Parliamentary hostility, towards compromise with the old-type classes and areas which it formerly attacked. These in turn are ready to compromise with it, because they have been tamed down and partly transformed, and the N.W. is now faced with the desire of the bourgeois form of society to expand fully over the whole country.
7. This mutual drifting together is favoured by the dynastic change (James's previous experience of politics in Scotland), and the international situation.

6. THE 'BOURGEOIS REVOLUTION'

1. Bourgeois revolutions, like 'bourgeois art', are made for the more or less reluctant bourgeoisie by the radical petty-bourgeoisie.
2. The work compressed into a few months in 1789 or 1917 was in England spread over several centuries. There was no 'peasant programme' in 1642, because there was no 'peasantry'. This part of the work of a 'bourgeois revolution' had been accomplished long before.
3. 1642-1660 is not a decisive turning point, but only an important incident, in the history of capitalism in England. In so far as it is composed of specifically bourgeois interests and activities, it is a sordid and dingy incident.
4. It is wrong, in this context, to draw any sharp distinction between merchant capital and industrial capital as 'progressive'. Capitalism in all its forms has a natural bias towards the parasitical, predatory, destructive, reactionary; in all its forms it can be relatively, conditionally, temporarily progressive. The various types of capital to a great extent interpenetrated one another.
5. Merchant capital ruled London, which was the stronghold of the opposition. The complainers in Parliament were very often mercantile. The expansion of England from 1650 to 1815 was organised by mercantile, not industrial, capital.
6. The growth of industrial capital in its newer forms before 1640 was far too recent to explain in any appreciable degree the growth of a revolutionary situation. Industrial capital did not dominate England before 1850.
7. It is very doubtful whether the Stuart government hampered industry. The monopolies may probably have stimulated it. They injured chiefly the consumer, and agitation against them was largely demagogue.
8. Industrial capital, like usurer-, merchant-, and finance-capital, can adapt itself perfectly well, in certain conditions, to the forms of an autocratic, conservative State.
9. It is wrong to suppose that capitalism had to burst through the cramping forms of 'mediaeval law'. As observed above, the intricacies of tenurial law were particularly favourable to the unscrupulous businessman, aided by a sharp lawyer. From c. 1450 to c.1650 is the period, in English tenurial history, of maximum fluidity and freedom of transfer (Johnson).

10. It is wrong to suppose that the tenurial framework left behind by feudalism was abolished in 1646. It was abolished in 1926. Nothing was cut off by the Revolution except the two still surviving incidents of tenure by knight's-service.
11. In general, no overhauling of the 'mediaeval' law-system was carried out. The Parliamentary Party had, indeed, always declared itself the champion of this law-system, against the far more 'modern' tendencies of the prerogative courts. The old law was a huge bourgeois vested interest. Capitalism is very rarely in a Benthamite frame of mind.
12. The only people who demanded reform of the law, especially tenurial law, were the Levellers and their allies – i.e., those who had *suffered* under the aggressive advance of capitalism.
13. The governing factor, for the bourgeois groups, was probably the slackening of the price-inflation and the tendency of real wages to force themselves up, added to unfavourable circumstances in the world market.
14. The solution they really aimed at (as became apparent under Cromwell) was a programme of militant imperialism. England's great potential military strength (like that of France in 1789) could only be deployed by the stirring up of popular energies – as far as possible via religion.
15. The Revolution is the greatest transaction in English history because of the extraordinary revolutionary energy, and advanced ideas, of the radical petty bourgeoisie – which, though too small in numbers to seize power, was *not* looking back to the middle ages, but forward to the *whole modern* struggle against class exploitation.

DOCUMENT 6 (1947/8)

Brian Pearce

Theses for Discussion on Absolutism, 4: A note on Feudalism

1. The discussion on absolutism revealed considerable unclarity and disagreement on the meaning of 'Feudalism'. This is a

fundamental question which must be settled if the discussion on Absolutism is to continue in a profitable way. Here is a small contribution to the clearing up of this question.

2. Stalin writes: 'Five *main* types of relations of production are known to history: primitive communal, slave, feudal, capitalist and socialist' ('Dialectical and Historical Materialism': *Short History of the GPSU (b)* p123).
3. I take this to mean that all the forms of society known to history belong to one or other of those categories, that they are all variants of these five main Types. Any or all of these types may assume different aspects in different countries and also may pass through different stages of development, but it would be misleading to see in every variant a new and distinct type of productive relations (The famous 'Asiatic mode of production' is classified by Soviet historians as a kind of Feudalism. See e.g. editorial footnote, *Selected Works of Marx* Volume 2 p. 658: 'Ancient Asiatic Society was an oriental form of Feudalism, marked by the following characteristic features...')
4. It is well known that capitalism has undergone great changes, especially in the epoch of imperialism so that it has been possible for some writers in the 20th century to argue that our current society is not capitalistic, because it is in so many ways different from the capitalism of 100 years ago. Yet we know and insist that, in spite of the many and important changes which it has undergone, it is still capitalism (cf. *Lenin, Imperialism, the highest stage of capitalism*). The same is probably true of the other types of productive relations, including Feudalism. We should not expect the Feudalism of 1600 to be the same as that of 1400, or rule out 'Feudalism' as a correct characterisation of English society in 1600 merely because it is in many ways so very unlike English society of 1400.
5. In reply to Kiernan I would say: Yes every form of society between primitive communism and capitalism except slavery, is a variant of Feudalism.
6. In my opinion, the fundamental distinguishing feature of Feudalism is the *extraction of surplus value by non-economic compulsion from producers who possess [the] means of production*. Upon this foundation is necessarily built up the structure of inequality, privilege and monopoly which is characteristic of feudal societies.
7. Lenin discusses in his *Development of Capitalism in Russia* the

conditions under which the 'barschina' system prevailed in Russia, and writes: 'The third condition for such a system is that the peasant must be personally dependent on the landlord. If the landlord did not exercise direct power over the person of the peasant he could not compel him, as possessor of land and a tiller on his own account to work for him. Hence "non-economic compulsion", as Marx calls it in describing these economic regimes, must be employed ... The form and degree of the compulsion may vary very considerably, from the state of serfdom to the system of estates in which the peasant occupies an inferior position' (*Selected Works of Lenin*, vol. 1, pp 243-44).

8. Noting that the abolition of serfdom in 1861 did not mean the end of the old order in the Russian countryside, by any means, Lenin observes: 'The possibility of exercising non-economic compulsion also remained: temporary bondage, collective responsibility, corporal punishment, forced labour on public works, etc. (*ibid* p. 245).
9. In the same context, Lenin points out that feudal dues can assume the forms of money-rent without losing their feudal nature. Money-rent is 'a mere change of form of rent in kind ... (A strict distinction must be drawn between money-rent and capitalist ground-rent; the latter presupposes the existence of capitalists and wageworkers in agriculture, the former dependent peasants) ... The basis of this form of rent remains the same as that of rent in kind, the direct producer is still the traditional possessor of the land ...' (ibid. p 229).

DOCUMENT 7 (1947/8)

Rodney Hilton

Comments on V. G. Kiernan's Theses on Absolutism as far as these discuss Feudalism[1]

FEUDALISM

1. What this definition says is true but inadequate. It describes some of the characteristics of most feudal societies. A satisfac-

tory definition of feudalism must describe precisely the nature of the exploitation by the ruling class of the ruled class (or classes) showing how surplus value was appropriated. B. Pearce's definition in his note 6 is in my opinion correct; though (as he realises) it is only partial. It is in fact a definition of serfdom, which might apply to the prevalent form of exploitation in the Late Roman Empire.

2. Until common agreement on the nature of serfdom is reached, this statement cannot be discussed. It would appear from later remarks that the performance of forced labour services is an essential condition of serfdom, in Comrade Kiernan's view. To assume this, or at any rate to assume that the payment of money rents brings about the end of serfdom, begs the whole question at issue.
3. It is true that feudal societies easily degenerate into anarchy, especially when the feudal ruling class has not as yet created a state machine to enforce its class interests as a whole. The most important contradiction in feudal society is not between 'rigid discipline' and 'anarchism' (this is in itself a somewhat idealist formulation) but between lords and serfs.

   The concept of necessary expansion is not clear (whatever the direction) in the same way that the driving force behind monopoly capitalism is. Nor is it clear why 'it' (feudalism – the system begins to assume a conscious personality) must utilise its surplus energy (what is this?) in civil war.

   Of course the lord-serf contradiction is not the only one in feudal society. There are tensions which cut across class divisions, or at any rate do not entirely coincide with them, such as religious and ideological divisions, antagonisms within the ruling class, antagonisms due to the continuance of tribal institutions etc. But these should be analysed concrete[ly] not left as 'tendencies'.
4. Of course the intensification of the exploitation of one class by another is limited by these factors. Of course the feudal ruling class during its life history transformed itself (and to a certain degree the world around it) during the course of its struggles. The question at issue is not that this occurred, but how and when. The answer to this is the answer to our problem.
5. Agreed. The principle form of class exploitation in feudal society was that of the serfs by the nobility. The burgesses were

from the beginning as much an exploiting as an exploited class.

6. This is not clear since it is not stated exactly what internal contradictions in feudalism helped the development of the money economy (i.e. presumably of production for the market – I feel that this favourite phrase of the bourgeois historians should be avoided). The attempt to increase production for the market certainly intensified the lord-serf contradiction in that the lords increased their feudal methods of exploitation (e.g. in England in the 13th century). The opportunities for the richer serfs and the 'free' peasants to participate in commodity production also produced a rather different sort of contradiction – feudal lord-rural bourgeois. But it is important to note that production for the market did not expand continuously during the feudal period. One of the features of the crisis of feudalism was a falling off of production for the market.

PRE-TUDOR ENGLAND

1. [2]...
2. It is true that the character of English feudalism changed in 1066. It is only relatively true to say that the collective tendency of the unusual features produced by the Norman invasion was towards the early commutation of military and servile obligations. Compared with E. Europe and Russia servile obligations were commuted earlier. But compared with France – a much more reasonable comparison in view of the many similarities of social and political structure – they were commuted late. Both in England and in France the large seigniorial demesnes worked by labour services of serfs began to disintegrate in the 11th and 12th centuries. This process was reversed in England in the 13th Century but not in France. In England there was an intensification of servile exploitation. But in any case the commutation of various services for money varies in significance according to the wider context of the character of the class relationships existing at the time. It should not be necessary to point out that commutation could take place in a purely feudal context.
3. I presume that the 'opposite affect' referred to must be a movement away from commutation. There may well have been a re-imposition of labour services in view of the shortage of wage

labour. This was Thorold Rogers' view and has been supported by recent Soviet commentators on Petrushevski's work on Wat Tyler, so I am informed. We are not entitled to equate the wage labour of the 14th and 15th centuries, enforced by the sanctions of the Statutes of Labourers and directed by the manorial administration, with the labour power which is a commodity in capitalist society. It is not true that the peasant insurrections 'effectively' threw off manorial serfdom – it is true in the chaotic internecine struggles of the nobles during the fifteenth century the system of manorial exploitation was not working normally. But anybody reading the Paston Letters must realise that if anything the serfs were doubly or trebly exploited through the machinery of the manor court.

4. and 5. There is no proof for the first sentence of this thesis. The point made by Comrade Pearce that feudal money rent and capitalist ground rent are not identical is particularly relevant here. If (as was the case) the nobles' income was obtained by compiling [compelling?] the payment of rent, of commutations for services, entry fines, tallages, profits of courts, through the machinery either of the manor court alone or with the help of the King's Courts, then that income was derived through feudal exploitation.

The stratification of the peasantry was of course the essential precondition for the growth of the rural bourgeoisie but this process occurred within the framework of feudal society and the feudal state. A typical example of this is to be found in the semi-industrial Wiltshire village of Castle Combe (c. 1450) where a group of rich peasant-clothiers farmed land, made and sold cloth at great profit, and were mercilessly mulcted, mainly by fines and heriots, by the lord of the manor, Sir John Fastolfe.*

It would therefore be interesting to know how the mode of production (the instrument of production and the relations of production) was *radically* affected. Admittedly there were in agriculture some interesting tendencies towards the diminution of the area of the annual fallow. But the old village community is not yet broken up, in spite of increased tenurial fluidity, and the beginnings of the stratification of the peasantry. Furthermore I believe it is true to say that there were no important technical advances in the weaving industry (crucial for the economy as a whole) between the invention and widespread adoption of the fulling mill (13th Century) and the introduction of the new draperies.

6. The purchase of land by merchant capitalists does not necessarily mean that capital enters the productive process. Men who had made their pile as merchant capitalists (e.g. the Poles) were constantly entering the ranks of the feudal nobility and gentry. They only used their merchants' profits in a non-feudal way when the relations of production in the countryside were in any case becoming capitalist rather than feudal; viz, after the Dissolution.

   The new class of farmers using wage labour is of course very important. They are the precursors of the rural bourgeoisie, of the new gentry. But significant as they are in the 15th century *as precursors* they do not yet transform the feudal character of agrarian society. Enough work has been done to show the extent to which labour services had been commuted by the middle of the 15th century, and personal serfdom in the sixteenth century (in the legal sense at any rate). What has not been clearly shown for lack of work on the subject, is the extent to which the fifteenth and early sixteenth century demesne farmers were able, directly or indirectly, to exercise feudal forms of compulsion on their workers, i.e. to what extent they took over the local powers of the lords of the manor. A mere study of leases will not give the answer. I believe that here again we shall find conditions very different from those of capitalist farming.

   The political and economic control of merchants over craft guilds was established in the 13th and 14th centuries (especially in the old cloth weaving centres), without any real change in the mode of production being achieved. There seems to be little reason to question the essential truth of the picture painted by Unwin and supported by Dobb, of the real beginnings of capitalist industrial expansion in the country cloth industry, untouched in the 15th century by the big merchant capitalists.
7. This statement requires proof.
8. To call the 15th century nobility 'defeudalised' is again, begging the question. It is of course true that tenure and military service, interdependent in the Anglo-Norman state, were now dissociated – and had been since the end of the 13th century. It is also true that the feudal nobility had divorced

itself from production. This is also true of the monopoly capitalists today but we reject the theory of the managerial state. In the 15th century the feudal nobility was still the ruling class and, faction fights or not, the state machine was the instrument of their power.

* *The manor and Barony of Castle Combe*, by G. Poulette Scrape, prints a Rental and Survey of 1453, with Court Rolls of the same period.

NOTES

1. The numbering here corresponds to that in Kiernan's theses in Document 5.
2. Hilton is here declining to comment on Kiernan's view that Absolutism was unknown in English history.

DOCUMENT 8 (1947/8)

Victor Kiernan

Note on Merchant Capital

1. Rigid separation between M.C. and I.C. (industrial capital) is undesirable; so is the term 'parasitical' to describe the relation between M.C. and the rest of the economy. In practice, all sorts of forms of association between M.C. and I.C. are found. M.C. cannot be highly developed without modifying the mode of production, though this modification may or may not be 'progressive'.
2. There is no question of either M.C. or I.C. being intrinsically 'progressive' or 'retrogressive' or incompatible with a State form like that of Absolutism. What is 'progressive' (i.e. what tends to drive history forward towards big scale machine-industry) is the recurrent conflict between the two, which is partially resolved at each stage into a more advanced fusion. This process may come to a halt at any stage; passage from each to the next requires a series of conditions to be fulfilled.

3. In W. Europe, M.C. played a revolutionary role, perhaps because here it grew up in the framework of a social-economic system (that of High Feudalism – old sense) peculiarly unstable and liable to internal contradictions. M.C. accelerated step by step the disintegration of feudalism, though its disintegrating influence may in some ways have been only indirect.
4. Miscellaneous remarks –
   a) In Tudor England, competition of large-scale London M.C. forced provincial town cloth traders to identify themselves with the cloth finishing crafts (still urban, unlike weaving), and draw these together into an industrial complex, strong enough to secure legislation in favour of town industry. If such legislation was 'reactionary', it was anti M.C. (See Unwin, *Industrial Organisation* ch.3: 'Industrial Capital versus Commercial Capital').
   b) Early Stuart grants of incorporation to craft bodies, combined with monopoly grants, had the effect of stimulating a rapid development of industrial capitalism. (*ibid.*, chs .5, 8, 9: 'Gilds & Companies of London', ch.17).
   c) After 1642-88, the dominant form of capital was capital invested in land. Next stood M.C. especially as organised in monopoly overseas enterprise (EIC). Industrial capital (largely to be identified with Nonconformity) emerged with a precarious tolerance, legally excluded from all direct share in State power. Things continued to progress because of the interaction and mutual stimulus between M.C. and I.C.

DOCUMENT 9 (1947/8)

Maurice Dobb

Note in Reply [to Kiernan on Merchant Capital]

It is, of course, an elementary principle of Marxism that there are no hard and fast dividing lines in the real world (whether it be between organic and inorganic matter, between classes, between social systems or between merchant and industrial capital). Yet this recognition does not prevent Marxists from distinguishing qualitative differences, e.g. between classes or between systems, and characterising each in terms of its dominant element. Nor should this prevent Marxists from distinguishing turning-points and decisive moments in development. I feel that V.G.K. in his approach has been so obsessed with the complexity of events, and so concerned (and rightly so) with the need to avoid too slick and schematic a treatment, as to come dangerously near to denying that you can draw any dividing lines at all.

Thus, if in the first sentence of his (1) the key-word is 'rigid', I would entirely agree. But because no rigid separation between M.C. and I.C. is possible (admittedly they shade off into one another), that is no reason for saying they cannot be distinguished at all. Admittedly M.C. was never entirely lacking in influence upon the mode of production: the difference here is one of degree. But so long as it confined itself to acting as a trading intermediary, this influence, I believe, was relatively slight and was indirect: moreover, M.C., being remote from production, had no interest in revolutionising the mode of production, and was predominantly parasitical, and hence much more frequently entered into partnership and alliance with the feudal ruling class (even merging with the latter) than with the progressive bourgeois elements that came increasingly into opposition with feudal power. But I am far from wishing to represent M.C. as a 'homogeneous reactionary mass'.

In my *Studies* (pp123-4 et seq.) I tried to show that a section of M.C. did attempt to penetrate the mode of production, and by bringing petty production (chiefly in the form of the country handicraft industry) under its control started to transform the character of this petty industry (c.f. pp143-5). This I suggested was a later, parvenu section of M.C. which was excluded from the export trades and hence was brought into antagonism with the powerful merchant monopolists, entrenched in the export trades, who were the main allies of the feudal nobility at this time. Here, indeed was a transitional form between M.C. and I.C., expressed in the name 'merchant manufacturer'. Even so, as Marx pointed out, these sections did not provide 'the really revolutionary way' of transition; they were, I suggest (though more research is evidently needed here), a vacillating element in the 17th century revolution; and they subsequently became 'an obstacle to a real capitalist mode of production.'

Hence I cannot agree with V.G.K.'s point (3) even as applied to these transitional and hybrid strata of M.C. I would not, however, deny to M.C. a disintegrating influence upon Feudalism; but would emphasise his admission that this influence 'may in some ways have been only indirect.' What I feel that V.G.K. has no right to do is to assume that having an 'indirect disintegrating influence' is the same thing as 'playing a revolutionary role.'

As I see the general picture, the three centuries preceding the 1640 revolution were transitional in the sense that the disintegration of the feudal mode of production was proceeding fairly fast. In other words, petty production (of small producers on the land and in the town crafts) was partially emancipating itself from exploitation by feudal overlords. This process was assisted by the growth of trade (although the growth of trade did not under all conditions result in emancipation, and in some cases produced the converse); and by giving scope for class differentiation within the petty mode of production the growth of trade helped to fertilise the soil from which the capitalist mode of production later grew. But this transformation of the mode of production onto a capitalist basis was not yet. It was far from being a simple product of the spread of monied exchange; and so long as M.C. remained purely merchant capital, confined to the sphere of circulation, it did not achieve or encourage any such transformation. This transformation required the direct subordination of the small producer to capital, and eventually his dispossession: i.e. subordination to an erstwhile merchant who began to invest his capital in the organisation of production or to the kulak-type which arose from within the petty mode of production itself and turned back upon the latter to exploit it.

I am inclined to believe that confusion of indirect influences of the growth of trade with direct influence of M.C. and of (partial) emancipation of petty production from feudal exploitation with the subjection of petty production to exploitation by capitalists, is largely responsible for V.G.K.'s tendency to advance the date both of the transformation of the mode of production and of the appearance of a bourgeois State. I suggest that here may lie a large part of the difference between us.

DOCUMENT 10 (1947/8)

Victor Kiernan

Note on the Origin of the Tudor State

1. In the 15th c. the feudal ruling class was undermined by the decay of manorial economy. There was a significant growth of production and trade, which prepared the establishment of a national market and required a centralised State power to protect it.
2. In the Wars of the Roses, the Lancastrian party was reactionary, anarchical, feudal. The Yorkists, beginning as an opposition group, had to seek the support of the middle classes, and thus became (no doubt in a primitive sense) a revolutionary party.
3. Owing to the unequal development of trade and production, these civil wars had in general the form of a struggle between the North and West (Lancastrian reactionary) and the South and East (Yorkist progressive) exactly as in 1642.
4. The 'Tudor State' began under Edward IV [d.1471]. That the ruler finally emerging (Henry VII 1485-1509) was a 'Lancastrian' is accidental and unimportant. He had no hereditary claim, and could acquire popularity only by marrying a Yorkist, and consolidate his success only by adopting and extending the 'Yorkist programme.'
5. Among the essential characteristics of the State thus inaugurated are these –
   a) Its geographical basis was the progressive South and East
   b) Its new coercive machinery was directed against what remained of feudalism, which was entrenched in the North-West
   c) It soon carried out a Reformation, which was welcomed by the progressive classes and resisted by the feudalists (the division again being South-East against North-West)
   d) It studied public opinion and propaganda, and could not function without the cooperation of Parliament
   e) Its international alignment was pro-bourgeois, anti-feudal.

None of these characteristics can be explained on the hypothesis that the Tudor State was only a 'revised edition' of a feudal State.

6. All this did not exclude the possibility of a situation emerging later in which capitalism, further matured, would have to seize direct control of the State and remould it more thoroughly. But the occurrence of the main phase of the bourgeois revolution in 1641 should not prevent us from seeing in 1485 a necessary preliminary phase of that revolution.

DOCUMENT 11 (1947/8)

Rodney Hilton
Brief Definition of Feudalism

1. Feudal society was determined by the feudal mode of production. This mode of production had the following characteristics:
   a) The vast majority of the population was engaged in, or immediately dependent on, agricultural production
   b) Technique was primitive and stationary (1) compared with even early capitalism
   c} The means of production, the land, was owned by a class of big landowners
   d) These landowners exploited a class who differed from slaves and wage-labourers in that they had been either allotted or allowed to retain holdings providing for their own subsistence
   e} The surplus beyond subsistence produced by the serfs was forcibly extracted from them in the form of feudal rent which might be food, labour or money or a combination of all three
   f) The bulk of industrial products was made in closest association with agricultural production (village and manorial craftsmen). Towns where industrial production (still handicraft) and marketing were more specialized were controlled in the interests of the nobility.
2. The main political characteristics of feudal society were:
   a) Monopoly of political power by the landowning class. It was exercised through both local (manor barony, liberty)

and central (Courts of Common Law, Parliament) institutions in varying ratios at different periods, according to the degree of the organisation of the ruling class.

b) Feudal legal and political institutions in their formative days were directed to ensure the maintenance and exercise of military power by the ruling class. Therefore military characteristics remain important even after the development of mercenary armies. (Restraints on land alienation, feudal aids, knighthood chivalry). (2)

---

1. Although primitiveness of technique must be considered relatively, it was thought right to stress it here. Crop yields were low *during the whole period* (seldom more than 4-fold), leaving little surplus. Only in the 17th century do yields go up to 8-fold, in early 19th century, 9-fold.
2. The military aspect of feudalism is stressed as an *essential* characteristic, both because of the important role of the military aspects of the feudal superstructure in hindering capitalist development, and because of the important part played by the barbarian war bands through whose impact feudalism received those characteristics which distinguish it from the serf state of the late Empire (cf Seljuk feudalism, the result of a similar impact).

DOCUMENT 12 (1947)

The Basis and Character of Tudor Absolutism

A discussion held in Marx House on July 5th and 6th by the Historians' Group of the Communist Party of Great Britain[1]

The Chairman (Com. Douglas Garman) introduced the discussion with a few remarks on the origin of the controversy within the Party on the question of Tudor Absolutism and the significance of the English Revolution of 1640. He reminded the group that it was the publication of Com. Christopher Hill's book on the English Revolution in 1940 which first brought the controversy into the limelight in England. The book was reviewed by a certain 'PF.' in the current issue of *Labour Monthly*. PF did not confine himself to criticising the book in detail but questioned the validity of its basic argument. He maintained that 1640, so far from being a bourgeois revolution, was in fact a frustrated counter revolution; that the English bourgeoisie had won a considerable amount of power under the Tudor monarchs and had been, indeed, an essential pillar of Tudor Absolutism; that feudalism cannot be said to have existed in any real sense in Tudor times, but had, on the contrary, been fatally weakened by the rapid expansion of 'Merchant Capitalism'; that, therefore, to speak of 1640 as a struggle between the old feudalism and the new, growing capitalism was historically incorrect. The Chairman pointed out that the controversy had, as it were, been nipped in the bud and had remained suspended in the air ever since. The recent publication of Com. Maurice Dobb's brilliant *Studies in the Development of Capitalism* had, however, brought into the light of day a whole host of relevant new material which enabled Marxists to carry forward the discussion with profit and might help towards the resolution of the controversy. It was for this purpose, he said, that this meeting had been called together.

Com. Christopher Hill opened the discussion by elaborating the 'Theses' which had been circulated among members beforehand. The adherents of the 'Balance Theory', he said, took to heart the famous sentence from Engels' 'Origin of the Family', without taking into consideration the numerous qualifications which it contained. The Tudor Monarchy was merely strengthening its own power as against the feudal lords, a process which *under the circumstances* led to a great development of an industrial bourgeoisie which in time itself became a challenge to the absolutist state, a challenge more formidable than the feudal lords because it represented a new mode of production. Hence, in self-protection, the state 're-feudalised' itself. This could be seen in a) the alliance between Crown and nobility, and b) the new Catholicism of the Anglican Church, i.e., Arminianism and Laud.[2] The 'Arminianism' of the Calvinists was irrelevant because among them it meant a real independence from outside the monarchical state. The independence of the Anglican Church was a pure fetish

– absolute right of bishops meant absolute right of the king. The final conservative settlement of the bourgeois revolution was due to the widespread interpenetration of the new bourgeoisie with the land-owning class.

Com. A. Leslie Morton who had been expected to oppose the line taken by Com. Hill announced to a surprised audience his general concurrence with the 'theses'. He merely pleaded for more emphasis on the fact that the Tudor Monarchy was not *purely* a feudal landowners' state. Equilibrium was itself a form of movement. Feudalism both existed and did not exist. Before it became fully itself it began to disappear. It was true that the king was the greatest feudal land-owner; but it was also true that the very existence of a state on a national scale was a stage in the disintegration of feudalism. (Henry II?) Therefore, although the king was a feudal monarch, he developed something contrary to feudalism. 1640 was the culmination of a long process.

Com. Brian Pearce, although a firm adherent of 'Hillism', attempted to liven up the discussion by putting forward what seemed to him some of the difficulties in the way of the interpretation in which he himself believed. He wanted to be a little more certain as to why he believed what he did believe. Could it really be, he asked, that the ruling classes of 1400 were the same as those of 1600?

Com. Geoffrey Lee then proceeded to elaborate his own solution to the apparent mystery. In this military factors played an important part. One of the features of the Tudor Monarchy was its monopoly of war. The feudal classes of England had gradually lost their warlike nature ever since Henry II made Scutage[3] into a general practice. (Hundred Years' War? Wars of the Roses??) This presented a striking contrast to Spain where the ruling feudal class retained its warlike nature till a very late stage in the development of feudalism. Just as this lessened the English Crown's dependence on the nobility, so the big strides of Merchant Capital increased its financial dependence on the bourgeoisie.

Com. Andrews, with a very learned contribution, brought his audience from the sublime realms of theory down to the brass tacks of solid facts concerning the 'changing character' of the English bourgeoisie between 1540 and 1588, a change, as he called it, from alliance to antagonism, which made any attempt to generalise about the period as a whole pointless. It was when the new capitalist traits became dominant in the bourgeoisie that the antagonism to the Tudor state first emerged. The monarchy was ever trying to hold back the specifically capitalist progress of production (e.g., Weavers Act, 1558; Apprentices Act[4]). Northumberland encouraged capitalists to concentrate on producing – for export. He urged Marxists not to forget that Merchant Capital did play a progressive role in disintegrating feudalism, particularly by its extension of the world market.

Com. T. A. Jackson astounded all present by the sheer brilliance of his remarks. All facts seemed to fit into their place in the clearness of his exposition. He pointed out that absolutism completed feudalism in the same way as fascism completed capitalism. The essence of feudalism must be sought, not so much in the ownership of land, but rather in sovereignty over men. Here the rights of the local lord were in continual conflict with the rights of the king. Absolutism can be said to have turned the state into one great feudal manor. As the earlier local feudalism was based on local self-sufficiency its transformation into a 'national' system necessitated the extension of an exchange economy. Commodity production was a necessary supplement of later feudalism. The Statute of Apprentices, the Monopoly Patents, etc. were nothing but an attempt to foist the old methods onto a new system. This gave rise to the great bourgeois struggle for the rights of the individual.

At this point Com. Hill intervened in the discussion to try and sum up what had been said so far. He recognised the necessity to divide feudalism into several stages. Com. Jackson's analogy with fascism he accepted as 'frightfully helpful' with but one proviso, viz. that it must be remembered that absolutism was at first progressive as compared with feudalism while fascism was never progressive. This suggested to him yet another analogy which might help to see absolutism in a better perspective, viz. the Labour government; this was undoubtedly progressive but its tenure of office was not likely to lead to any fundamental changes. Obviously the ruling classes of 1400 were not the same as those of 1600 but what did that say. The ruling classes of today were hardly the same as those of 1850 but we were still living under the same capitalist system. The change from feudalism to capitalism was not so much the growth of a money economy as the change from the power of men to the power of money. In this light it was as well to remember that no wage-relationships existed on a large scale until the 17th Century and that in Tudor times a mere 3% of all arable land was subject to enclosures. This led among other results to a considerable limitation of the proletariat.

Com. Eric Hobsbawm drew a number of illuminating parallels with the far more clear-cut continental absolutisms. These reveal a very definite hostility to the bourgeoisie (e.g., the expulsion of the Huguenots from France, the suppression of the towns in Austria and Prussia). But such a policy could not be carried out consistently. The very existence of an absolute nation-state gave the bourgeoisie a bigger chance because it was necessary to it and the state had to adopt bourgeois methods (Joseph II).[5] In some cases the state acted as a creator of capitalism (Colbert).[6]

Com. John Morris urged the importance of defining the various ways of pumping out surplus value. He mentioned three ways whose significance must be assessed; (a) direct labour services; (b) rents in kind; (c) money-rents. While he described the first two as essentially similar, he regarded the third as different in kind. Above all money-rents represented something entirely new in history; the ancient world had failed to evolve such a system. However, in the later Middle Ages money-rents had become characteristic. This was the distinguishing mark between the 13th and the 15th centuries. It helped to put an end to local economy and to a fundamental change in the character of trade.

Com. Pearce then pointed out the fallacy of regarding all money-rents under one heading. He quoted Lenin to support the contention that a money-rent did not automatically mean a capitalist rent; it might merely represent a changed form of the old. Arthur Clegg in a recent article in the *Communist Review* had contrasted the feudal money-rent in the countries of the Far East with the capitalist rent of the West. Money-rents, therefore, were no criterion by which to identify the basis of an economic system.

Com. Jack Lindsay warned of the danger that beset any attempt to be dogmatic about feudalism. Ancient Babylonia, 16th century England, 18th century France, were all feudal in their own way; yet who would deny the tremendous differences between all these? There was a certain complexity in the development of economic systems which could not easily be swept aside by facile generalisations.

On this point Com. Maurice Dobb had one or two useful

things to say. It was imperative to distinguish between money-rents which themselves represented a *qualitative* change and money-rents whose emergence merely facilitated the appearance of circumstances under which 'dissolving factors' could grow. Russian feudalism had been strengthened by the emergence of money-rents. Exchange, etc, developed in response to the needs of feudal society. It could not, and did not, act as a solvent of feudal society until that society had for various reasons reached an *advanced stage of disintegration*. This was very relevant to a consideration of the basis of Tudor Absolutism but it by no means solved the problem of why it arose. After some vague and unconvincing remarks about the peasant threat the discussion ended on a note of uncertainty.

The present writer had the misfortune to lose his way to Marx House on Sunday morning. The following is therefore unlikely to do justice to the contribution of Com. Kiernan who valiantly opposed the Hill-Dobb line. It is gathered from remarks made by other speakers with reference to Com. Kiernan's contribution. In his view it would be entirely incorrect to class Tudor England as a feudal state. Bourgeois commerce had made great and important strides in England ever since the 13th century. By the time of the accession of Henry VII, the bourgeoisie had become the *chief* financial prop of the monarchy. Tudor policy recognised this fact and was therefore aimed primarily at the advancement of the bourgeoisie. The real class character of Tudor England could be illustrated by the famous Essex rising [1601]. Essex realised that if he wished to have any chance of success he would have to win the support of London, the centre of the bourgeoisie. Shakespeare, too, in fact all Elizabethan culture, strikingly testified to the bourgeois character of Tudor England.

When the present writer finally arrived at Marx House, Com. Hobsbawm was in the middle of some remarks on continental absolutism. He stressed the need of the absolute state, however hostile it might be to bourgeois aspirations, to assume bourgeois forms of organisation – it had to introduce modern methods (e.g., Joseph II, Frederick II).[7] This led to an impasse. The efforts of the enlightened despots almost always failed. It was a fallacy to think that any monarchy could be above classes.

Com. Pearce had in front of himself a prepared statement, but before he came to that he wanted to take up one or two controversial points which Com. Kiernan had raised. The chief financial source of the Tudor monarchy was not the bourgeoisie but the Crown's own feudal estates. Absolutism was, as it were, a joint stock company of the great nobles – it was the application of mediaeval methods on an unprecedentedly wide scale. The Essex episode served precisely to illustrate how strong feudalism still was in Elizabeth's time. The fact that he sought support in London did not say very much. London had been an important centre of political power since well back in the Middle Ages. On the whole Essex was not popular with the bourgeoisie. Coming to his own prepared statement, Com. Pearce urged the importance of first understanding continental absolutism. During the period that was under consideration the feudalists were confronted with two co-incident dangers, (a) the peasantry and (b) the bourgeoisie. In Poland, however, only one of these dangers had any significance, viz. (a) Poland was the scene of serious peasant disturbances. The bourgeoisie, on the other hand, had declined (Turks along the Black Sea; shifting of trade routes to the West). No absolutism arose in Poland; this was even the period in which the Polish Crown became elective. It was reasonable to conclude from this that the threat from a restive peasantry was not a sufficient cause for the emergence of absolutism. But its importance must not be underrated – it was Kett's rebellion [1649] which had led to the institution of the Lords Lieutenant of the counties. The Midland Revolt of 1607 had had a considerable effect on the feudal class of landowners. In France the bourgeoisie's refusal to make common cause with the peasants and its alliance with certain purely feudal sections of the nobility had compromised its chances of success. The Huguenot nobles were not analogous to the bourgeoisified gentry of England; there had been no bourgeois penetration of agriculture.

Com. Joan Cook was dissatisfied with the sense in which the word feudalism was being used. According to her conception of feudalism (which gradually turned out to be just 'natural economy'), it had ceased to exist to all intents and purposes by the 16th Century. The extension of commerce weakened feudalism because of the consequent rise in prices. It led to a qualitatively new class, i.e., the capitalist gentry which constituted the chief prop of the Tudor monarchy.

Com. Dobb considered that it would not help to formulate abstract definitions of feudalism. What was wanted was a more concrete examination of feudalism in its different forms. On the question of the mode of production he warned against over-simplification. The mode of production was not to be confused with the technique of production. Relations were the key factor. The mere existence of a class of merchants did not necessarily (though they might) threaten the feudal class. By saying that at any given point of time feudal production continued, one really said that the relations involved were still essentially feudal, i.e., stationary labour, 'tithings', obligatory payments, etc. Feudal obligatory payments could not be identified with the classical Ricardian 'rent'. A money economy did not affect production until it *penetrated* it.

Com. Hill began his reply by expressing his appreciation of Com. Kiernan's contribution. But he warned Marxists against the danger of swallowing the bourgeois 'special English' legend. The absolutism of the Tudors and Stuarts must be seen as essentially comparable to other absolutisms. Once more he stressed the point that merchant capital 'did a job for feudalism'; there was a Third Estate in all classic feudal societies. On the question of Tudor finance he agreed with the previous remarks of Com. Pearce. Tonnage and Poundage he called a feudal tax, laying himself open to attack by advancing as sole justification for this statement that it had originally been granted some centuries before Tudor times. 1642 marked a far-reaching change in methods of taxation. Feudal aids were abolished and a completely new type of tax was introduced, viz excise. The position of the bourgeoisie under the Tudors could be compared with the position of the Trade Unions in England today. Their influence was undoubtedly very great, but they were very far from being the *basis* of state power. Nor was the bourgeoisie under the Tudors, and it could not be until after a revolution.

Oddly enough the last word in this discussion was left to Com. Kiernan who announced his disagreement with everything that had been said. Merchant capital had penetrated agriculture already in the 16th Century. The restriction of the movement of the peasantry could not be carried out very effectively and such restrictions of the movement of labourers was in any case also in the interests of the bourgeoisie (capitalist). Feudal human relations had become money relations in Tudor times (see Elizabethan literature). On the question of Tudor finance he found himself astounded by Com. Hill's formulation as to what constituted a feudal tax. He admitted, however, that he found himself on uncertain ground here and stressed the necessity of further research into the composition of Tudor finance. His thesis, he claimed, was not incompatible with a revolution in 1642. There had been co-operation between feudalism and capitalism prior to that date, a co-operation epitomised by Shakespeare.

The Chairman wound up the discussion by saying how clear it was that a great deal more careful work was necessary on the study of the questions which had been under consideration by this group. With this in mind, Comrades proceeded to enjoy a very good lunch in the Garibaldi Restaurant.

NOTES

1. The anonymous writer of this summary evidently did not differentiate between the Historians Group and the 16th/17th century section.
2. Archbishop Laud was executed in 1646; he shared the Arminian opposition to the idea of Predestination but the term 'high church' perhaps better explains why his policies were widely perceived as 'popery' by the Puritans.
3. A fee paid by knights in lieu of military service.
4. An act touching weavers was passed in 1555 and was designed to protect them from the abusive practices of 'rich and wealthy Clothyers'. The Statute of Artificers, imposing amongst many other things seven years apprenticeships, dates from 1563. For both see R.H. Tawney & E. Power, *Tudor Economic Documents* (London 1924).
5. Joseph II of Austria (1741-1790), Holy Roman Emperor and ruler of Austria from 1765.
6. Jean Baptiste-Colbert (1619-83), Louis XIV's Controller General of Finance and foremost Secretary of State.
7. Frederick the Great of Prussia (1712-86), King of Prussia from 1740.

DOCUMENT 13 (1947)

Minutes 6/7 July 1947
Discussion on Absolutism

The Chairman opened the discussion by sketching the history of the controversy over the historical role of absolutism. Pokrovsky explained it as the state form corresponding to the economic stage [of] 'merchant capitalism'. Soviet historians subsequently rejected his theory of merchant capitalism as a separate stage of economic development and with it his explanation of absolutism as based on merchant capital. Hill's *English Revolution* led to the revival of Pokrovsky's view by 'PF' in a review in the *Labour Monthly* in 1940 and to a controversy cut short by the war. The discussion on Morton's book showed however that complete clarity has not been achieved on the subject. Fortunately recent work by Soviet historians and Dobb's *Studies in the Development of Capitalism* now enable the discussion to be resumed on a better foundation. The chairman emphasised that the controversy involved not only a question of terminology, but the Marxist theory of the state as a whole.

M. Dobb introduced the discussion with some remarks on the economic background of absolutism. The main issue in the 1940 Controversy had been the character of the state in the 16th and 17th century. The theory of 'merchant capitalism' as a separate mode of production with its corresponding state form had been widely accepted at one time but evaporates on closer analysis. The type of society prevailing depends on the mode of production which varies according to the method of extracting surplus value from producers. The substitution of money payments for labour does not necessarily involve a change in mode of production. The fact that in the 16th and 17th centuries merchants obtained a share of power misled Pokrovsky and P.F into thinking that a fundamental change in mode of production had taken place.

C. Hill, developing the theses he had prepared as basis for discussion, drew attention to Engels' carefully-worded statement about absolutism. Loose interpretation of this ignoring Engels' careful qualifications had led to the idea that the Tudor monarchy was above classes. The unique feature of English absolutism was that parliament, the old feudal assembly, came to represent the bourgeoisie. This came about because capitalist relations grow up in the countryside. Many of the gentry turned wool producer and domestic employer and the split between feudal and bourgeois came within the ranks of the gentry. This explains many of the peculiarities of the English revolution. At the same time Hill emphasised the need for more detailed study of the actual development of English absolutism.

B Pearce declared that the views of Hill's thesis presented difficulty to many people because they could not recognise English society in the early 17th century as feudal. To many the disappearance of serfdom signified the disappearance of feudalism. It was necessary to explain why the 16th and early 17th century were to be considered essentially feudal.

G. Lee stressed the importance of changes in the techniques of warfare as a cause of the transition from estates monarchy to absolute monarchy. The feudal lords lost their military functions earlier in England than elsewhere and those became concentrated in the greatest feudal magnate, the King.

K.R. Andrews drew attention to the subtly changing character of the bourgeoisie in the 16th century. There was a gradual change in the relations of the bourgeoisie to the state and a section of it became a 'revolutionary pole' attracting to itself all opponents of the feudal state. The essentially feudal character of the C16 state is shown most clearly by its policy aimed at restraining the development of capitalist industry. Andrews outlined in some detail three crucial stages in the development of the bourgeoisie in the mid-sixteenth century. During the middle stage 1559/1569, something approaching equilibrium between feudal and bourgeois forces was attained.

T.A. Jackson suggested a parallel between Fascism as the final stage of capitalism and absolutism as the final stage of feudalism. Both represented attempts to arrest development at the stage it had reached. Absolutism was the completion of feudalism not its abolition. Feudal power became centred in the crown; the whole state became like one huge feudal manor. Feudal economy was essentially a natural, subsistence economy but for all that exchange and the merchant class had been a necessary supplementary part of it. It was a mistake to think of the feudal class as only a landowning class. Town and merchant corporations were also feudal lords, part of feudal society.

C. Hill, answering the points raised, said that Soviet historians had attempted to distinguish various stages of Feudalism: tribal monarchy, estates monarchy, absolute monarchy. The latter was in most countries the last stage of feudalism, preceding the bourgeois revolution. The analogy with Fascism was useful up to a point, but absolutism, unlike fascism, was progressive in its earlier stages. He than attempted to define feudalism, stressing the factor of service as opposed to money. The wage-relationship was not yet common in the 16th century and military and other forms of feudal service were commoner than it is often supposed.

E. Hobsbawm said that in continental countries the character of absolutism was much clearer than in England. As soon as the rise of the bourgeoisie had produced a certain 'equilibrium' the absolute monarchy had been concerned to check the further growth of the bourgeoisie and the towns.

J. Morris quoted Marx's description of three ways of extracting surplus-value from the producer: produce-rent, labour services, money-rent. The adoption of money-rent completely changed the character of the mode of production. The ancient world had failed to develop money-rent and thus to put purchasing power in the hands of the producer. Thus merchant capital affected only the towns. But in the 16th century money-rent became the prevailing form of tenure for the first time in world history, involving a fundamental change in the character of society.

B. Pearce quoted from Lenin's *Capitalism in Russia* to the effect that money-rent might only be an alternative to produce- or labour-rent. Capitalist rent was fundamentally different, but a money-rent was not necessarily a capitalist-rent.

M. Dobb, answering the economic points raised, agreed with Pearce's view on rent. Kosminsky had shown that there was an element of money-rent in England throughout the feudal period. In Russian feudalism, money-rents had alternated with labour-services without in any way endangering feudalism. As a pointer towards a definition of feudal economy he recalled Soviet historians' descriptions of it as a system 'in which the exaction of surplus value from the direct producers takes place to a significant degree through extra-economic forms of compulsion'. He emphasised the point that towns and trade were not incompatible with, but a necessary part of, feudal society. Those who failed to recognise the ruling class of 1600 as a feudal class must recognise that a ruling class may change in composition and personnel and yet remain the same class. Finally he drew attention to a question which had not been posed. Why did absolute Monarchy arise and what was the basis of the transition from one form of feudal state – estates monarchy – to another – absolute monarchy? Was it due to the need to defend the feudal classes against peasant revolt, against the rising bourgeoisie, or was it due to other causes. And if it was against the peasantry that Absolutism had first arisen, why was it that the peasantry played a relatively minor role in 1640 – was it that the Kulak stratum of the peasantry had become by the 17th century a fully-fledged rural bourgeoisie?

V.G. Kiernan explained the grounds of his disagreement with Hill's thesis. Quoting the first sentence of the thesis, he declared that the Tudor state was not a 'feudal landowners state'. Tudor revenues were not essentially feudal. The crown revenue as a feudal landowner was relatively unimportant, and in any ease consisted mainly of ordinary bourgeois rents. The same applied to the relations of other landlords and their tenants. Tenure was only nominally feudal, only in its formalities, and by 1600 the basic relationship was a modern one, founded on money-rent. As far as any feudal element was present, it continued until the end of the 18th century. The Essex rebellion of 1601 showed the character of the C16 nobility. Essex tried to rally not tenants but the London populace. He was no more a feudal magnate than is Lord Rothermere. The definition of feudalism is important. It is absurd to use it [to] cover everything lying between primitive communism and developed capitalism. It should be used in the strict sense customary among historians and confined to Western Europe. To fill in the resulting gap we must have separate categories – and 'merchant capitalism' [is] a good category. Pokrovsky's conception was right; but by it we must not understand that there was a state dictatorship of the merchant capitalist class, only that the absolutist state could not exist without the support of merchant capitalism. Dobb, in denying that merchant capital is a separate category tends to make the 'mode of production' a kind of abstraction. Merchant capitalism only functioned in the sphere of exchange, but nevertheless tells us much about the mode of production prevailing. The mode of production itself is not independent but a product of the class struggle. Morris was right to say that money-rents were fundamentally new. They did indeed exist in the 12th century – but only on a very small scale. By the 16th century they had become general, with two consequences. Firstly, to create a home market for industrial goods. Secondly, to enable landowners drawing money rents to engage in merchant-capitalist activities. Extra-economic forms of compulsion exist in every society. Nor were they especially characteristic of the 16th century, when large numbers of cultivators were paying a merely nominal rent and were far from having all their surplus-value 'skimmed off'. Paragraphs 5 and 6 of the theses amount to admitting that there was no real absolutism in England since there was no police, no standing army, no bureaucracy. What there was, was an alliance of the gentry with merchant capital, usurers' capital and industrial capital. It was not a balance of conflicting class forces but a fusion of interests. This is shown in the sphere of ideology. Elizabethan culture is unique in world history. Such a great outburst of culture could not be produced accidentally. It was a product of a whole society and its class structure, and arose from a co-operation of classes not from a precarious balance. In short there was an alliance of the post-feudal gentry with merchant capital.

B. Pearce took up Kiernan's point about Essex. He was a typical feudal noble of the time. His monopoly of sweet wines was only an extension on a national scale of the medieval lord's rights over trade. Kiernan's views amount to saying that the Tudor state was already a bourgeois state. Hobsbawm was right to draw attention to continental absolutism. In Poland in the 16th century no absolutism arose and the monarchy went to pieces. Owing to the weakening of the bourgeoisie, the feudal aristocrats were able to deal with the peasant revolts without the help of a strong state. In France the bourgeoisie was strong enough to defend itself but not strong enough to take power. The French bourgeoisie was weaker than the English owing to the weaker development of industry. The key to the English developments was the growth of capitalism in the countryside.

Joan Crook agreed with Kiernan. The 16th century was marked by the economic decline of the feudal classes and the rise of the gentry which she regarded as a capitalist class. The Tudor monarchy was based mainly on the bourgeoisie and it was the old feudal nobility which struggled against the monarchy.

M. Dobb, summing up, stressed the need for a more concrete examination of the different forms and types of feudalism, before any abstract definition could be attempted. Perhaps a committee might be formed to study the question. Answering Kiernan's criticisms about the use of the term 'mode of production' he denied that it was a 'mystical entity'. It was not the same as 'technique of production' but referred to the social relationships in the process of production. It was possible for trade to grow without seriously changing the relations of the direct producer to his immediate overlord [...].[1] To establish that the bourgeois mode of production exists it must be shown that the exploitation of the producer is by the money relation alone. This is not to deny that trade had important reactions on the mode of production. But this reaction only becomes significant when merchant capital begins to get a grip on the processes of production and to change them, for instance when it began to organise country industry 'from outside'. Characteristic of the various transitional types of relationship lying between legal dependence and money-dependence was the debt relationship so typical of the 16th century. Referring to Kiernan's remarks on Elizabethan culture and ideology, Dobb agreed that Elizabethan ideology was clearly not that of a decaying class, but rather of a class conscious of its future. At the same time, it was an ideology not turned against the state, but glorifying the state. These features point to the importance of progressive elements within absolute monarchy itself, as paragraph 9 of the theses suggest. Possibly it might be considered that the monarchy played on the whole a progressive role up to 1588.

C. Hill, concluding the discussion, said that Kiernan's points were very real points. He had been aware of some of them and had tried to fit them into his thesis. The vital point of disagreement was the role of Merchant Capital. Dobb's *Studies* had thrown much light on this role and on the function of merchant capital within feudal society. Taking up Kiernan's detailed points, Hill reaffirmed that the Tudor financial system was still essentially medieval. Subsidy, tonnage and poundage were feudal taxes. It needed the bourgeois revolution of 1640 to introduce a bourgeois form of taxation. Pokrovsky did not really hold the Marxist view of the State at all. That the bourgeoisie should in the 16th century have a strong influence on what was still essentially a feudal state is no more surprising than that the Trade Unions should now influence the policy of what remains essentially a capitalist state. Absolute monarchy was a 'feudal landowners' state, although the merchant capitalists fitted happily into it at first. It is true that the gentry played a big role in the absolutist state – and no-one denies that there was a significant and growing capitalist sector in this class in the later C16 – but it was not yet the basis of state power, and could not become the basis of state power without a revolution. Referring to Kiernan's remarks on Elizabethan culture, Hill suggested that the peak period of literature and culture generally seems to occur at a similar stage in the historical development in many different countries – in the peak period of absolute monarchy. This may arise out of a tension between backward-looking feudal ideology and forward looking bourgeois ideology, a tension existing within the minds of the individual artists.

V.G. Kiernan, answering Dobb and Hill, declared that by the later 16th century money-relations were the decisive factor in class relations on the land. A kind of semi-feudalism existed in border areas but was not the basis of the Tudor state. He does not maintain the Tudor state was a bourgeois state, only that it was a mixed state in which elements of the old feudal classes still existed, but in which the bourgeoisie was important. It was ludicrous to describe tonnage and poundage as 'feudal taxes'. Elizabethan drama drew its strength from a feeling of solidarity, from an attempt to fuse the class values of the two elements, the old feudal class and the merchant class. The fusion later broke down in the 'Jacobean tragedy period'.

The Chairman, adjourning the discussion, underlined the necessity of careful preparation if future discussion were to be fruitful.

NOTES

1. Sentence omitted, unreadable.

DOCUMENT 14 (1948)

Minutes 10/11 January 1948

Discussion on Absolutism (cont)

Maurice Dobb, opening the discussion, referred to the questions raised in the two notes on Merchant Capital. It had not been suggested that Merchant Capital had no influence at all on the mode of production, or even that it was exclusively parasitical. What he had suggested was that Merchant Capital tended to be parasitical in the degree that it was *remote* from production and acted as a *pure* intermediary. There were, it was true, sections of the merchant class who came to be quite closely linked to production and these undoubtedly performed a progressive role. A leading example was the hybrid type of London merchant who in the 16th and early 17th Century was already beginning to organise the country domestic industry. It was in this connection precisely that Marx spoke of Merchant Capital penetrating production as one of the ways – the 'not really revolutionary way' – of transition from the feudal to the bourgeois mode of production. Further research is required with a view to forming some estimate of the quantitative importance of the newer forms of production and to discover whether or not J.U. Nef has exaggerated the development of industry in this period in contrast to the older view which ignored it. Other points needing further investigation are:

a) What was the character of the feudal ruling class in the earlier 17th Century?
b) How are we to define the mode of production represented by the leasing of land by 'feudal landowners', mainly at money rent, to small peasants who do not employ wage labour to any significant extent? How strong were the feudal coercive powers of the lord in practice in this period; and when exactly do we draw the line between feudal and bourgeois rent?
c) The role of Merchant Capital in the Netherlands Revolt.

K.R. Andrews drew attention to the double and contradictory aspect of Merchant Capital in this period. It was parasitic within the feudal mode of production; but at the same time, by widening markets and accumulating capital, it acted as the 'midwife of capitalist production'. In this connection one must distinguish between the earlier and later halves of the 16th century. In the first half, merchants played a positive role, although they had relatively little influence on the Tudor feudal state: in the second half, and particularly after 1549, which marks a turning point, they played a largely parasitic role, as is seen in the growth of monopolies etc. In this later stage too, the Tudor State itself became aware of the danger from the bourgeoisie.

Brian Pearce, taking up the questions posed by Cde. Dobb, said that the term 'feudal rent' was applicable to the money rent paid by a small peasantry. Hilton had shown that money rents occurred as early as the 13th Century; there was 'non-economic compulsion' in this rent-relationship in the 16th century however subtle its form, and the rent did not represent a 'market price'. For similar reasons Marx had referred to 'feudal farmers' in Ireland in the 19th century. 'Capitalist rent' presupposes the employment of wage labour on a decisive scale in agriculture. It is this which marks the decisive change in the made of production. After it had occurred, Marx referred to the English landlord as an 'industrial capitalist' because he employed, or drew his surplus from the employment of wage-workers. To avoid confusion when speaking of merchant capital and industrial capital, we should remember that 'industrial capital' is capital which is invested in production, whether 'industrial' in the narrow sense or agricultural – it is capital which controls production and not the producers. Down to the 16th Century in England there was only merchant and usurer capital. In the 16th century, when the merchant began to 'put out' work, a new relation arose: the merchant ceases to be a mere buyer and becomes a contractor. This is the first stage in the transition to industrial capitalism.

Dona Torr considered that the importance of 'non-economic forms of compulsion' in the exploitation of the peasantry in the 16th century could not be overstressed. To understand it, it is necessary to consider the peasantry as a class, not only as individuals, and to bear in mind that the landowners still held state power and were able to maintain the conditions of exploitation. Thus they were able to turn to their advantage the fact that the peasantry possessed means of production, to produce conditions in which the peasant 'exploited himself' to the uttermost, obtained low prices for his products, was hindered by low technique and low productivity and bore heavy taxes. Through the action of the State, the peasantry was forced to cede surplus value to the ruling class as a whole.

Christopher Hill also agreed that the small peasantry, working on their own account, were feudally exploited. In any case, what could in any real sense be called a 'free', 'independent' peasantry was small and in constant process of transition. By 1600, on the other hand, there was already quite an important 'kulak' element, already capitalist. Thus the 'independent' peasantry in the 16th century do not, as had been suggested, in any way form a basis for a new form of state power.

Maurice Dobb, referring to the distinction between 'feudal rent' and 'bourgeois rent' drew attention to the distinction made by Marx between 'differential rent' (varying as between good and bad land – the rent familiar to bourgeois economists) and 'absolute rent', arising from the landlords' monopoly of land. Was it not possible to consider that 'pure bourgeois rent' would only exist if the land were nationalised and that the element which Marx called 'absolute rent' was a survival of feudal rent? The monopoly of land in the hands of the landlord class in fact constituted a kind of compulsion against the peasantry. In speaking of the feudal ruling class, Cde. Dobb considered it important to stress the distinction between the big baronial feudalists and the smaller knights and squires. It was the latter who came to form especially close relations with merchant capital and who may at certain periods have played a relatively progressive role.

Rodney Hilton made a detailed reply to V.G.K.'s thesis on the Origin of the Tudor State. Dealing first with the disintegration of the feudal economy in the later middle ages he traced the results in a fall in feudal profits and in consequent competition and anarchy among the ruling class and, combined with the effects of dynastic struggles, in a reduction in their number by executions and attainders with the consequent concentration of estates in fewer hands, especially into the hands of the crown. This disintegration was, however, also part of a general agricultural depression which caused impoverishment of sections of the peasantry too. A kulak class emerged, but still only on a small scale. Enclosures began, but, as the reports of 1517 show, only as yet on a petty scale. Thus in this period the makings of the rural bourgeoisie were visible, but it was still far from fulfilment. As far as effective class forces were concerned, this situation is probably reflected in the increased power of the feudal state based on the concentration of feudal property. From the mid 15th Century onwards there are signs of the increasing power of the Government as against the Commons in Parliament. The bulk of legislation was initiated by the Government, even when disguised in 'Common Petitions' and conciliar organs were being strengthened, especially in the North and in the Welsh marches.

At the same time it is not true that there was very significant growth of production and trade, at least before the last quarter of the 15th Century. As late as 1481 wool and cloth exports combined were still less than they had been in 1310. Nor was there any compensating growth in the home market, for although the populations of London and Bristol increased, that of most towns declined. There was, it is true, an increase in the total value of foreign trade in the last half of the 15th Century. But in the thirty years following 1450 the increase in exports was only 19% and the export surplus fell. This represents only the beginning of a recovery and it is not until the 1530s and 1540s that the increase in trade and production became significant enough to provide the basis for the development of a powerful bourgeoisie. Certainly, it is impossible to speak of an 'industrial revolution' in the 15th century.

Turning to what he called V.G.K's 'geographical theory of the 15th Century Bourgeois Revolution', Hilton admitted that the South-East was more economically advanced than the North-West of England in the 15th Century. But this had always been the case, even in 1086, as Domesday Book shows. It was true too, that a good deal of the military strength of the Lancastrian party came from the North; but again, this was partly because of the Franco-Scottish alliance, which meant that, as the Lancastrians had become the 'peace with France' party, they were able to fall back on Scotland, and recruit there. Also the Percys happened to be Lancastrian, and Lancaster and Cheshire were crown appanages. But it should be noted that the Nevilles, other leading northern magnates, were Yorkists.[1] In fact the territorial alignment is so unclear, and in any case determined by factors other than class alignments, that analogies with 1640 are as meaningless as would be analogies with 1086. Anyone wishing to prove that the civil war of the 15th century had a bourgeois-revolutionary character must above all be able to demonstrate that the bourgeoisie was a positive political force, fighting for power. The Yorkists were admittedly – amongst other things and in the early stages – a war party, seeking allies against France. Hence those merchants interested in trade with the Low Countries supported the Yorkist policy of alliance with the Duke of Burgundy against France. But this support did not make the Yorkists a bourgeois revolutionary party any more than the merchant support which Edward III had enjoyed for the same reason had made the Hundred Years War [1337-1453] against France a bourgeois democratic war. Typically enough, one of Edward IV's first acts on seizing power [1471] was to refuse to ratify the security held by the Merchants of the Calais staple for the payment of the garrison.

Summarising his objections to V.G.K's thesis on the nature of the Yorkist-Tudor State, Hilton pointed out that the question we should ask is not whether this state was based on South-East or North-West, but what class interest it represented; who wielded state power, and for whom? The power of the Yorkist-Tudor state

– which was certainly more effective than that of the Lancastrians – was based on a progressive concentration of feudal property and jurisdictions into the hands of the crown. It was this power and wealth which enabled the crown to ignore the bourgeoisie, in so far as, in Parliament, it had any political voice at all – as is shown by the fact that, from 1450 onwards, almost all Parliamentary legislation was initiated by the crown. The organs of state power, the council and its offshoots, and the JPs, locally, were in no way controlled by the bourgeoisie as a class. The use of non-noble bureaucracy does not represent bourgeois power, but was in fact a perennial device used by feudal Kings at such times as they had achieved a concentration of feudal property and jurisdiction – e.g. Henry 1, Henry II. The state power was of course used against dynastic rivals; but its main function was to maintain the system of exploitation. The Tudor JPs were directly descended from and performed similar functions to the Justices of Labourers of 1350. In short, none of the political crises of the 15th Century, 1454, 1461, 1469-71, 1483, 1485, can be shown to have been participated in to any important degree by the bourgeoisie or to have resulted in the acquisition of power by the bourgeoisie.

Christopher Hill summing up the discussion clarified the Marxist conception of Revolution in general, and of the Bourgeois Revolution in particular. A revolution in Marxist theory is the adoption of politics to economics, not vice-versa. Thus the evidence recently revealed of considerable industrial development in England in the later 16th Century does not imply that the Bourgeois revolution had occurred, but suggests that the conditions for it were maturing. A revolution, furthermore, represents a movement of *classes* against existing institutions, the new class feeling itself frustrated by the state forms and *ideology* of the old ruling class. Thus the Bourgeois revolution occurred *after* a significant development of the bourgeoisie has taken place, not before. It could not for that reason take place in the 15th century. Any violent change, any *coup d'état*, or civil war, is not a revolution. Nor is the identity of the ruling class merely a question of personnel or of policy. Louis XIV staffed his court and administration with many bourgeois but that did not make the bourgeoisie the ruling class. To become the ruling class means control of the main centres of power. Under Feudalism of the

Estates-Monarchy these had been mainly local; their centralisation under the Tudors was a necessary prerequisite of bourgeois development.

The bourgeois revolution differs from the Socialist revolution in certain respects. Lenin put it thus: 'The difference between socialist revolution and bourgeois revolution lies precisely in the fact that the latter has ready at hand the forms of capitalist relationships, while the Soviet Power – the proletarian power – does not inherit ready-made relationships' (*Selected Works* vol. VII p.286).

Bourgeois revolutionary ideology is always inadequate, whether it is Puritanism or Rationalism. But a new ideology is none the less essential to give the rising bourgeois class confidence for its task. No such ideology had developed in 1485; to portray that event as a revolution is to ignore that a revolution is not just a small shift in the balance of class forces, but a profound transformation of society and of all values.

The first task of the Bourgeois Revolution is to overthrow the feudal state. Thus it is aimed at destroying absolute monarchy (or in certain cases foreign domination) and at establishing a representative assembly controlling finance, the executive and the church. Secondly, since the Bourgeois Revolution is based on an already developed bourgeoisie, it has to use its control of the state only to remove obstacles to capitalist development, such as feudal taxes and tenures, monopolies etc. Thirdly, it has to take positive steps to encourage capitalist production such as, in England, the Navigation Acts, colonial wars, sales of land, and the subordination of petty production to capital.

V.G.K.'s conception of a revolution by stages is incorrect. It is true that 1688 and 1832 carried forward the Bourgeois Revolution in England, just as 1830 and 1848 carried forward the Revolution of 1789 in France. But always there is a nodal point, when power is really transferred; and in England this point was 1640, not 1485. The bourgeois revolution is not a ladder up which one advances, step by step. State power at any time is either bourgeois or it is feudal. Marx and Engels, it is true, spoke of a balance in exceptional circumstances (which they carefully defined). But all V.G.K's examples of Bonapartism, which he tries to equate with the Tudor monarchy, are taken from periods when the emergence of a working class threat had inclined both exploiting classes – feudal and bourgeois – to compromise with one another. In

England, the prerequisites for any such 'independence' of the State Machine – bureaucracy, a standing army, an arbitrary system of taxation – were inadequately developed before 1640. The only period of English history when such a 'balance' might be said to have existed was 1654/58, when it was based on Cromwell's army. After the bourgeois Revolution of course, there may be 'unholy alliances' like that of 1660 in England, or 1815 in France. Under working class pressure Bonapartism may even come before the full Bourgeois Revolution – but not before such pressure has arisen. Thus in England, the only question is: when was the nodal point. In Hill's opinion it was 1640. If V.G.K. thinks it was 1461 or 1485, the onus of proof lies with him, for all the Marxist classics, as well as common sense, are against him.

This controversy is of great political importance, because the bourgeois revolution is still a real political issue in Asia, South East Europe, Spain and other parts of the world. Pokrovsky, by ante-dating the Bourgeois Revolution, in fact played into the hands of Trotskyism. His view leads to under-rating the role of the State, to the assumption that bourgeois politics always reflect economic development and thus to a denial of the role of the party and of leadership. Pokrovskyism is fundamentally reformist because it assumes that a transfer of power is possible without revolution or at least it has a blurred idea of what a revolution is, conceiving the bourgeois revolution as somehow obtaining a share of power without ousting the feudal ruling class.

In regard to England in particular, two things had evidently puzzled V.G.K: that the Tudor Monarchy was different in important aspects from the state-forms preceding it, and was in a real sense progressive; and that the bourgeoisie prospered under the Tudors. In view of these two facts V.G.K. concluded that the Tudor State was bourgeois. Thus he was led to postulate a quite imaginary Bourgeois Revolution in the 15th Century, for which he can find no evidence. In fact, no-one denies the 'progressive' character of the Tudor State, just as no-one denies that the capitalist regime established in 1832 was in important respects progressive. But 1461/85 only represent a reshuffle, designed to consolidate the state, which was in danger of breakdown, and to consolidate it primarily against the threat of the peasantry; and the edge of the organised state was turned, not against the capitalists indeed, who represented no threat as yet, but against the peasantry, as in 1536, 1549, 1569, 1607, 1631 (cf. Louis XIV and Catherine the Great). A 'revolution' of the serfs was an important component of the Bourgeois Revolution of 1640, represented in part by the Leveller movement.

V.K.G. reads the significance of the Reformation Parliament of 1529 backwards instead of forwards. Hilton has shown convincingly that English society was still feudal in the period 1450-1529 and that the influence of the House of Commons in this period was small. In any case the Commons did not *yet* represent the bourgeoisie. A section of the gentry was to pass over to the bourgeoisie in the 16th century, but had as yet done so on no significant scale.

The conciliar machinery of the Tudor State was directed, not against 'what remained of feudalism', as V.K.G. asserts, but against individual feudal magnates, and against the military aspects of their rule, which were disintegrating the State. Henry IV of France and Peter the Great of Russia pursued a similar policy. But there was no attack on Feudalism as a mode of production, nor on feudal social relations. Nor did the opposition between North-West and South East play a central role; even in 1642 there was a class struggle in every county.

The Tudor monarchy concentrated the State power, in the first place against the peasantry; and it centralised the state power against localism, especially in the backward north and west. To these ends it used the Prerogative Courts in much the same way as Chancery had been used earlier. All this *objectively* helped the bourgeoisie, which was for the winning side and which benefited by the enforcement of law and order and the development of a bureaucracy. Thus the 16th Century saw an alliance of the gentry, the merchants and the monarchy. This alliance was not something absolutely new, but a development of the old Parliamentary alliance, going back to the 14th Century and to Edward l. (A similar alliance existed in France under Louis XIV and in Russia under Peter the Great). The English Reformation under Henry VIII was a process primarily of land-grabbing, not the victory of Protestant (i.e. bourgeois) ideology, which developed on a significant scale only later.

The need for national defence against international reaction, represented by Spain and the Pope, made absolutism progressive in England, as it was to be under Richelieu in France, for a similar reason. This situation again *objectively* helped the bourgeoisie, which pushed on the government.

The Tudor State pursued a policy of protection of trade in order to promote national wealth and develop the sources of taxation (cf.14th Century England, 17th Century France, Peter the Great's Russia) because it was not afraid of capitalism as a mode of production. It only began to be afraid of it in the course of the 16th Century, after merchant capital had 'spilled over' to a significant degree into industry. Thus in 1563 it began to check free industrial development; thus in 1571, the House of Commons is found insisting on legalising interest in face of government opposition; and the government's policy of checking enclosures could not be carried out because of local opposition. The essentially feudal character of the Tudor Monarchy is clearly shown by its Statute of Uses (1536) and its establishment of the Court of Wards (1540) both measures aimed at guaranteeing the *feudal* rights of the Crown. In the latter part of the century too, and more clearly after 1588, the Crown attacked bourgeois ideology, as represented by Puritanism.[2]

V.G.K's view is dangerous because it plays into the hands of those bourgeois economists and historians who push the origins of capitalism further and further back into the past in order to show that it is really an eternal category; and secondly, because it plays up to and is in fact identical with the old bourgeois heresy that English development is in some sense peculiar, peaceful, non-revolutionary. The Tudor Monarchy is indeed complicated and difficult to analyse. But do the Marxist categories apply to it, or do they not? If they do, let us refine our analysis within their terms of reference, which is what the original theses tried to do. If they do not, let us say so frankly and abandon Marxism.

V.G.K. says that the Tudor monarchy is an absolute monarchy in the Marxist sense, yet not feudal. In doing so he is in fact implying, either that there is a mode of production to which absolutism is the corresponding structure (as Pokrovsky asserted); or that the state power can be simultaneously feudal and bourgeois (which implies reformism). It is absurdly insular to oppose all the Soviet Historians, and Marx and Engels, who admit the peculiarities and difficulties of England, but try to discuss them within the Marxist categories. We as Marxist historians find strong (bourgeois) resistance to the Marxist categories, naturally. All the more reason for refining our analysis *within* those categories, not for abandoning them, and with them all the revolutionary traditions of 1640 and of our own party.

Cde Kiernan at the conclusion of the discussion withdrew his main contentions, while drawing attention once more to a number of points which appeared to require further attention.

NOTES

1. The Percys and the Nevilles were the most powerful of the medieval northern barons, the former based in Northumberland and the latter in Durham and Yorkshire. 'Many historians', it has been said, have perceived their bitter feud 'as the critical element in converting factionalism at court into civil war in the kingdom at large', Anthony Pollard, 'Percies, Nevilles and the Wars of the Roses', *History Today*, 43: 9 (September 1993) pp42-48.
2. The Statute of Uses was designed to stop evasion of the inheritance tax payable on the estates of feudal dependents of the Crown. So great was the resentment which it aroused that it was replaced with the much milder Statute of Wills in 1540. However in the short term at least the Crown secured an increase in its revenues from feudal perquisites including its right of wardship when estates were inherited by minors. See above p92-3; see also p98, point 10.

DOCUMENT 15 (1948)[1]

Victor Kiernan

Postscript (Absolutism)

1. My contribution to the discussion may be summarised in this way:
   a) My starting point was the feeling that there were objections to the view brought forward in C. Hill's 'Theses on Absolutism in England' and in the original discussion on it; principally that
      i. The mechanism of the bourgeois revolution (1642) was being over-simplified.
      ii. The progressive aspects of the Tudor Monarchy were underrated.

iii. Absolutism was characterised as a phase of the feudal State without a satisfactory definition of feudalism being provided.

iv. Too sharp an antithesis was being made (representing too extreme a reaction from Pokrovsky's views) between Merchant Capital as a conservative force and Industrial Capital as the driving force of the bourgeois revolution.

b) I was led from this to maintain that neither the mode of production and the social-economic structure in 16th Century England, nor the Tudor Monarchy, were really 'feudal'.

c) This involved an over-emphasis of their 'bourgeois' aspects, which made 1642 unintelligible. I therefore had to suggest that the mode of production was a distinct one, neither feudal nor capitalist, and that the Absolute State rested on a balance of class forces. In this connection I quoted Marx's statement, in 'Revolution in Spain', that 16th century Absolutism 'presents itself as a civilising centre, as the initiator of social unity', making possible 'the general rule of the middle classes, and the common sway of civil society.' (I withdrew at an early date my statement, in my theses on Absolutism, section 3 paragraph 1, that the Tudor monarchy was not an absolutism of the same general type as the Continental).

d) This mode of thought in turn involved the argument that the bourgeois revolution in any country proceeds by distinct stages, of which in England 1485 would be one and 1835 another, and 1642 only the biggest of a number of leaps.

2. At the end of our closing discussion I abandoned the general case I had tried to build up, and recognised that the view put forward by C. Hill was the more logical and consistent, and was approved by the remaining participants in the discussion. In particular I recognised

a) That I had been unable to bring forward real evidence in favour of my view of 1485.

b) That there were objections to any theory of the bourgeois revolution proceeding by stages.

c) That it was necessary to stress the character of 1642 as the English bourgeois revolution.

d) That in the light of the definition of Feudalism that had been brought forward by this time, there was nothing illogical in the thesis that the Tudor State remained 'feudal' while under its framework there went on in the 16th century a rapid accumulation of bourgeois elements in the economic system.

3. I still think, however, that certain of the points which I raised in the course of the discussion deserve some further consideration, and should be taken account of in the formulation of the historical process in England. Some of these are –

a) With regard to Merchant and Industrial Capital –

i. The often-repeated idea of Merchant Capital being essentially parasitical is liable to be misleading. As Engels says: 'When the trade in products becomes independent of production itself, it follows a movement of its own, which, while it is governed as a whole by production, still in particular cases and within this general dependence follows particular laws contained in the nature of this new factor; this movement has phases of its own *and in turn reacts on the movement of production*.' (Letters 27.10. 1890)

ii. There was a growth before 1642 of Industrial Capital, in some old (wool) and various new (mining, glass etc) fields. But the extent of this tends to be overstated, and its role in the bourgeois revolution tends to be made too simple and dominant. We must be realistic about the actual changes brought about in State power. Engels points out that even after 1688 power was still in the hands of the big landowners, though these now had to pay attention to the interests of 'the financial, manufacturing and commercial class ... and the bourgeoisie was a humble but still recognized component of the ruling classes of England'. Moreover, the most powerful bourgeois element up to 1832 was commercial and financial capital; industrial capital was a very junior partner, and in fact the manufacturing class, being largely Nonconformist, was to this extent legally excluded from all direct share in State power.

b) Our picture of a revolution like 1642 is mainly of new productive (capitalistic) energies 'breaking through the integuments of a feudal structure. But in elaborating this picture, it is necessary to be on guard against falsifying the details of an extremely complex process.

i. The precise ways in which existing institutions impeded the development of the new forces have to be defined exactly and estimated realistically. It has then to be shown precisely how the new energies were liberated by the institutional changes brought about by the revolution. These changes were not so extensive as is sometimes supposed.

ii. One question of this sort is: How far did the early Stuart policy on industrial monopolies, and on the incorporation of new Companies in London of a manufacturing (as distinct from commercial) character, impede or accelerate the growth of capitalism?

iii. In regard to the cloth trade: Was the main need of the bourgeoisie one of freeing production from fetters imposed by the existing State, or was it one of creating a stronger State-machine to secure access to bigger foreign markets for an industry already tending to overproduction?

c) We should take fully into account the degree to which the bourgeois groups were forced into a revolutionary programme by the pressure of mass discontent. By about 1600, the main 'enemy of the people', as recognised in popular literature and left-wing religious literature, was not the feudal noble, but the capitalist, especially the usurer and the capitalist farmer. The bourgeoisie had to fight on both fronts. In order to get the masses behind it, it had to build up an elaborate propagandist picture of the situation, suffering from many distortions. In 1789 the bourgeoisie had an 'agrarian programme' offering immediate and considerable benefits to the agricultural masses. This was not so in 1642, because in England the spread of capitalist relations in the countryside had already gone very far. Hence the ideology of 1642, unlike that of 1789, was very largely distorted into a theological shape.

d) It is especially important to be precise as to the changes desired and effected by the bourgeoisie in the field of tenurial law. There is no sharp absolute breach between feudal and capitalist rent. As Marx says: 'The transition of capital to landed property is also historical, as the modern form of property in land is a product of the effect of capital upon feudal, etc. landed property' (Letters, 2.4.1858). On the great areas of land acquired by the moneyed classes before 1642, they actively maintained all those features of feudal tenurialism (such as fines-at-will) which were useful to them in exploiting and expropriating the cultivators. These features fitted in very well with capitalist relationships, and indeed served as the lever by which capitalist relationships were firmly established. Capitalism arose *on the basis* of feudalism, by taking over from it the rights of exploitation which feudalism had conveniently created for it. It was only for propaganda purposes that the bourgeois reformers talked of making a clean sweep of the 'Norman tyranny' represented by medieval feudal law. When they were in power, and the Levellers called on them to do so, they immediately refused. What was feudal in *form* in this 'obsolete' system was already largely capitalist in *essence*.

e) While fully admitting the importance of the bourgeois revolution as a historical category, I still think we should be careful not to put it in the same order of importance as the proletarian revolution, and not to impose on it characteristics that only properly belong to the latter. The bourgeois revolution is a redistribution of class power, not its abolition. Capitalism is overthrown by the proletariat, feudalism is *not* overthrown by the peasantry.

f) Although a common denominator may be found among all social forms intermediate between primitive communism (or slavery) and capitalism, and these may all be brought under the term 'feudalism', it is none the less important to take into account the great divergences between different types of feudalism. It is to be noted that:

   i. Out of all parts of the world, only W Europe evolved capitalism. W. Europe previously had a peculiar (I think a peculiarly unstable) type of feudalism (cf. 3d above).

   ii. Of all non-European regions brought into contract with the West in the 19th Century, Japan adapted itself far the most readily to capitalism, after previously having a feudal structure resembling in many ways that of western Europe.

iii. M. Dobb raised the question, which I think extremely important, of what is the mode of production in an agrarian system worked by peasant proprietors and/or tenant farmers paying money rents, not visibly burdened by 'non economic compulsion', and not employing hired labour. Such a system does not appear to be either feudal or capitalist. It has often made its appearance; in particular it prevailed in China for 2000 years, and the superstructure based on it was very different from that in, for instance, Japan.

g) While recognising the general validity of the argument for classing Absolutism as the final phase of the feudal State, I am not sure that the reorganisation, reconstruction, or reshuffling of feudalism involved in this phase has yet been defined accurately enough, in such a way as to enable justice to be done to the 'progressive' aspects of the Tudor Monarchy. Absolutism seeks to preserve feudalism by freezing it, rendering it static, but by doing so it radically alters its nature, and unintentionally ensures, in the long run, the decay of feudal society (I was blamed during the discussion for confusing society with State; but the feudal, or any other, State must be seen as having a positive part to play with regard to the preservation or otherwise of a certain social structure.) The best illustration of this process is, perhaps, the period of the Tokugawa Shogunate in Japan [1600-1868]. The transition from the older feudal to the Absolutist State requires the presence of such a factor as development of money-economy.

4. I should like to repeat that the above points are only raised as detached comments or questions of detail, not as part of a general criticism of the point of view put forward by C. Hill, M. Dobb and others.

NOTES

1. This is dated 28 February 1948 although it is clear that Kiernan delivered a statement at the meeting on the 10/11 January. Presumably it was written up for circulation with the minutes.

DOCUMENT 16 (1948)

The 16th-17th century section of the Historians' Group of the Communist Party (Communist Review July 1948, pp207-14) State and Revolution in Tudor and Stuart England

The Political Committee of the Communist Party has decided to celebrate next year the three-hundredth anniversary of the first English Republic, 1649, as an event of major political significance.

Marx and Engels devoted much attention to the English bourgeois revolution, as can be seen from the study of their writings on this subject recently published in *Science* and *Society* (Winter, 1948). But when Christopher Hill's pioneer essay, *The English Revolution,* appeared in 1940, British Marxists were largely unfamiliar with the view that the bourgeois revolution of 1640-49 was 'perhaps the most important event that has yet occurred in English history.' The question was raised to a higher theoretical level by the publication, in 1946, of Maurice Dobb's *Studies in the Development of Capitalism*, which, besides drawing attention to often neglected material in writings of Marx and Lenin (such as *Capital Vol. III,* and *The Development of Capitalism in Russia)* contains invaluable original discussions of the problems involved, based on recent economic research interpreted by Marxist method. Within the last year, Party historians have had discussions on the English bourgeois revolution and the State form which it overthrew (the absolute monarchy which grew up under the Tudors and was destroyed in 1640). The present article, without entering on every question or repeating the story of developments outlined by Hill and Dobb, attempts only to indicate some main general points arising from the discussion which maybe of interest not only to teachers and other specialists, but to all Party members.

The discussion revealed unclarities about fundamental questions of historical development which are no less important for the present than for the past. The reformist and gradualist notions still dominant in the British Labour movement are linked up with mistaken ideas about British history, especially about the transition to capitalism and the political victory of the bourgeoisie (for example, Ramsay MacDonald, quoted by Harry Pollitt, Report to Twentieth Party Congress: 'In human history, one epoch slides into another, individuals formulate ideas, society gradually assimilates them and gradually the accumulation shows itself in the social structure').

The two main questions at issue in the discussion were: (1) How do we decide what are the class relationships determining the basic character of a given society? and (2) What is a social revolution, and how does it happen?

The first question arose in the concrete form: What were the predominant relations of men in production in England at the beginning of the seventeenth century? Was it a feudal or bourgeois society? Some of the points of method which emerged in thrashing out this question are also relevant to the question: what is a capitalist and what is a Socialist society? – where clarity is so greatly needed today.

The second question arose in the concrete form: what class controlled the State between the accession of the Tudors in 1485 (or of the Yorkists in 1461) and 1640? Did the State serve the bourgeoisie and combat feudalism, or not? The underlying questions of how we determine the class character of a given State and what is the role of the State in the transition from one social order to another are very topical indeed.

II

On the first question; some comrades contested the picture given by Hill of England, 1640, as a land wherein 'the structure of society was still essentially feudal', in the sense that the growth of capitalist relations was still cramped by an overall framework of feudal relations which were upheld and enforced by a feudal State. The discussion of this point necessitated both an examination of the actual facts and also a consideration of what Marxists mean by feudalism, as against the conventional legal-academic usage.

The English feudalism of 1600, based on the exploitation of the free and semi-free peasants and other small commodity producers by a rentier aristocracy, naturally bore a different aspect from that of 1400 where the feudal lords exercised a more brutal and direct control over the life and labour of their serfs. The social order was in an advanced stage of decay, owing to the growth of capitalist relations and to peasant revolt, and its extreme dependence on the central government reflects this decadence. Basically, however, feudal relations still prevailed; power depended on the monopoly of land and the legal rights of the landlord over the direct producer, from whom the tribute exacted still largely reflected the older conditions of labour service, with the direct producer in customary possession of the land, rather than those of 'economic' rent required by the new capitalist class (Hill, pp. 35-36.)

It was also noted that exploitation through local power is not a necessary feature of feudal society. There was a high degree of centralisation of power as early as the fourteenth century in England, compared with many other West European countries (wide competence of the royal jurisdiction, with a central bureaucracy, control of the Justices of the Peace, and of wages, etc.). Exploitation of the people by the feudal landlords (together with their merchant and financial hangers-on) was in the England of the early seventeenth century carried on to a very great extent through the central government, especially by means of the monopolies granted by royal favour. Such a lucrative privilege as the Earl of Essex's monopoly of the sweet wine trade raised to a national scale the medieval lord of the manor's right to take toll of all traders operating in his little territory.

In short, the social order was still one which suited the feudalists, much as the imperialist-monopoly capitalism of 1948, whilst differing in important respects from the capitalism of 1848 (owing, again, to the advanced stage of contradiction between productive forces and social relations) is nevertheless the same social order at bottom, and has not become Socialism or 'something else' non-capitalist.

III

What led certain comrades to doubt the feudal nature of English society in the 1600s was some confusion not only about feudalism, but also about capitalism. The ordinary academic view of 'the new monarchy' in England has something in common with the mistaken notion of the Soviet historian, the late M. N. Pokrovsky, that there was a special epoch of 'merchant capitalism' lying between early feudalism and what he called 'industrial capitalism' (the factory system). Marx proved that merchant capital is not a new mode of production, but 'the historical form of capital long before capital has subjected production to its control' (*Capital*, vol. III, pp. 384-396). Though he dated the capitalist era from the sixteenth century, treating previous economic and social developments (for example, the abolition of serfdom) as the 'prerequisites' for this stage (*Capital*, vol. I, p739), he showed that it was only with the changes made by the industrial revolution that the direct producer as a class became completely subordinated to capitalist relations, losing all control over his product and over the means of production.

The long drawn-out process which converts the decisive body of producers into proletarians is to be traced through transformations in the kind of exploitation; at the lower level of production the direct producer must be in possession of land; later, at the higher level, he must be divorced from it. At one pole we find surplus labour extracted as tribute or tax ('non-economic' rent) paid by direct producers to landowners, at the other, surplus value extracted through wages, paid to direct producers by capitalists. In the one case a relation of servitude or personal dependence, in the other a relation of 'free' contract. Intermediate stages are tested by questions as to how far the producer is in possession of some or all of his means of production, how far, as a wage labourer, he is solely dependent on wages, how far the products of his labour go direct into a consumption fund (his own or his master's), how far he controls their exchange, etc., etc. In sixteenth and seventeenth century England, despite the increasing grip of merchant capital on production (reflected in the differentiation inside the gilds and among the peasantry) the decisive labour force remained in possession of their means of production and the mobility of labour was discouraged (Elizabethan Poor Law, Statute of Artificers, Act of Settlement).

In the economic transition of the sixteenth century the dominant tendency was for already-established merchants to turn towards production, financing and exploiting domestic handicraft production in the suburbs of towns or in the villages outside the reach of urban gild regulations. Thereby a section of the merchant class broke away (at least partially) from that landowner-merchant alliance which had been developing since the fourteenth century and involved powerfully conservative elements; and the interests of this section came to be associated with the growth of industry.

At the same time there was a growing tendency for more well-to-do craftsmen, accumulating capital and taking to trade, to organise production on a capitalist basis by employing poorer craftsmen to work for them (what Marx called 'the really revolutionary way': *Capital*, vol. III, p. 393; Dobb, 120-4, 134-5). This tendency came to a head at the beginning of the seventeenth century in the rise of a democratic movement among the craft element inside many of the big London Livery Companies (or gilds); a movement that was evidently an important lever in the bourgeois revolution. While some of the merchants were becoming capitalists, therefore, organising domestic industry and a few 'manufactories', others, especially those who monopolised foreign trade, were hand in glove with the feudalists to soak the capitalist sector through 'controls' like Alderman Cockayne's disastrous project for the cloth business. Lucy Hutchinson describes the groups around the King which, together, made up the feudal ruling class of the England of Charles I: 'the needy courtiers, the proud, encroaching priests, the thievish projectors, the lewd nobility and gentry.' All these thrust their hands deep into the pockets of the whole people, from the capitalists, urban and rural, down to the humblest peasant, and by their extortions and privileges held back the full development of capitalism. A large, wealthy capitalist class had arisen, both in industry and in agriculture, a section of the gentry and yeomanry having gone over to capitalist methods, running their small estates as units organised for commodity production by wage-labour. But the capitalists found themselves mulcted and penalised in various ways, and the expansion of their way of life obstructed by the feudal elements in control of the State.

IV

In examining the way in which the feudalists exploited the rest of the community we were brought from a consideration of the structure of society to a consideration of the State. Not only did the State serve directly as a means of transferring surplus product to the feudalists, it also, through the monopolies, etc., protected and upheld feudal privilege and inequality against capitalist encroachments, as well as against popular revolts. For instance, the Statute of Artificers (1563) was an attempt to freeze the status quo by restricting the mobility and free recruitment of labour, regardless of the interests of expanding capitalism. This is typical of the way in which the absolutist State worked. It is wrong to see in the struggles between the monarch and certain groups of nobles, or in Henry VIII's dissolution of the monasteries and assumption of control over the Church, a fight of the monarchy 'against feudalism'. The King was the biggest feudal landowner, his revenue and the 'prerogatives' which safeguarded it were based on feudal rights: revenue from crown-lands and from feudal courts (such as the Court of Wards), customs and excise, purveyance for the armed forces, etc. (Customs dues were like feudal tolls in that they were imposed on exports and imports primarily to produce revenue for the King.)

The fact that the Tudors' revenue was collected and administered more efficiently than the Lancastrians' had been did not alter its feudal character. All that the monarch aimed to do in relation to the minor feudalists was to establish his ascendancy over them as fully as possible and make them closely dependent upon him. The period sees a *concentration* of feudal property and power in the hands of the monarchy, with a corresponding transition of the feudalists from local semi-sovereigns to courtiers – a transition to which in the early stages they resigned themselves very unwillingly. (This process of concentration has a certain limited analogy with the growth of the great trusts and of State capitalism in our time.)

The new sources of land and wealth, the greater unification and internal order which the absolute monarchy brought about, were more favourable than previous conditions for the growth of capitalist production. In our own age the concentration of capitalist production has prepared the basis for Socialism and created better conditions for struggle to overthrow the capitalist order; the form of State power, however, still harmonises with the interests of monopoly capital and imperialism. The Tudor and early Stuart State was essentially an executive institution of the feudal class more highly organised than ever before. In the second half of the sixteenth century there was as yet no serious conflict of interest between the rising bourgeoisie and the Crown, which needed their economic strength in the fight for national existence against the reactionary power of Spain: this is shown in the new national pride and the rich flowering of music, drama and poetry under 'Good

Queen Bess'; but before the end of Elizabeth's reign the bourgeoisie were outgrowing this relation. In the Stuart period, in order to create conditions for free and full development of their own social order, they had to seize State power. This meant destroying the organs of absolutism (Star Chamber, High Commission) and the personification of the old regime in Charles I. The executive and organs of force were subordinated to the control of the 'Commons House of Parliament'. Parliament was an institution dating from feudal times, but it represented mainly the landed class, and in England, where capitalism had grown up largely in the countryside, many of the gentry had capitalist interests in industry or agriculture. The English bourgeoisie represented in Parliament was able to smash the absolute monarchy before the latter could build a great apparatus of bureaucracy and militarism like that in France – an apparatus which Laud and Strafford consciously strove to reproduce in England.

Only after the revolution of 1640-49 does the State in England begin to be subordinated to the capitalists. This revolution was something qualitatively different from such changes within the feudal framework as had occurred in 1461, 1485, 1529, and so on, though these had in some ways improved conditions for capitalist development. The revolution of 1640 replaced the rule of one class by another. This was the answer to our second question. The change accomplished can be seen in the abolition of crown monopolies and feudal tenures, in the Navigation Act, the fight to wrest world trade from the Dutch, the development of the navy, the forward colonial policy (Ireland, Jamaica), the establishment of the Bank of England (1693), and in fiscal policy; taxes falling on production replaced by taxes falling on consumption, and a consistent protectionist system which has the effect, in Marx's words, of 'manufacturing manufacturers'.

From fear of the militant and democratic petty bourgeoisie the English capitalists did not carry through the complete transformation of the political structure heralded by our first republic; the monarchy was revived in 1660, and retained 'under new management' in 1689, after James II had been punished for failing to appreciate that a revolution had occurred. Now, however, the feudal-absolutist monarchy had given place to the constitutional monarchy, and the State was at the service of the new landlord-capitalist alliance, though the defeat of the revolutionary-democratic forces, and the preservation of feudal elements through the continued dominance of merchant over industrial capital, prolonged for 140 years the rule of an oligarchy.

V

In the course of the discussion, two main trends of non-Marxist thought revealed themselves. On the one hand was economic determinism, which sees 'politics' more or less automatically adjusting itself to 'economics', identifies the State with society, underestimates the role of man's conscious struggle and smoothes out the course of history into an evolutionary process where social revolutions, if such they can be called, happen gradually and spontaneously without people being aware of them, all under the relentless drive of 'economic forces'. On the other hand, was the trend of ignoring the ultimate economic basis of social relations. The first school of thought forgets the *dialectical* aspect of dialectical materialism; the second forgets that it is dialectical *materialism.* It is the relationship between men in production, the presence or absence of exploitation of some by others, and the means by which exploitation is achieved, that provides the clue to the basic structure of any society. The change from one mode of production to another, involving the substitution of one predominant type of production relations far another, takes place through class struggle, in which the exploiting class of the old order fights hard with all the means at its command (including State power) to retard the change and retain economic ascendancy.

The English Revolution of 1640-1649 fulfilled the function of every bourgeois revolution: it swept away the main barriers to capitalist development. It produced remarkable creative developments in science, philosophy and the arts: the Royal Society and Newton, Hobbes and Locke, Milton, Bunyan, Defoe, Vanburgh and Wren. It made possible the agrarian and industrial revolution. The England born in 1649, for all its bourgeois limitations, had a most powerful influence in world history: it showed the way to the American revolution of 1776 and with it to the great French Revolution of 1789. The forces in the New Model Army and the Leveller movement that were defeated in our revolution constituted the most vigorous and self-confident assertion of popular democracy ever known in the world up to that time, and not seen again until the uprising of the common people in France in 1789-94. With Winstanley and the Diggers, a Communist theory was for the first time associated with the democratic movement.

During the long reign of capitalism the bourgeoisie has come more and more to deny its revolutionary past; a century ago the *Communist Manifesto* showed that only the working class can complete the conquest of freedom begun by the bourgeoisie in its prime. Today only the working people can worthily celebrate the tercentenary of the revolution since they only can carry that revolution through to its end in Socialism. In this celebration, led by Communists, the nation can learn a lesson in democracy and dictatorship. To understand what happened in 1649 is to understand better what is happening in Eastern Europe today.

Absolutism

DOCUMENT 17 (1949)

Maurice Dobb

Some Notes on the Changes in the Mode of Production in the First Half of the Seventeenth Century

1. The mode of production at the beginning of the 17th century in England was in a complex state of transition; marked by great unevenness of development as between different economic sectors (e.g., village economy in the South and South East and in the West and the North). More important than the *state* of technique and social relations at any given time is the way in which these were *changing*. This is particularly significant for understanding the class alignments of the period, which were complex and subject to rapid shifts. Only when this has been studied (and much more research on it is needed) and understood in its many-sided character, as a *process* of revolutionary change, will the reflection of that process in the ideological conflicts of the period become comprehensible. Schematic attempts neatly to label everything and put it in its separate box once and for all must be avoided.

If any justice at all can be done to the situation by a bald summary, one can say this of the situation in general. By this period the 'petty mode of production' (production by small commodity producers), had to a large extent but still incompletely (and far from completely in the more backward agricultural districts of the West and North) emancipated itself from feudal exploitation (compulsory exaction of the surplus product of the petty production for the benefit of feudal overlords). This petty mode of production was in process of being penetrated by capital and subjected to capital. At the same time it was being itself disintegrated by this subjection to capital and by the burgeoning of capitalist relations of production.

2. The survival of feudal exploitation and feudal relations of production is seen in agriculture, not only in the survival of feudal dues (payable by force of law or custom) and service obligations, but also in much of the money-rent payments of tenants, which still bore many of the characteristics of feudal rent, and which at any rate had not completed the transition into capitalist rent (implying a free-market in land and unfettered right of movement on the part of the tenant farmer). It has been a common fallacy among bourgeois economic historians that commutation of feudal services for a money payment represents the end of feudalism and the transition forthwith to bourgeois 'money economy'. Such a view has led to the predating of the end of feudalism as an economic form, and to a neglect of the surviving elements of feudal relations in Tudor and early Stuart times. In this connection it is well to remember the following statements of Marx: 'In all forms in which the direct labourer remains the "possessor" of the means of production, the property relation must at the same time assert itself as a direct relation between rulers and servants, so that the direct producer is not free. This is a lack of freedom which may be modified from serfdom with forced labour to the point of a mere tributary relation ...'. Speaking of money rent, distinguished from capitalist rent, he says: 'By money rent we mean here ... that ground-rent which arises from a mere change of form of rent in kind, just as this rent in kind, in its turn, is but a modification of labour rent. Under money rent the direct producer no longer turns over the product, but its price, to the landlord (who may be either the state or a private individual). A surplus of products in their natural farm is no longer sufficient, it must be converted from its natural form into money.' Having said this, however, he at once goes on to show that this kind of money rent is itself transitional in character – that it represents compulsory or feudal exaction of the surplus product in a state of dissolution. 'The character of the entire mode of production is thus more or less changed. It loses its independence, it remains no longer detached from social

connections ... Money rent, as a converted form of rent in kind and as an antagonist of rent in kind, is the last form, and the dissolving form, of that form of ground-rent which we have considered so far ... In its further development money rent must lead – apart from all intermediate forms, such as that of the small peasant who is a tenant – either to the transformation of land into independent peasants' property, or into the form corresponding to the capitalist mode of production, that is to rent paid by the capitalist tenant' (*Capital*, [1905] Vol. III pp, 918, 925, 927). It is the fact of feudal relations *surviving*, but in changed and *disintegrating forms*, that, I believe, affords a key to understanding much which has been obscure about the 17th century class struggle and bourgeois revolution.

3. A further development in village economy is of importance: the growing social differentiation within the petty mode of production itself. This was of long standing; and evidence of richer peasants employing some hired labour and of poor peasants ('cotters') offering themselves for hire is to be found as early as the thirteenth century. It was a process that was much accelerated by the growth of production for a market (and its concomitant money-rents), and tended to be more advanced in those areas where commodity-production (for the market) was most developed. In this growth of kulak-farming (seen, e.g. in the improving-peasant and the peasant-enclosure) in Tudor and Stuart times, accompanied as it was by the growth of a rural semi-proletariat of impoverished peasants, we see the beginnings of capitalist relations in agriculture, disintegrating and transforming the petty mode of production.

Two features of this development are of special importance. Firstly, the new type of 'improved farming' represented important changes in productive methods in agriculture, and brought with it an increase of productivity (both of labour and per acre of land?). Secondly, a considerable section of the smaller gentry (the squirearchy) took to commodity production on the basis of wage labour, both arable and pasture, on the basis of the new enclosed farming, and the financing of village cottage industry (chiefly cloth). The fact that the dividing line between yeomen, or kulak-peasant, and the squirearchy became increasingly blurred (the latter investing in bourgeois forms of production, and the former buying manors and gentility) is a crucial feature of Tudor England. (Cf. for this the writings of Christopher Hill; especially his article on 'Land in the English Revolution' in *Science & Society*, Winter, 1948-49).[1]

4. The urban and suburban-handicrafts represented the earliest examples of the petty mode of production emancipating itself from feudal dependence (e.g., the struggles of the towns against feudal overlordship in the thirteenth and fourteenth centuries); as they also represented early examples of class differentiation and the first embryo-stage of the bourgeois mode of production. This latter took the form of the 'putting-out system', under which work was given out to poorer craftsmen by the richer, who came to be separated from direct production and assumed the role of trading intermediaries and entrepreneurs (for details, see my *Studies in the Development of Capitalism*, Ch III section II). Indeed it seems to have been these nascent bourgeois elements who took the lead in the struggles against feudal overlordship.

By the first half of the 17th century it is clear that this growth of bourgeois relations of production (in the still incomplete and transitional form of the putting-out system) had reached considerable maturity, especially in the cloth industry (but also in certain other handicrafts, such as leatherwork and some metalwork trades). This development had followed along two main lines: (i) the growth of a class of *kulak*-capitalists from among the craftsmen themselves to become organisers and financiers ('merchant-manufacturers') of the urban and suburban handicrafts; (ii) the turning of a certain section of merchant capital towards industry, to organise handicraft industry in the villages (out of reach of urban gild regulations, and often in competition with urban handicrafts), also in the putting-out system. This was done extensively in the 16th century by the merchants of many of the London Livery-Companies, such as the Drapers, Clothworkers, Haberdashers, Girdlers, Leathersellers, Cutlers (details are given in *Studies in the Development of Capitalism*, Ch. IV, pp.126-138). The first of these developments was spoken of by Marx as 'the really revolutionary way'. Of the second he spoke as 'serving historically as a mode of transition', but becoming later 'an obstacle to a real capitalist mode of production and declining with the development of the latter' (*Capital*, vol. III, pp388-96). It seems clear that it was the smaller capitalists associated with the farmer (e.g. the clothiers of the provincial towns and the country clothiers) who provided (along with yeoman and squire-farmers of the new type) the principal driving force of the bourgeois revolution; although the sections of merchant capital which had links with production were allies-up-to-a-point of the Parliamentary cause (if vacillating allies who later compromised with reaction, and paved the way for the Restoration).

Much confusion and false interpretation has been caused by a tendency to treat 'Merchant Capital' as a homogeneous entity, neatly pigeon-holed as 'bourgeois' and 'revolutionary'. While important sections of the larger merchants – those who (as we have seen) had invested capital in production (indirectly via financing the putting-out system) – played a progressive role, at least in the early stages of the revolution, this is not true of merchant capital as a whole. Merchant capital at the time was composed of various strata. In particular, those merchants who dominated the export trade seem to have played a reactionary role. As parasites upon the Crown and the feudal State, on which they relied for their privileged position, they tended to be allies of the Crown in preserving the old State-form and the old order. They exploited the existing mode of production in their own way – a *feudal* way, *via* trading monopolies which they acquired through political influence and power. In fact, it is important to realise the extent to which the *form* of feudal modes of exploitation (monopoly rights, dependent on political privilege and power) pervaded all productive relations at this period – even those where the relations of production were becoming predominantly bourgeois in *content*. The reflection of this contradiction in the ideology of the period must, surely, be a highly important subject for investigation and discussion (although here I cannot offer any constructive suggestions)?

5. It should be noted that a proletariat in the full sense of the word was still little developed at this period. There had been the 'sturdy vagabonds' of Elizabethan times, victims of Tudor rack-renting and enclosure. But the basis of the domestic handicraft industry was still the small (if impoverished) owner, and much of the wage-labour of the countryside was done by the cottager or squatter on the waste who still had, at least, a parcel of ground. Sometimes the capitalist invested directly in the

means of production, as with the capitalist-owned fulling-mill in the cloth industry (also in the examples given in the paragraph); but on the whole this was still rare. What limited the full maturing of bourgeois relations (and formed a basis for the domestic system) was that *the direct producer was still joined to his means of production*. His hold on them was precarious: soon he was to lose them altogether through indebtedness or forcible dispossession. But the process of 'primitive accumulation' had to advance much further before bourgeois production could mature into the 'factory stage'.

6. There were, however, one or two lines of production where the technique of production had progressed sufficiently even at this time to lay the basis for something like factory production. Precisely because of the scarcity of wage-labour (at least, of its immobility), such industries often had to rely on forced labour. Thus a further contradiction of this period: some of the most technically advanced industry depended an compulsory, instead of 'free' labour, and was run by capitalists who depended on royal privilege (monopoly patent-rights) and were apt to be royalist in sentiment and alignment by reason of this feudal tie. This was the case in mining, where the invention of improved pumps enabled deep-mining which required capital running into tens of thousands; in salt-making, with the invention of a new process of dissolving rock-salt; in paper making and powder-making; in brass and ordnance and sugar refining. Similarly ironworking was very soon to see a new type of furnace replacing the old small-scale bloomeries or forges; in west-country nail-making the new slitting-machine was coming to replace handicraft nail-making; and in the Birmingham district the blade-mill, driven by water-power, was influencing sword and dagger making (although these latter developments belong rather to the second half of the seventeenth century than to the first).

NOTES

1. This is a very curious citation as the yeoman or kulak barely appears in Hill's article prior to the 1640s and only then obliquely in the guise of the Levellers' vain attempts to preserve peasant property rights. See above pp52-3.

DOCUMENT 18 (1949)

Christopher Hill
The English Bourgeois Revolution and Ideology

(I assume that the reader will have carefully studied Caudwell's *Crisis in Physics*)

1. The English revolution of 1640-9 was a bourgeois revolution. The absolute monarchy, the persecuting state church, the feudal nobility were defeated and never restored to their old positions (for amplification of this statement, see *The English Revolution, 1640*).
2. The restoration of 1660 was a compromise between victorious bourgeoisie and defeated feudalists, dictated by their fear of the revolutionary petty bourgeoisie, of a threat to big property. King, House of Lords, Bishops were restored to give dignity to the new order. But monarchy, House of Lords and church were subordinated to the bourgeoisie in the House of Commons. This was fully confirmed in 1688, when a would-be absolute monarch (James II) was ejected and some of the Bishops, who till then had preached passive obedience to divinely-constituted authority, took the lead in opposing James.
3. This vast economic and political revolution naturally had its ideological counterpart. Modern science and modern political thought reflect the needs and interests of the bourgeoisie. These notes are concerned particularly with political thought.
4. The ideology of the revolutionary bourgeoisie was Puritanism. Only a very few thinkers had emancipated themselves from the traditional religious modes of thought. But to say that Puritanism was the ideology of the revolutionary bourgeoisie does not get us very far. Puritanism is a loose word, covering a great deal. It will perhaps help if we look back at the main achievement of the reformation, which Engels called the first of the three great decisive battles of the bourgeoisie against feudalism. This may help us to see how Protestantism and Puritanism (its more radical development) prepared for materialism and modern science as well as for theories of democracy.
5. The reformation proclaimed the rights of individual conscience

against ecclesiastical authority. Luther's 'priesthood of all believers' was an egalitarian democracy of the faithful. The individual entered into direct relations with God, spurning the mediation of priests, saints, the Virgin. It was a denial of the hierarchical order of feudalism.

6. In attacking priestcraft the reformers attacked the magical elements in religion. The bread and wine was not *really* changed into the body and blood of Christ. The priest ceases to be the indispensable maker of magic, consecrated and marked out by his vestments: he becomes a *minister*, the servant of the congregation, indistinguishable from them by his clothes and possibly even elected by them. (The attack on magical modes of thought affects not only the official religion, Catholicism, but also the unofficial, underground, witch-cult, which was wiped out in protestant countries in the sixteenth and seventeenth centuries.[1] In one sense Protestantism was directed against crude materialism, image worship etc. (Caudwell, 78-9, 82-6)). God became at once more personal and more remote: he spoke directly to the conscience of each believer, but he also became [an] abstract and absolute moral law. He ceased to be involved in the social fabric. The transition from (catholic) justification by works to (protestant) justification by faith is the transition from a religion based on the performance of formal duties and ceremonies (payment of tithes, confession, contribution of candles, etc) to a religion based on purity of intention and motive. God still stands for that part of reality which cannot be explained. But now he is confronted not by agricultural communities trying to propitiate him in the only way they know, through mediators, but by atomized individuals, who are conscious of their helplessness in face of the blind forces of nature and the market, but yet have learnt the great lesson that God is more likely to help those who help themselves. Protestantism and Puritanism emphasize effort, thrift, self-control – virtues by which capital is accumulated.
7. The reformation destroyed the authority of the church. What was to take its place? In practice the king did: the early reformers were perforce erastian. They could win the opportunity to preach their doctrines freely only if they could persuade the head of the feudal state that the church was worth plundering and that the position of the monarchy would be strengthened by controlling

the church propaganda machine. The early reformers distinguished between matters essential to salvation and 'things indifferent': with the latter the secular state might deal. So in this sphere the principle of expediency was smuggled in. And there was never an agreed definition of what things were fundamental: the area of 'things indifferent' tended to expand.

8. But whatever the practical erastianism of the early reformers, it was difficult to work out a satisfactory theory of the Divine Right of Kings which had not already been undermined by the attack on the church. Authority in all spheres came in question: increasingly men appealed to reason, expediency, utility, against accepted conventions and established authorities. In science, this tendency is best illustrated by Bacon. (I am here discussing this only at the ideological level: the real motive force in the ideological revolt against authority is the reaction of the bourgeoisie against its frustration by the feudal social order and state.) This development in thought was enormously expedited after 1640, by the processes of revolution. Before the outbreak of the civil war the parliamentarian leaders always tried to justify their actions by quoting precedents from past English history; after 1642 they began to do things for which no precedents could be found.
9. Similarly, the establishment of complete toleration for all religious sects – the necessary condition for unity of the progressive forces against the old regime – showed that there was no political system to be found in the Bible on which all could agree. Men began to see that text-swapping was as unremunerative as precedent-hunting. Each way *reason* came to the fore: problems could be solved by *discussion*, by ascertaining what was *expedient*.
10. That is where Hobbes came in. Hobbes is thoroughly protestant in his attitude to the magical elements in religion, and in his emphasis on the fundamental equality of natural man (no longer of Christians only). Hobbes tries to find rational laws for politics, starting by assuming a world of atomized individuals recognizing nothing but their own interests (cf. Adam Smith's later economic man).
11. But Hobbes raises an interesting question. Philosophically a materialist, he was in politics a royalist, or at least a neutral. Similarly Bacon, very influential though his ideas were among

the parliamentarians after 1640, made his career through the absolute monarchy, and remained its supporter in principle until his death in 1626. Materialism was not necessarily revolutionary in the seventeenth century.

Why not? In part the answer can be found in biography. Hobbes was a tutor in the great feudal family of the Cavendishes. But there is more to it than that.

12. Seventeenth century materialism was *mechanical* materialism; it was static, allowing for no change. God was still necessary to introduce change; the great watchmaker could put the hands on an hour or two. For Hobbes (and for other political reactionaries) the claim to divine inspiration was the greatest danger to established political order; for Oliver Cromwell and Milton (and other revolutionary leaders), as well as for lesser Fifth Monarchists and Quakers, their belief in the direct interest of God in the affairs of man, possibility of his direct intervention, was essential. Their sense of co-operating with God's purposes was a source of moral energy to the revolutionaries. With Bacon, as Marx put it, 'materialism still includes within itself the germs of a many-sided development'. It 'pullulates with inconsistencies imported from theology'. But with Hobbes 'materialism becomes one-sided ... Knowledge based upon the senses loses its poetic blossom, it passes into the abstract experience of the mathematician; geometry is proclaimed as the queen of the sciences. Materialism takes to misanthropy ... From a sensual it passes into an intellectual entity; but thus ... it evolves all the consistency, regardless of consequences characteristic of the intellect' (Cf. Caudwell, 102-5).[2]
13. It was only the democratic petty-bourgeois revolutionaries, the Levellers, and the extreme left-wing group of the Diggers, who begin to work *through* religion to a materialist theory of politics that is not static; and here the ideas of Walwyn the cheese-monger and Winstanley the bankrupt merchant were uninfluential because of the defeat of the left after 1649. Pacifist quietism wins out among the petty-bourgeois democrats, especially after 1660: pie is sought, if anywhere, in the sky.
14. Harrington perhaps comes nearest to a materialist theory that also allows for history, for change: political power is based on

economic power, and the political superstructure must change when the economic basis changes. Harrington had a good deal of influence in the later seventeenth century, notably on Locke, the Whig theorist of 1688. But Harrington again was politically ambiguous: a friend of Charles I as well as a theoretical republican. And it is not the revolutionary elements in Harrington's theory that survive. By the end of the seventeenth century the bourgeois-aristocrat alliance which dominated society and political thought no longer wanted a revolutionary theory. Harrington's theory of revolutionary change had sunk to Defoe's: 'There can be no pretence of government till they who have the property consent'. It merely justified the ruling class in possession. Locke's theory justified the revolution of 1688, in defence of property; but left no room for revolt by 'the lower orders'.

15. Other intellectual activities contributing to the new outlook should be noted. The hunt for precedents stimulated historical research and criticism: Selden's scholarly *History of Tithes* undermined the church's claims to divine right as effectively as more emotive arguments. Difficulties in explaining away texts led to textual criticism even of the Bible. Hobbes pointed out that the evidence for any miracle must rest on the word of one 'who (being a man) may err and (which is more) may lie'. Within a generation of the 'Puritan Revolution', Wycherley's Lady Brute, when confronted with the Biblical adjuration to love our enemies, replied 'That may be a fault in the translation'.
16. The scepticism of the restored aristocracy after 1660 had its economic roots. The idealists of both sides, Puritan and Cavalier, were sacrificed in the class compromise of the restoration. Materialism came easily to those who were compelled to adjust themselves to the demands of the new society. They had to get capital somehow, whether by marrying into aldermanic families or by stimulating industrial development on their own estates. The atmosphere was favourable to the development of the sceptical-materialist amateur scientist.
17. But this science had no deep roots in productive activity. And materialism was a court luxury: all the propertied classes appreciated the uses of religion as a means of keeping the lower orders in place. Although the scientists of the Royal

Society were originally supporters of Parliament, they adapted themselves quite easily to the restoration. And this adaptation was ideological as well as political: deism rather than materialism is the dominant note even in 'advanced' thought during the century after 1660.

18. Some problems I should like to hear discussed:
    a) 'The categories of science ... always reflect in a class society the particular conditions of functioning of the working class as seen by the ruling class' (Caudwell p89). Can we accept Caudwell's account of the class roots of mechanical materialism and the dualism of bourgeois thought?
    b) Is my explanation of the necessity of God for the revolutionary bourgeoisie (12 and 13 above) acceptable?
    c) What were the ideological assumptions of the practicing scientists of the seventeenth century (Gilbert, Harvey, Boyle)?[3] Do we get an oversimplified picture by studying mainly Bacon – Hobbes – Locke? Was Newton's interest in the Book of Revelation a personal idiosyncrasy or a sign of intellectual degeneracy in old age; or something more.
    d) The relatively limited influence of materialism in eighteenth century England needs explanation. The works of Bacon, Hobbes, Harrington were accessible; but there is only a thin trickle of radical republican materialism (atheistic or deistic). English ideas are developed in France. Blake, one of the greatest radicals in politics, proclaimed himself a Berkeleyian idealist.
    e) In eighteenth century England nonconformists are closely associated with scientific advance. Yet politically nonconformity after 1660 seems to me to act as a sort of lightning conductor away from revolutionary politics.

NOTES

1. These themes were to be developed by Hill's student Keith Thomas in his hugely important *Religion and the Decline of Magic*, London 1971.
2. K. Marx & F. Engels, *The Holy Family or Critique of Critical Criticism. Against Bruno Bauer and Company* (1845) Chapter VI, Marx and Engels Collected Works, Vol 4, 1975.
3. For Gilbert and Boyle see Document 19.

DOCUMENT 19 (1949)

Stephen Mason
Notes on Science and the Battle of Ideas in the English Revolution

1. Modern science originated and developed with the economic and political power of the bourgeoisie. This is illustrated by two points; firstly, science grew in the geographical areas of mercantile prosperity, and developed or declined with that prosperity. It grew first in the Medieval centres of trade, Northern Italy, and the towns of the Hansa League, but the geographical discoveries brought the centres of trade to the Atlantic seaboard, and with trade came science, first to the Netherlands, then Northern France and Southern England. (See maps in Pledge's *Science since 1500*). Secondly, interest in science quickened with the political triumph of the bourgeoisie in England (see Morton's statistical analysis of the *Dictionary of National Biography* for the seventeenth century in *Osiris*, 1936, 4 p. 360).
2. The works of the early modern scientists show in their content the stimulus of the technical problems experienced by the bourgeoisie of the time, chiefly in war, industry, and navigation; these were of such a character, like the longitude problem, that they could only be solved by a scientific approach, as opposed to trial and error, or magical methods. (See Hessen, *The Social and Economic Roots of Newton's Principe*).
3. The form that early modern science took upon itself was determined by past history and in ever increasing measure by the character of the new bourgeois mode of production, or more specifically by the attitude of the bourgeoisie to that mode of production. The past history of ideology soon ceased to have any great formative effect upon the character of modern science, since a conscious break with the past was made, but it remained of importance so long as the Ancients-Moderns battle of ideas was waged.[1]
4. From the Middle Ages came two ideological traditions, one the orthodox religion of Catholicism; the other the underground

magical witch-cult in which may also be included astrology and alchemy, though they were not always underground even if they were magical. In Gordon Childe's words, magic is a supposed means of enabling men to get what they want, whilst religion serves to persuade men to want what they have got. Thus most forms of magic were underground in the Middle Ages since the ruling class sought to maintain a static society with power in their own hands. The early bourgeoisie of the 16th century took to alchemy and astrology as well as science to achieve their wants, and perhaps express their opposition before they had developed their own distinctive world view. No distinction was drawn between science and magic by the Medieval schoolmen, both were the prerogative of the devil, (Faust legend), hence taken over *in toto* at first by the bourgeoisie. The witch cult proper was much more popular than alchemy and astrology, and hence was the first to be suppressed. It was also more primitive and irrational, and perhaps degenerate (no longer corresponding to communal realities). Alchemy and astrology on the other hand were intellectual systems, and though often rejected by the schoolmen, were embodiments of the scholastic categories. They were rejected by the bourgeoisie when they became conscious of their own distinctive world view (mechanical atomism) in the 17th century, though they had become sceptical on practical grounds sometime before.

5. Caudwell in his *Crisis in Physics* remarks, 'The categories of science ... always reflect in a class society the particular conditions of functioning of the working class as seen by the ruling class' (pp.89). This statement is questionable. The early bourgeoisie seem to have derived their categories from their own mode of production as seen and practiced by them. The mode of production afforded not only the content of early modern science (through technical problems), but also the methodology of that science and its theoretical forms.
6. The determinants of the content of early modern science are discussed in Hessen (above), navigation, war, industry etc.
7. In seeking to improve the means of production and transport (forced upon them by the profit motive), the bourgeoisie became practical, inventive, developed the trial and error crite-

rion of the experiment (or rather took it over from the crafts, and made it both a theoretical and a practical criterion of a hypothesis).

8. In commerce the bourgeoisie became mathematical, conducted extensive computations to determine profit and loss. This approach was extended to nature, all things were measured and correlated mathematically. Then the mechanical view developed, momentum was seen as the coinage of natural transactions; bodies had each a certain amount of momentum which determined their action and motion.
9. Interest in the improvement of technology gave rise to this mechanical point of view in a characteristic form. The world was understood by analogy in terms of the machines that then existed as seen by the bourgeoisie. The bourgeoisie brought about the first effective and fertile union of theory and practice as the method of science, but only as the method; in the theory of science the world was contemplated as an independently active entity. To the bourgeois, man's control of the world was the result of his god-like knowledge, not of his activity; by the second half of the seventeenth century, the bourgeoisie had become a ruling class in England, and suffered, in theory, the contemplative illusion of all such classes. The machines that existed at that time may all be described as machines of transport. Ships and carts were obviously such. Pumps transported water from one position to another. Windmills and water wheels transferred mechanical energy from the winds, waters, to grindstones etc. They were machines that saved man from the brute task of labour, but there were at that time very few machines that could reproduce the creative actions of human skills, or transform one form of energy (heat) into another (mechanical, as in the steam engine); these came later with the industrial revolution. So the world was seen as a static world, one without development or evolution. Change took place, but it was only the transport of bodies, mechanical motion. History could be unrolled, backwards or forwards; all was predetermined, for there could be no emergence of novelty. This only came with the creative, transformative machines of the industrial revolution, which also transformed society, and led thither to the evolutionary cosmology of the 19th century.

10. Summing up the last four points we may say that the bourgeois viewpoint of the seventeenth century, as expressed say by Newton, was a reflection of the contemporary mode of production as seen by the bourgeoisie. It was a world of independently moving bodies viewed contemplatively from without. These bodies suffered only transport in space and time. They possessed no inner activity, and on meeting exchanged only externally given momentum.
11. In the battle of ideas of the seventeenth century a distinction must be drawn between the men with the scientific method and attitude, (the scientists proper), and the men imbued solely or mainly with the mechanical cosmology, (the philosophers like Descartes and Hobbes) though of course there were men who were both (Newton, Leibnitz). The scientists generally speaking were active, politically progressive and dissenters in religion, (with considerable qualifications). The philosophers imbued with the contemplative viewpoint of the new cosmology tended to timidity and fence sitting in practice. They contemplated the world, rather than changed it, their theory determined their practice, or rather the lack of it. The scientists were active in spite of their general theory, the scientific method determined their practice, and this was experimental and active. Another possible reason for the political inactivity or ambiguity of the philosophers was the lack of the idea of history or evolution in the seventeenth century mechanical cosmology. They could not identify themselves with the forces that held the future in their hands, since theoretically speaking from their viewpoint, there could be no novel future, only a rearrangement of the *status quo* (Hobbes).
12. The scientific method agreed with later Protestantism in assumptions and attitude. In the Protestant creed man looked to his own individual religious experience for religious truths, he interpreted the scriptures for himself just as the scientist interpreted nature for himself, relying on his own experimental knowledge. Both were opposed to the authority of the Roman Church and both were persecuted by that body in consequence. There was also a positive stimulation, since scientific acclivity was numbered amongst the good works that signified salvation. Candolle, *Historie des Sciences et*

Savants, [1873] claims a 6/1 predominance of Protestants to Catholics amongst the famous scientists of Europe between 1660 and 1860. This figure is too low since he counts the French atheists of the eighteenth century as Catholics.

13. These general points may be illustrated by the early English scientists, John Dee, 1527-1608, alchemist, astrologer, mathematician, William Gilbert, 1540-1603, first English experimental scientist, anti-Aristotle, anti-alchemy, but still in part an astrologer, William Harvey, 1578-1657, royalist, anti-Aristotle, responsible for the analogy of the heart as a pump. The next significant persons are the group of young Protestant scientists who found the 'Philosophical College', precursor the Royal Society, in 1644, notably Wilkins, Wallis, Patty and Boyle. Their main concern at first is with the scientific method and the utilitarian aspects of science. They effectively establish science in England, and through their efforts the Royal Society is founded at the Restoration. Most of them adapt themselves to the compromise, though they vigorously defend the place that they have secured for science against the attacks of divines, the universities and the litterateurs.

From the 1670s interest in the utilitarian aspects of science wanes. Solutions to the problems of the mercantile phase of capitalism have been solved in theory, though not in practice, (particularly the longitude problem, solved by the 18th century watchmaker John Harrison). Interest in scientific theory remains, and is crowned by Newton's work of 1687 *Principia*, though his ideas had been worked out by 1670. With the great Newtonian synthesis interest in scientific theory wanes somewhat, until revived with the stimulus of the industrial revolution (1750s). Newton takes to interpreting the Book of Daniel, whilst Boyle, the one time 'Father of Modern Chemistry' in the 1650s and 1660s takes to alchemy in 1678.

NOTES

1. An allusion to the dispute over the respective merits of ancient and modern learning which affected both England and France in the late seventeenth century.

DOCUMENT 20 (1949)

Stephen Mason

Notes on Science and the Battle of Ideas in the Sixteenth and Seventeenth Centuries

Trends towards and within science during this period:

1. Mathematical neo-Platonism of the humanists. This for the most part was backward-looking and superstitiously archaic, closely associated with magic, witchcraft, and astrology, the search for magic numbers, perfect geometrical figures in nature, etc. Men try to do new things in old ways by these means, but do not succeed and produce little or no science. The one positive strand in this movement occurs in sixteenth century astronomy (Copernicus [1473-1543] and to some degree, Kepler [1571-1631]). This was a science associated with the priesthood and ruling class from antiquity.
2. A purely qualitative experimental method emerging from a craft source in technically backward regions that were developing economically, like southern England in the sixteenth century. This expressed in the work of the English craftsmen, (Norman) and scholars, (Gilbert) on magnetism, and finds a generalised philosophical expression with Bacon. Prominent in the science of magnetism, in connection with navigation, and chemistry, in connection with medicine, (Paracelsus in Basle), and mining, (Agricola in the Harz mines).[1]
3. The non-mystical use of mathematics, (i.e., distinct from 1) by merchants, surveyors, navigators, etc., relying on passive observations rather than active experiments, (sixteenth century).
4. The development of a fully mathematical experimental method by the craftsmen, engineers, and scholars of technically advanced areas (Simon Stevin[2] in Holland), that were not necessarily advancing much economically, (Galileo [1564-1642] in Italy). Turn of the sixteenth century. Descartes [1596-1650] tried to do for this methodology what Bacon had done for (2), give it a full philosophical expression, but he dropped the idea of active experimentation, developing only the passive contem-

plative method of rigorous mathematical demonstration as the road to certain knowledge.

5. The rise of the mechanical materialist ideology from the craft traditions (2 & 4). In a qualitative form, from (2) as seen in Gilbert and Harvey, and in a mathematical form, from (4) as seen in Galileo. The latter the more influential strand, on which Descartes builds a speculative mechanical world view. He envisaged the world as an assembly of atoms, possessing no inner activity of their own, ordered only by external forces, a viewpoint with which scientific problems were approached later, by scientists proper and into which solutions to those problems were fitted. Descartes' world was one contemplated from without, mastered by the understanding as it were, not by the activity of the observer. This viewpoint is expressed clearly in the political theory and position of his disciple Hobbes.
6. Another trend was keen experimentation directed towards immediate utilitarian ends. It was [a] short sighted, untheoretical trend, or where theories were developed, they took old medieval forms. The chemical trend originating from Paracelsus at the beginning of the sixteenth century took this form. It was a new chemistry expressed in the theoretical forms of alchemy.

The trends towards and within science were based on more deeply lying social and economic movements, to which they gave methodological and ideological expression. The experimental attitudes (2 & 4) came fundamentally from the craftsmen, from whom also came the 'truly revolutionary source of capital'. The differences between (2) and (4) seem to have been mainly due to the differences in technique between the areas in which they developed, England & Italy respectively, in the sixteenth century. The experimental attitude was of petty bourgeois origin, and was associated with the radical sects in protestant countries, particularly in its one-sided form of trend (6). Paracelsus in Basle was associated with Zwingli, whilst the radical puritans during the interregnum lauded the experimental method to a greater extent than the moderates, wishing to push science into the universities, particularly the still alchemical chemistry in which trend (6) was prominent, (see, [Samuel] Hartlib; [John] Dury; John Hall 1649; Noah Biggs, 1651; John Webster, 1654; the last named also wanted to introduce astrology into the universities).[3] Chemistry was of course very much a craft science dealing with drugs, metallurgy, soap and glass making.

Much of the mathematical method of science came from the big merchant interests, for their occupation demanded calculation, and in some aspects was dependant [on] the applications of mathematics, the geometry and astronomy that were involved in navigation and surveying, connected with foreign trade and changes in land ownership respectively. The merchants also provided the complementary source of capital, but their economic and political role was more equivocal than that of the craftsmen, finding a religious expression in the more moderate sects of Protestantism, such as English Presbyterianism during the interregnum. When the two groups providing the two sources of capital came together in England against their common royal enemy and secured victory, the two aspects of scientific method came together, and interest in science took a qualitative leap forward in the country. The scientists of the interregnum and the restoration were keenly experimental, reviving the views of Bacon, but they were also mathematical, measuring all things ('I have taken upon myself the course of expressing myself in Number, Weight, and Measure,' Petty). Bacon's views were regarded as the basis of science, whilst those of Descartes were regarded as useful in tackling particular problems, but speculative ('The mechanical hypothesis', Boyle, as opposed to 'The Baconian Philosophy').

Most of the affective English scientists of the interregnum were moderate puritans, in some cases connected with the grandees personally, Goddard was Cromwell's physician, Wilkins, his brother in law, or were given appointments at Oxford by the commonwealth, (Wallis, Willis, Ward, Petty, besides Wilkins and Goddard).[4] They were more theoretically minded than the radical puritans, and more experimentally minded than royalist 'scientists' such as Digby[5] and the non-partisan philosopher Hobbes. The latter followed Descartes, developing mechanical speculative views. Hobbes was never a F.R.S.

The radical puritans, in the revolutionary experimental tradition of the craftsmen capitalists, wished thoroughly to reform the universities and introduce experimental science, particularly chemistry. The moderate, Wilkins, and royalist, Ward,[6] replied to these criticisms, justifying the position at Oxford. The moderate puritans of the mercantile, mathematical trend in science were politically equivocal, and compromised easily at the restoration, whilst the radicals were dropped (the Hartlib-Boyle correspondence ceased 1659). Hobbes represents the extreme of this trend, an inactive non-partisan position in politics, and a non-experimental, speculative-mathematical attitude in science. But even so the moderate puritan scientists were more positive politically and more experimental and realistic in science than Hobbes. Boyle, one of the most experimentally minded of this group, succeeded in giving a scientific theoretical foundation to chemistry, that was so much supported and pushed by the radicals, for the latter with their narrow empiricism could not do it themselves (one of Boyle's small following, Lower, was however a Quaker). Moreover, scientific chemistry died with Boyle and his school; alchemical notions re-emerged, and it was not until Lavoisier and the French revolution that scientific chemistry was finally established. Thus the moderates were the most effective group in science, the group whose theory was the most closely related to practice, as we see also in Petty's political economy. They were more realistic than the atheistical followers of Hobbes, that thronged the restoration court, on the one hand, and the radical puritans, now become nonconformists on the other. The moderates lost some favour at the restoration, they were mostly purged from the university posts given to them by the Commonwealth, but they quickly became prominent again. Wilkins for example became bishop of Chester.

Towards the end of the restoration period, and particularly after the expulsion of James II, English science loses much of its earlier insistence upon active experimentation and utilitarianism, though those were never dropped completely. There is with Newton's *Principia*, 1689, a trend towards the abstract and mathematically theoretical in science. This coincides with a slight decline of interest in science towards the end of the century in England, and also with the virtual disappearance of speculative Cartesian views on the one hand and blind empiricism on the other. The viewpoint and method of science were tightened up as it were, strengthening the realistic and positive elements, though there was this tendency towards the abstract, and the slight decline of interest in science. It was a process that paralleled the tightening up of the state apparatus with the expulsion of James II, securing the dominion of parliament.

Both Newton and Locke are more realistic than their respective predecessors, Descartes and Hobbes. Locke and his views were rooted in the social movement of his times, whilst Hobbes was a non-partisan, isolated individual, and his views were speculative, though he was the first to work out a secular political theory from first principles. In the same way Newton's theories were genuinely scientific, rooted in the real world, whilst Descartes' views were unrealistic speculations, though they were the first generalised expressions of mechanical materialism that provided a fruitful point of view for later experimental workers. Both Newton and Descartes conceive of the world as atomic, each particle tending to continue as it is, moving uniformly along its own straight line, unless ordered by some external force or mutual gravitational power. In the same way Hobbes and Locke conceive of society as an assembly of anarchic individuals that are ordered by external force or mutual contract. The atom world mirrors the individualistic society, society as seen and understood by the bourgeois.

With Newton also a protestant-scientific world view crystallised out. It was thought that God had created the world in the beginning exactly as it is now, but thereafter it continued on governed by natural mechanical laws, like a perpetual piece of clock work. Newton thought that God had to make adjustments now and again like an engineer, but the world was mostly self sustaining. How far this was generally accepted in the 1690s and thereafter it is difficult to say, but it constituted a rigid Anglican orthodoxy. Attempts to suggest evolution were resisted as atheistical, and they came effectively only towards the end of the 18th century, from the historical heirs of the radical puritans, men associated with the dissenter industrial-liberals of the provinces (Erasmus Darwin in Birmingham, Hutton in Edinburgh).[7] It was this group of men that now became effective in science, reviving the experimental chemistry advocated by the radical puritans of the interregnum, aiding the 'Revolution Chimique' effected by the French.

NOTES

1. For Gilbert see Document 19; Theophrastus Paracelsus (c1493-1541) was a Swiss physician who spurned conventional medical wisdom and engaged in experimental observation; Georg Agricola (1494-1555) German scholar and experimentalist sometimes called 'the father of mineralogy'; the identity of Norman is not clear.
2. Simon Stevin (1548–1620) Flemish mathematician and engineer.
3. For discussion of this group see C. Hill, *Intellectual Origins of the English Revolution Revisited*. The works alluded to are: John Hall, *An humble motion to the Parliament ... concerning the advancement of Learning*; Noah Biggs, *The Vanity of the Craft of Physick; or, a New Dispensatory, wherein is dissected the errors, ignorance, impostures, and supinities of the schools ... With an humble motion for the reformation of the universities ...*; John Webster, *Academiarum Examen: or, the Examination of Academies: Wherein is discussed and examined the matter, method, and customes of academick and scholastick learning, and the insufficiency thereof ....*
4. For more information about the fortunes of this group see Mason, 'The influence of the English Revolution on the development of modern science', *Modern Quarterly* 4, (1949).
5. Sir Kenelm Digby, embryologist, foundation fellow of the Royal Society; see Hill, *Intellectual Origins Revisited* p.44.
6. Presumably Seth Ward, who became Bishop of Salisbury.
7. Erasmus Darwin (1731–1802), physician, natural philosopher, physiologist, inventor and poet, grandfather of Charles Darwin; James Hutton (1726-1797) was a geologist, naturalist, chemist and experimental farmer.

DOCUMENT 21 (1950)

Christopher Hill

Bourgeois Ideology after 1660

1. The question I was asked was 'Was there a single bourgeois ideology after 1660?' So expressed, the answer can only be 'No'. The bourgeoisie is never a homogeneous class in the

sense that the proletariat was to become one; and after 1660 there were many groups of the bourgeoisie with conflicting interests, to say nothing of other classes.

2. On the other hand, the compromise settlements of 1660 and 1688 were reflected in ideological developments. For present purposes 1660 saw, on the one hand, the restoration of monarchy, state church, defeated feudal landlords, to positions of prestige and some power within a predominantly capitalist society; on the other hand, the suppression of bourgeois-democratic revolutionary elements, the triumph of the less revolutionary capitalist trend. 1688 recognised the fact that the interests of ex-feudal landlords were now identical with those of the bourgeoisie. Both classes (and the church) combined against James II's attempt to restore the old monarchy and the old religion. The Glorious Revolution demonstrated the secure tenure of power by the alliance of landlords and non-Revolutionary bourgeoisie; the monarch could be changed with no fear of revival of bourgeois democratic revolutionary movements.

The consequences for ideology of the settlements of 1660 and 1688 include the following:

a) The overthrow of the feudal-absolutist state and of the feudal landowning class whose interests it represented is reflected in ideology by
   i. the reversal of the tendency to join the Roman Catholic church fashionable among the aristocracy in the 1630s and in James I's reign;
   ii. the effective end (as contrasted with sentimental and academic hangover) of divine right and non-resistance theories. The non-jurors after 1688 were not a politically significant group, except possibly in Oxford.

b) With the triumph of capitalism, the distinction between 'the landed interest' and 'the monied interest' remains, and is the basis of the division between Tories and Whigs; but its real economic significance progressively diminishes. Many ex-feudalists adapt themselves to capitalism; those others who had survived 1640-60 were gradually extruded. This dual process seems to have its reflection in
   i. the Cambridge Platonists, and other attempts by Anglicans to meet science half way;

ii. the snook-cocking, sceptical-materialist Hobbism of a group of court aristocrats, forced to accept the material basis of the new regime, but utterly cynical about the bourgeoisie's pretensions to ideals. It is significant that this group disappears within a generation or so as the 'process of adaptation is completed; restoration comedy is cleaned up not by Collier but by the disappearance of its social basis in the country and of its focal point of support at court after 1688.

c) The acceptance of the monarchy, the House of Lords, the established church, by the conservative (commercial) sections of the bourgeoisie. This involved in ideology:

i. the abandonment of revolutionary Puritanism, hostility to 'fanaticism', whilst retaining the other face of Puritanism – discipline for the lower orders. (cf. Engels: 'The Calvinist reformation ... provided the ideological costume for the second act of the bourgeois revolution, which took place in England. Here Calvinism justified itself as the true religious disguise of the interests of the bourgeoisie of that time and on this account did not reach full acceptance, as the revolution was completed in 1689 by a compromise between one part of the nobility and the bourgeoisie' (Engels, 'Ludwig Feuerbach').[1]

ii. The abandonment of republicanism, of the revolutionary elements in the thought of Milton, Harrington, Sidney, whilst retaining their real class content and the concept of parliamentary sovereignty (Newton's God is like king, bound by the law which originates from him and which he sanctifies).

iii. The sloughing off of their parliamentarian connections by the scientists; royal and aristocratic patronage for the Royal Society; Royal Society scientists play down materialism, emphasise their respect for authority and established institutions; abandon schemes for educational reform, lay stronger emphasis on God and the 'argument from design'. This was the heavy price paid for official recognition of the Baconian scientific attitude.

d) The exclusion from political power, from polite society and from higher education of the radical bourgeois and petty bourgeois democrats, and their utter failure to make any come-back. This is reflected in ideology in:

i. the conversion of Puritanism, a revolutionary creed, into nonconformity, a petty bourgeois ideology, sectarian, often pacifist-quietist; nonconformists evolve their own separate educational system, turn more and more away from politics and concentrate on the economic activity for which their creed peculiarly fits them; and later turn to science.

ii. The driving underground of the Levellers and their ideas, and their gradual disappearance in the materialisms or deism of Tolland, Mandeville, Collins etc. (who also look back to Hobbes – see 2 b ii above)

(e)

i. The whole of England is subordinated to capitalism; the witch-cult is stamped out, even in outlying areas.

ii. The temporary triumph of commercial over industrial capital, of the less revolutionary elements in the bourgeoisie, leads to diversion of capital to investment in overseas trade, land purchase, etc. There is a short-run stabilisation of the domestic system, producing a somnolent, non-revolutionary mentality among many of the direct producers.

iii. Over a longer period, the process of expropriation of the peasantry and the formation of a proletariat is facilitated. It is accompanied by sporadic machine breaking and other forms of primitive proletarian resistance, not associated, so far as can be seen, with any independent ideology or form of organisation. Disappearance of the Diggers. Failure of nonconformity to establish control of the new urban and rural proletariat creates the problem with which in the next century Wesleyanism grappled. The new radicalism, when it emerges in the second half of the eighteenth century, is bourgeois-democratic, not proletarian. (Note the existence in the 18th century of 'Tory democracy', the backward-looking sentimental sympathy for capitalism's victims of a Goldsmith, the hatred for the bourgeoisie of a Cobbett, which might take the form of Toryism before the rise of radicalism as an independent bourgeois-*democratic* trend with working-class support. Early eighteenth century Jacobites apparently hoped to draw support from working-class elements like the Midlands miners.

3. The ideological developments listed in 2 (a) and (e) are largely negative. Those listed in 2 (b) and (c) are to a large extent synthesized in Locke, who comes nearest to formulating an ideology acceptable to the bulk of the ruling-class (see (4) below). 2 (d) (i) suggests the existence of a separate – though not fundamentally opposed – petty bourgeois nonconformist ideology. 2 (d) (ii) provides some link with late eighteenth century radicalism, but radicalism owes more to the industrial revolution, and to the influence of the American and French Revolutions. (But note the nonconformist origins of most early radicals).
4. Some points about Locke, 'both in religion and in politics the child of the class compromise of 1688' (Engels, in *Selected Correspondence*, p. 483).
   a) Of bourgeois origin himself, at Oxford during the revolution, close dependent of the Whig leader Shaftesbury, political exile in Holland, then in government service under William III.
   b) Reflects the new economic set-up in his emphasis on property as the basis of political power – the economic aspects of Harrington's thought without Harrington's sense of the possibility of revolutionary change, of economic developments upsetting the superstructure. Even Locke's contradictions are revealing, e.g. the famous naiveté about the right to property being founded on labour: 'the turfs my servant has cut ... become my property. The labour that was mine, removing them out of that common state they were in hath fixed my property in them' (*Second Treatise*, Everyman, p.130). The state of nature is an abstraction from bourgeois society; the right to property is founded on the right to exploit the labour of others. *Some considerations of the consequences of the lowering of interest* shows clearly enough that by 'property' Locke is thinking of big capitalist property, and not, as bourgeois commentators often suggest, of the small independent property of the petty-bourgeois. For Locke property is justified by appropriation. 'As much land as a man tills, plants, improves, cultivates, and can use the product of, so much is his prop-

erty. He by his labour does, as it were enclose it from the common ... God gave the world to men in common, but he gave it to the use of the industrious and rational' (p132). This justifies enclosure and the grabbing of colonial territory. The 'industrious and rational' bourgeoisie's ability to produce more abundantly is made the moral justification of its domination.

c) In the *First Treatise on Civil Government* Locke directs his main fire against Filmer's *Patriarcha*. Rightly: for he is finishing with feudalism, establishing the bourgeois free-contract state in place of feudal hereditary monarchy and feudal landed property. Those commentators who express surprise that Locke did not direct his argument against Hobbes misunderstand the class content of both Hobbes's and Locke's theories. Locke is adapting the all-or-nothing Hobbesian theory of sovereignty to the needs of the class compromise reached after the English revolution, and at the same time toning down Hobbes's irreligious materialism; but he is not confuting Hobbes.

d) In the *Second Treatise on Civil Government* Locke is specifically the defender and ideologist of 1688, of the Glorious because bloodless Revolution, the revolution to end revolutions, the revolution made without calling in the masses. Here Locke castrates the revolutionary theories of Milton and Sidney whilst retaining their class content; but makes the important advance of distinguishing between 'society' and 'the state', showing that (as in 1688) the government can be changed without society dissolving into 'anarchy'.

e) He establishes the tradition of the perfect British constitutional system, evolved by continuous development and compromise, the as-little-as-possible revolutionary path leading to class harmony; and also the view that liberty is negative, means being left alone, depends on a 'separation of power' which reflects the division within the English ruling class.

f) in his *Essay on Toleration*, and *The Reasonableness of Christianity* Locke synthesizes and sums up the various approaches to 'rational Christianity' made by Milton, the Cambridge Platonists, the broad church Anglicans, the

Royal Society scientists, the Quakers, the Deists; and so robs Protestantism of all those elements which had seemed to Hobbes dangerous because politically subversive – direct contact with God, claims to inspiration, 'fanaticism'; the anarchy of the inner-light. Thus Locke came nearest of anyone to solving the problem which had bothered the European bourgeoisie ever since the Reformation – how to get rid of the bath-water (Anabaptism, left-wing sectarianism, lower-class protest) without throwing out the baby (rugged individualism, 'Christian liberty', the ideological reflection of private enterprise) (cf. Marx: 'Cromwell and the English people had borrowed speech, passions and illusions from the Old Testament for their bourgeois revolution. When the real aim had been achieved, when the bourgeois transformation of English society had been accomplished, Locke supplanted Habakkuk' ('Eighteenth Brumaire', *Selected Works* [1942 ed] I p.317). At the same time Locke's acceptance of toleration *as a principle* recognizes the fact that the bourgeoisie is not a homogeneous class, that the separate nonconformist petty bourgeois ideology (in its various forms) also has its social role to play now that it has ceased to be revolutionary and the bourgeoisie is no longer afraid of it.

g) In the *Essay on the Human Understanding* Locke fuses this 'rational Christianity' with the new scientific outlook, its mechanical materialism, its emphasis on experiment, experience, the senses; and so puts the ideological coping stone on to the practical acceptance of the Church of England (as a buttress of law, order and property) by the bourgeoisie and the scientists in 1660. Cf. Marx: 'Hobbes had systematized Bacon, without, however, furnishing a proof for Bacon's fundamental principle, the origin of all human knowledge from the world of sensation. It was Locke who, in his *Essay on the Human Understanding* supplied this proof' (Quoted by Engels, *Preface to Socialism, Utopian and Scientific* p. xii).

5. Sabine remarks in his *History of Political Philosophy* that Locke defeated his enemies by the supreme weapon of indifference. The bourgeoisie's scale of values was not established merely by

rational argument, but by the economic triumphs of capitalism. Both Filmer and the Levellers had asked questions about the right of the bourgeoisie to speak for the whole people that were never answered at all.

6. By the 18th century, then, Locke dominates English thought, which is bourgeois thought, and indeed progressive thought throughout Europe. Bolingbroke, the leader of the great Tory fiasco in 1714-15, the *reductio ad absurdum* of divine right Jacobitism, then sold out to Locke and Whiggery on the ideological front. Swift, the last protest of the old order, shows its political ineffectiveness.
7. Just because Locke arrived at a synthesis of bourgeois thought which claimed to be universal, i.e. to speak for all humanity, his thought contains contradictions. As with Calvin and Hegel (who attempted syntheses before and after him) these contradictions allowed of different emphases among the right and left wings of his disciples. Thus Burke's conservative philosophy looks consciously back to Locke; but it is also directly from Locke that the political theorists of the American Revolution and the eighteenth-century French materialist philosophers derive.
8. Marx sums up: 'Locke is the classical exponent of the legal relations of bourgeois society in contrast to feudal society; the ideas of all later English economists are based on his philosophy' (*Theories of Surplus Value,* I A 3).[2] 'Locke ... was an advocate of the new bourgeoisie in all its forms, the manufacturers against the working classes and paupers, the commercial class against the old-fashioned usurers, the financial aristocracy against the state debtors, and ... went so far as to prove in his own work that bourgeois reason is the normal human reason' ([*Contribution to the*] *Critique of Political Economy,* p93).[3]

NOTES

1. See above pp27, 31 & note 95 for the full reference.
2. Karl Marx, 'Theories of Surplus Value', *Collected Works Marx and Engels*, Vol 30, pp348ff.
3. Cf *Collected Works Marx and Engels*, Vol 29, Lawrence & Wishart, p315.

DOCUMENT 22 (1949)

Christopher Hill & G de N. Clark
Calvinism and the Bourgeoisie

References:

For the Reformation generally see Marx 'Introduction to a Critique of Hegel's Philosophy of Law', *Modern Quarterly* vol. III no 2, esp p247.

For Luther, *Works*; and H. Pascal, *Social Basis of the German Reformation*.

For Calvin, *Institutes of the Christian Religion* (esp. preface and Book IV ch. XX).

Marx and Engels quoted by C. Hill in *Science & Society*, vol XII no. 1 pp152-5.

Some useful information in the 'Life' by Carew Hunt [presumably Carew Hunt: *Calvin*, 1933].

The central problem of the bourgeois revolution was always how to draw in the masses for attack on feudalism, and then, when victory was secured, to prevent them reaping the benefits. In conditions of 16th and 17th C. neither of these objects could have been achieved under banner of mechanical materialism. The new ideology had to be religious, both to defeat Catholicism on its own ground (to solve the question of *salvation*) and for discipline, to hold excessive popular aspirations in check. All that will be attempted here is to show in general way how Calvinism was adapted to the needs of bourgeois society as such, and how it served the specific needs of the bourgeoisie as a revolutionary class at this time. There was of course no rigid distinction between the two aspects; but in the first section we shall be concerned with much that is common to Luther and Calvin, in the second with the latter's special contribution.

1. FOR BOURGEOIS SOCIETY AS SUCH THE MAIN IDEOLOGICAL REQUIREMENTS WERE:

1. To break the power of feudal ideology over men's minds. Hence the attack on Pope, priest and monk; on the heavenly

hierarchy of saints, angels and archangels mirroring the feudal hierarchy on earth; on the role of the church as repository of authority and guardian of property – a function now to be fulfilled by the national state – and as monopolist of theory on economic questions; above all on *magic*, on the special role of the priest as intermediary between the individual and God.

2. A new ideology, clearly and logically formulated. This was supplied by Calvin in the *Institutes* – the Summa Theologica of Protestantism. The main features were to be:

a) Individualism – the direct relation of the individual to God; personal reading of the Bible; 'conscience', personal responsibility, and public discipline to replace the social 'sharing' of sin in the confessional.
b) It must be *relatively rational* – i.e. attacking the mysticism of the priest, altar, vestments, transubstantiation. The emphasis is on education and preaching as against ritual; there is room, later on, for revelation to be supplemented by scientific discovery, on which the old religion by now turned its back. But it must not be too rational; Zwingli's doctrine was clearly felt to be too democratic in its implications and was not revived after his death; while Servetus and the Anabaptists (even after they no longer represented a danger politically) were outside the pale. An element of dogmatism was always present, especially in Luther: and at Geneva in 1552 it was decreed that 'The *Institutes* are the word of God' and no one must controvert them.
c) Salvation is now by faith alone; the doctrine necessary to cut the ground from under Mass, pilgrimages, processions, prayers for the dead – as 'works' – no longer avail anything for salvation.
d) Asceticism has to be brought out from the cloister into the world, and a common moral standard (at least in theory) imposed on all men. 'Every Christian has to be a monk *all his life*'. Work is now sanctified in a new and special sense, and the obligation laid on all men to follow a 'calling'.

As this ideology emerges, it reflects exactly the ending of 'feudal, patriarchal, idyllic relations', and their replacement by the callous, invisible cash-nexus. Instead of a visible hierarchy there is now an invisible gulf between the Elect and the damned. This can also be seen in the Calvinists' attitude to sin, which is no longer to be pitied and expiated, but hated (in the damned) and overcome (by discipline) in the Elect. Predestination not only 'expressed the fact that in the commercial world of competition success or failure does not depend upon a man's activity or cleverness but upon circumstances uncontrollable by him'. It also reflected the division of society into two classes – a division which becomes strong and more absolute as bourgeois society develops, but which already existed in embryo in the sixteenth century. This division was 'both justified (from eternity) and obscured by the stress on the individual's spiritual behaviour as the sole criterion of social division'. Predestination also provided unanswerable justification for the imposition of discipline on the reprobate. On this central question there occurs perhaps the only obscurantism in the *Institutes*: we must not enquire *why* most us are damned.

3. Political independence. Where real independence was possible, the ideal of the bourgeoisie was a republic on the models of Geneva or Holland. Presbyterianism as generally recognised was the republican form of church organisation; no bishop, no king. But in any case Protestantism provided the flag for *national* movements (not necessarily under bourgeois leadership) as well as for the struggles of the bourgeoisie to become independent of feudal power in their own country.
4. Political theory is extremely vague in Calvin's own works. Various forms of government are lawful (cf Cromwell's view that it is lawful to pass through all forms to achieve the desired end); but aristocracy, pure or modified is best. Calvin's own constitutional reforms in Geneva (1541-3) tended to shift power from the broader to the more oligarchic representative bodies. The reason for this vagueness, it may be suggested, lay in the character of Calvinism as an international movement: the situation in different countries varied widely and changed rapidly; and Calvinism proved extraordinarily adaptable precisely because it did not involve any specific political system. Three points may be noted:
   a) the state exists (i) to prevent idolatry, blasphemy, etc; (ii) to maintain 'public quiet', 'protect every man's property', and permit 'innocent commerce'.
   b) 'It were a very idle occupation for men to discourse

what would be the best form of polity in the place where they live, seeing these deliberations cannot have any influence, in determining any public matters'.

c) The powers that be are of God: magistrates are His vice-regents, and must be obeyed even when they are tyrannous. 'It belongs not to us to cure those evils, all that remains for us is to implore the help of the Lord ...' But 'at one time he raises up manifest avengers from among his own servants, and gives them his command to punish accursed tyranny, and deliver his people'. These do not 'violate' the majesty with which kings are invested but are 'armed from heaven'. Here clearly is the germ of the thesis *Vindiciae Contra Tyrannos*, that rebellion maybe lawful if it is led by the magistrates i.e. by the bourgeoisie with a foothold already in the state machine.[1]

5. Economic and social theory.
   a) the so called 'economic virtues' of industry and thrift are of course those most conducive to the accumulation of capital. Labour, business, and ultimately moneymaking pure and simple are invested with positive ethical value. Moreover, success as such is evidence of divine favour. The sanctity of labour in one's calling provides a consolation for drudgery, replacing craftsman's pride as the division of labour proceeds; and perhaps tending against excessive mobility of workers from one 'calling' to another when feudal restraints were removed.
   b) the attack on 'idleness' in the form of monasticism comes early as it has a good mass appeal. It is soon followed by the attack on pilgrimages and Saints Days, and their replacement by the business-like regular Sunday rest. Thus Luther: 'men and maids ... ought to work with pleasure and delight, simply because it is God's commandment and be willing even to make payment themselves and be glad that they can obtain masters and mistresses and have such a joyous conscience, and know that they can do real golden works which until now were not done and were despised so that everyone in the devil's name ran into convents, to pilgrimages, and to indulgences'.
   c) the taking of interest is allowed in principle; though as Laski says, Calvin went no further in practice than St.

Antonine in the fifteenth century. But Calvin's safeguards and qualifications were ignored as soon as the bourgeoisie were in a strong enough position to do so. So long as they relied on the support of the petty bourgeoisie and artisans it was necessary to maintain the traditional economic doctrines by which the latter were supposed to be protected.

d) similarly with regard to the poor: all the early reformers are concerned with poor law provisions, e.g. at Geneva the 'Ordonnances' specifically appoint deacons to minister to the poor. It is only in the later phase of Calvinism that the inference is drawn from individualism and predestination, that poverty is due to wickedness and that society has no responsibility towards it.

II LUTHER AND CALVIN

In theology, Calvin followed Luther in most respects, adding little, but systematising, and making precise, sharp and logical what had been turgid and vague. What Calvin supplied above all was organisation and discipline; and in assessing the role of Calvinism in any country, forms of organisation are usually more important than theology. For Luther 'the church' was a society or fellowship including alike the just and the unjust: for Calvin, a highly organised vanguard to which only the Elect were admitted. When suitable allowance has been made for the difference of class basis, this may be likened in many ways to the international revolutionary movement of today. Generally speaking, Calvinism made headway in those countries where the bourgeoisie were strong enough to attempt the seizure of power, England, France, Holland, Switzerland (and by way of exception Scotland). In Germany the Erastianism of Luther marks the surrender of relatively weak and scattered petty-bourgeoisie to the absolute power of the Princes.

III NEEDS OF THE BOURGEOISIE FOR THEIR REVOLUTIONARY STRUGGLE

1. A definite code of beliefs (supplied by the *Institutes*).
2. Faith in the justice and success of the revolution; in the absence of a worked-out *political* theory of revolution it was

necessary to act 'blind', empirically, stage by stage. Here predestination plays a similar psychological role to historical materialism in assuring ultimate success; and, likewise it is not fatalist. Success is inevitable, but only because we are working for it.

Note in passing

a) that Calvinism at first subscribes to the unity of theory and practice. Good works were necessary, not for salvation but to 'glorify God' and 'to get rid of the fear of damnation'. Beza and much later Cromwell both recommended that doubts should be resolved in action.

b) that predestination assumed the central role in Calvin's theology only in the 1559 edition of the *Institutes* (first published in 1536). Hitherto he had consistently advised the Huguenots not to take up arms.

3. Class-consciousness and discipline 'producing men capable of standing up to kings'; above all, a *party* with definite head-quarters, organisation and trained cadres.

   a) the model organisation was laid down by Calvin in the 'Ordonnances' at Geneva. As generally adopted, these involved a kind of democratic centralism, the lower bodies electing delegates to the higher and all being bound by the decisions reached.

   b) with this organisation went the demand for independence of the Church from the State (i.e. from the State of the old ruling class), ultimately for a theocracy (i.e. a dictatorship of the bourgeoisie exercised by the bourgeois party machine). In either case the bourgeoisie scoured control of the machine by the key institution of lay elders whose powers and responsibilities were often equal to those of ministers. In Geneva they constituted a majority of the Consistory (the key disciplinary body) and were chosen from the leading citizens. In England, when the attempt was made to impose a system of 'classes' in 1645-7, the elders provisionally appointed by Parliament were for the most part drawn from the gentry; and by a resolution of September 30 1645, peers and MPs were automatically included for their areas (see Shaw's *English Church 1640-60* esp. vol. 11 pp. 393 seq., 404 seq.). In Scotland in 1638 the Covenanters' (new) demand for lay representation in the Kirk Assembly was seen by Charles I as a vital point at which to resist.

c) Ministers, because of their special role as a party leadership, were chosen and trained with great care. They had to satisfy the existing body of ministers of the sincerity of their convictions, and pass a rigorous examination; in Geneva they had also to be accepted by the city Council and, after preaching, by the body of the people. They were revocable at any time, the unworthy being reduced; they were responsible individually for the whole body and vice-versa; they held weekly 'colloquia' to ensure a uniform theoretical line, and quarterly meetings for self- and mutual- criticism, which were open to the public. Their primary duties were preaching and 'welfare' – house-to-house visiting.

d) Discipline had to be of the highest order, for example for illegal, underground work in France, 'the personal life of ministers had to be above reproach – contrast here the catholic priest, whose authority rested fundamentally on his magical powers. Calvin himself was keenly aware of the danger of careerism, and is said to have refused a cure to Castallio for this reason.[2] After the seizure of power, the discipline had also the function of suppressing popular movements; the upper bourgeoisie at the same tine sought to free themselves from it, not only from the familiar regulations of dress and deportment but in economic affairs (control of interest rates, poor law etc.). Its ultimate sanction in the first phase was excommunication (i.e. expulsion); in the latter the (bourgeois) state power could be and was called in.

e) Education was regarded as of prime importance from the start: Calvin and Beza gave personal attention to the school and university at Geneva, Calvin insisting that the schoolmaster should be a minister.

4. For the sake of mass appeal in the early stages the demand for toleration was regularly put forward, though the right of private judgment seems to have been peculiar to Luther (who soon abandoned it) and the Anabaptists. Democracy in Calvinism was for the most part an inner-party and therefore bourgeois democracy. But even in Geneva Calvin's 'Ordonnances' were published, discussed, and finally voted clause by clause in the

General Assembly of the citizens. And the final, though not the main, voice was left to the people in the election of ministers and in cases of excommunication.

IV

The general picture so far given obviously requires qualification in the light of detailed studies of the development in each country, which cannot be undertaken here. But in saying that Calvinism represented the ideology of the 16th and 17th C bourgeoisie organised for a revolutionary struggle, we should bear in mind:

1. The extreme adaptability of the ideology to the political needs of different times and different countries. For example after the Edict of Nantes the Huguenots justify passive obedience where previously they had justified revolt (C. Hill in *Science and Society*, Vol. XII no.3. p 23-5). In the Church of England Calvinism is orthodox *as theology* till the time of James I (himself a Calvinist at first); but not of course as discipline which suggests that here at any rate organization was more important than theology.
2. In almost every country a section of the nobility becomes Calvinist (or in some cases Lutheran) for reasons that have nothing to do with capitalism.
3. In England the situation was unusually complex because of the more advanced development of the bourgeoisie. Puritanism had to bind together the interests of widely separated strata; and individuals were rising (or sometimes falling) in the process of development. Therefore down to 1640 Puritanism is much 'broader' than continental Calvinism. But the Presbyterian *system* drew its main strength from the merchant oligarchy of the City, confident that they could dominate its 'democratic' machinery.
4. In Scotland, Presbyterianism gained unique hold over the mass of the population despite the extreme backwardness of economic development. Christopher Hill suggests that this may owe something to the surviving pre-feudal tribal organisation, allied with a new national consciousness; the lead coming from the burghers and lesser gentry, whose interests were not yet sharply marked off from those of the masses. 'To find an

earlier parallel to the Presbyterian organisation we have to turn to the (pre-feudal) witch-cult, here we find elected elders (the coven), a hierarchical organisation, a covenant with the God of the witches.' (Cf. Margaret Murray, *The Witch in Western Europe* and *The God of the Witches*. See Hill's paper).

5. In the Netherlands again the situation is complex. In the South, Calvinism made its first appeal to the bourgeoisie in the most advanced commercial and industrial centres, especially where, according to Granville, they imposed it on their work people by preferential distribution of alms and employment. (In the old industrial areas of Namur, Liege, etc, where the gild structure remained, Calvinism made little headway). After 1665 the lower strata carried matters further than the bourgeoisie wished to go: ultimately these preferred reconciliation with Spain to Calvinist-democratic regimes in Ghent, Brussels, Antwerp.

   In the North Calvinism becomes of decisive importance as the 'compact form' of national resistance, led by gentry and merchant bourgeoisie. After the victory of the revolt in the North, the big bourgeoisie favour Arminianism, while the petty-bourgeoisie and the masses adhere to strict predestination (the Counter Remonstrants).

V THE PETTY BOURGEOISIE

Calvinism is only the ideology of the petty-bourgeoisie in so far as these are drawn into the struggle of the progressive gentry and merchants against the feudal ruling class. When the petty-bourgeoisie and peasantry throw up their own ideology, it takes one of two forms:

1. Luther's rapidly changing standpoint reflects exactly the aspirations and the failure of the German petty bourgeoisie, at first revolutionary, but scared out of its wits at the peasant rising and immediately willing to make peace with absolutism. Thus Luther repudiates his previous teachings on the right of private judgment, the use of force, the priesthood of all believers; then finally becomes completely authoritarian and Erastian.
2. Anabaptism was the 16th century anarchism, the revolt of the masses against organised Church and state alike. The standard of faith is no longer the Bible but private inspiration, the

answer of the illiterate to the dictatorship (however democratic) of the literate; the priesthood of all believers carried to its logical conclusion, every man his own priest. The inspiration often came, nevertheless, from the Old Testament and the object, condemned by Calvin as a 'Jewish vanity', was to realise the kingdom of God on earth. Against the State, the Anabaptists taught that Christians should ignore its authority; while it could easily be inferred, if baptism was effective only with the consent and belief of the baptized, that government should be with the consent of the governed.

It was only in England with Winstanley that a genuine proletarian ideology could be developed. But the Anabaptists were the object of savage repression from all the Reformers at all times after 1522. Luther attacked them constantly. At Zurich it was decreed in 1526 that they should be drowned without mercy, 'whether man, woman, or girl'. Calvin himself wrote expressly to refute those who would overthrow society and 'live like rats in the straw, pell-mell'.

In this conflict it is Calvinism that represents the organised force of [the] main revolutionary class; and it is Calvinism that by virtue of its greater discipline and theoretical clarity absorbed the remnants of the Lutheran and Zwinglian alternatives in France, Switzerland and the Netherlands

APPENDIX – THEORIES OF THE EUCHARIST

It may be of interest to compare the main doctrines on the central question of theology in the 16th century.

Catholicism taught that in the Mass bread and wine were *really* changed into the body and blood of Christ – the 'essence' changing though the 'accidents' (sensory properties) remained as before. This is Transubstantiation.

Luther held that the body and blood were consubstantially present 'as fire is present in molten lead', and so were actually partaken of. Luther could reach no compromise with Zwingli, not as H.A.L. Fisher has it because both were dogmatic theologians but because *hoc est corpus meum* symbolized an absolutism that had no point of contact with Zwingli's more rational doctrine.

Calvin held that the body and blood were 'virtually' present and so 'spiritually' partaken of through faith.

For **Zwingli** and **Munzer** the Communion was merely a symbolic and commemorative feast, without mystical implications.

NOTES

1. P. Du Plessis Mornay, *Vindiciae Contra Tyrannos*, 1579.
2. Sebastian Castellio [1515-63], French preacher and theologian.

DOCUMENT 23 (1950)

Victor Kiernan
Calvinism and the Transition from Medieval to Modern

A. *Class Antagonisms of the Later Middle Ages*

1. The primary factor in the transition from medieval to modern is the resistance of the petty producers to feudal exploitation. All through the epoch of middle class revolutions, it was the revolutionary energy of the masses (not pro-capitalistic, but anti-feudal) which alone could supply the newer rising classes with the strength they required. This remains true of 1789, when peasant riots and Paris 'mobs' broke down the resistance of the *ancien régime* and allowed capitalism to come to power; the 'apocalyptic' (Hazlitt) character of 1789, the vision of Liberty, Equality, Fraternity, is the old popular Anabaptist vision of a new heaven and a new earth, clothed in middle class phrases.[1]
2. In the later middle ages there was both increasing resistance from below, and increasing pressure from above, with the growth of big merchant capital, money economy, changing military techniques, tendency towards concentration and monopoly, reflected also in the guild, Church, municipal government. Feudal counter-pressure threatened to reduce the peasantry further towards serfdom, and to stratify it. Free or semi-free peasants formed a rural 'petite bourgeoisie' actively

struggling in Catalonia, Bohemia, Sweden, England. In the Netherlands there was a species of 'industrial capitalism'. Anabaptism flourished here, but also in central Europe where towns were decaying and serfdom growing. Anabaptism flourished, not wherever there was oppression and resistance to oppression (cf. Valencia, Majorca, the French peasantry) but wherever oppression threatened the class basis and integrity of the poorer groups with a radical transformation.

3. In the detail of the process of transition, certain interrelated points should be kept in view as helping to form the complex set-up out of which the B.R. [British Road[2]] – a very exceptional and unique development – was to emerge.
4. Medieval Christendom at its most integrated had been militantly expansionist: this had helped to keep the social order together and religion in good health. In the later Middle Ages the expansion of the feudal culture halted. This was chiefly due, not to powerful resistance outside, but to feudal disintegration hastened by resistance from below; but the failure to expand further then hastened the disintegration (eg failure of the Kaldar Union imposed on Scandinavia by Danish-Holstein feudalism).[3]
5. Between 1450 and 1550 the situation was catastrophically changed by two 'external' developments (not 'accidental' but due to Christendom's weakness and strength respectively): Turkish occupation of the Balkans and penetration of the Mediterranean, and Spanish-Portuguese conquest of South America and parts of the Far East, with the resulting influx of colonial goods and bullion. With these events, the old, slowly developed, 'natural', regional integration of Europe was broken up. The old wealthy centres, N. Italy and Flanders, fell under outside military-feudal control; S.W. Europe was orientated towards the colonies; the Habsburg lands became a March, economically self-sufficient. The Flanders-Italy-Levant axis was, after an interval, replaced by the Baltic highway: northern Europe, at first impoverished, left out in the cold, developed a new regional-specialisation, chiefly as between north-west and north-east, exchanging manufactures for raw materials.
6. Within the feudal-agrarian ruling class, there had always been a broad though fluctuating division between higher and lower nobility – lords and squires, Magnates and gentry, Grandees

and Hidalgos. Feudal societies had emerged in different ways, and the concept of 'nobility' had important variations. It implied superiority over the classes below, but also the assertion of equality with those individuals above the ordinary 'nobleman' (including, as in Aragon, the King, who was merely one of the Magnates-*ricoshombres*). The idea of conquest, or of successful resistance to conquest, everywhere underlay the concept. Conquest might have been effected by small organised groups (Normandy; Norman England; – the 'pyramid' type of feudal structure), or by larger groups, whole 'nations' (Hungary, Spain; – the more 'democratic', less hierarchical type of feudalism). The latter regions too had tended to fall under the domination of great lords who grew up chiefly along the Marches (Poland, Andalucia); but a strong equalitarian sense persisted across the lower men, and the rise of the Magnates was resented. The small 'noble' might actually be a peasant – as frequently in the Basque lands; 'noble' meant *free*, entitled to full membership in the 'nation'. In. E. Europe 'parliaments' continued to be mass assemblies of the nobility; medieval Magyar history is the conflict between Lords and gentry. In the 'pyramid' areas also, when the hierarchy disintegrated as it lost its functional value and was shaken by peasant resistance, the ties of lord and vassal turned into competition over the inheritance. This 'democratic' element in the lower feudal nobility made an essential contribution to Calvinism, capitalism, and the modern European concept of democracy. (Cf Daimyo and Samurai in Japan.)

7. The 'middle class' of feudal gentry were more exposed and sensitive than the great lords to the pressure of peasant unrest, and were at the same time in danger of being engulfed in the great estates. (The Polish slachta, the threadbare Don, the Tudor gentleman waiting at table on Cecil or Bacon.) They were in danger of being squeezed out of the system, crushed between the two millstones. The revolt of the Imperial Knights in 1520 illustrates the feelings of the more desperate of them – the Knights were, in a manner of speaking, the Anabaptists of the feudality. For feudal society to have any chance of further evolution, it was indispensable that the feudal ruling classes should be divided against themselves. Where circumstances allowed their divisions to be reconciled, evolution was halted.

B. *The Absolute Monarchy*

8. Politically, the rise of monarchical State power on a revised basis is the most obvious bridge between late medieval and early modern. The new State always began with more or less of a 'popular' basis: 'popular' in feudal terms, not capitalist (rising bourgeois). This basis consisted in the support given to the Crown by the middle and lower-middle strata of mediaeval society, as against sections of both the highest and the lowest strata. These supporting strata were the burghers (eg France) free peasantry (NB Sweden), but above all the middle and smaller landed gentry (NB Hungary – Matthias Corvinus, backed by the gentry against the magnates with their troops of retainers). A new dynasty might be thrown up from the ranks of the gentry themselves (Vasa; Tudor). It was the smaller English landowners who primarily benefited from the disarming of the great lords by the Tudor State. Similarly Spain, where the Catholic Kings leaned on the mass of the Hidalguia; notice their distrust of great nobles in office, and the 'feudal-democratic' character of their 'Conciliar' administration.
9. The essential idea of the Absolute Monarchy was not at all to entrust unlimited, arbitrary power to an unfettered despot, a 'dictator' – except in the sole sphere of international politics, on which the Monarchs always (therefore) concentrated. It was, on the contrary, to set up, with a supreme judge or Arbiter at the top, a fixed, rigid, static social order; replacing the medieval order that had been a dissolving into Chaos, but preserving wealth and power in the possession of the middle landowners, seconded by the merchants and guildsmen; a social order in which every man should remain faithfully in the sphere to which God had called him (this was the original sense of the Protestant 'Vocation'). These classes had no heed for an active, dynamic, 'policy-making', State (except for war). Their assumption was that after a preliminary clearing away of rubbish (cutting off of Over-Mighty heads, etc) by King and Estates (Parliament, Cortes, Riksdag), and some re-codification of law, the system would be placed in an equilibrium which need never again be impaired. This was still the ideal of the 18th century Philosophes, and these men had a natural admiration for China, the land of eternal beatitude for the middle classes under a benign but retiring Emperor.

10. 'Absolutism' is therefore in some ways a misleading term. 'Quod principi placuit' was a later distortion. The true sixteenth-century Monarchy's laws extended to every sphere of life, but they were binding on the Monarchy itself. No *individual* could stand against the State; but the prescriptive rights of classes and corporations were guaranteed against interference – whereas the modern Sovereign English Parliament cannot proceed against individuals, but is (in principle) absolute as against all corporate interests. The Spanish monarchy, even in decay, preserved something of this original character: it was static, legalistic, hieratic, and the Divine Right of Kings was never preached by it. Here and in Portugal in the 19th century we find Carlists and Miguelites raising the cry of 'Viva el rey absolute', and meaning thereby, *not* royal dictatorship, but on the contrary the preservation from Liberal-Parliamentary interference of all traditional corporative rights, not only of Church and nobility, but also the democratic *fueros* [charters] of Navarre and the Basques: rights 'absolutely' sacrosanct under the 'absolute' Crown.
11. The new State represented a clearing of the ground, a breathing space for the middle strata of society. But since it rested on no radical transformation of the mode of production, but was only a re-shuffling of power within the same group of interests – only a 'feudal revision' – it could not be a final settlement. Instead of remaining perpetually fixed, it began at once to evolve through a new feudal cycle, with local variations determined by local balance of forces and circumstances. In practice the character of Absolutism in a particular context can be judged a good deal by its fiscal arrangements. Nearly everywhere, it was a firm principle that nobles should pay no direct taxation and privileged towns comparatively little. It was important that in England – where the high (titled) had marked itself off early and distinctly from the gentry – the lower nobility was not immune from taxation. The French Crown always depended mainly on direct taxation of the peasantry, which tended to draw off, partly for the benefit of the big noble, some of the surplus that might otherwise have been appropriated by the small land owner.
12. The establishment of the Monarchy was 'anti-feudal' in the sense of being directed on the whole against the greatest

feudal Magnates (and prelates). That is, it was not in origin the completion of the Magnates' drive towards concentration and monopoly, but the reverse. However, the Crown's supporters included from the first some of the old big nobles; and there was also the growth of a fresh crop of Magnates – either new Marcher Lords of the old type, as in the Habsburg empire, or in conquered Granada; or else great families connected with the State machine (Cecil; Montmorency; Xinenez, Oxenstierna.) These two types tended to amalgamate, though one could still distinguish them in the House of Lords of 1642. The administrative cadres of the monarchy had been provided partly (N.B. France) by burgher *gens de la robe*, but more generally by the more educated sections of the gentry (English lawyers, Spanish *Letrados*; also the J.P.s). These, however, tended to sink into subordination to the Magnates and the normal evolution of the Monarchy was to repeat the previous feudal cycle and move towards a modernised 'neo-feudal' hierarchy.

13. This happened completely, though silently and unobtrusively, in Spain, where the 16th century sees the high nobility crystallise out, from the large and *growing* mass of small nobles, in the form of the *Titulos de Castilla* and the *Grandeza de Espana*. The Revolt of the *Communeros* [1520-23] may be seen as the protest of the *hildaguia* [lesser nobility] including its urbanised wing, the town *Regidores* [municipal councillors], and pushed on by mass social unrest, against the tendency they already felt of the new State to slip out of their hands. It was suppressed, in the King's absence, by the big nobility. But the Crown acquired immense prestige by imperial conquest, and found a place for the gentry in colonies, armies, monasteries, while the great landed nobles, clustered round the Court, were the real beneficiaries, and the State began to die of dry rot. Imperial tribute made this moribundity peaceful and comfortable.

14. The Monarchy survived best in the Counter-Reformation areas, where this evolution was carried to completion. In the two foci of the Counter-Ref., Spain and Austria, R.C. fervour was kept alive even more by contact with Infidels (which gave religious fire and uniformity a functional value) than by hostility to Protestantism. Energies being directed outwards,

the neo-feudalism could develop at leisure. The Monarchy began later but retained its vitality much longer in Austria, where it served a genuine defensive need against Turkey till after 1700, than in Spain, where the defensive struggle (N. Africa) was a side-issue and the real external orientation was towards (colonial) regions offering little resistance to penetration. The monarchy everywhere aimed at expansion (England-Ireland, etc; France-Italy; Sweden-Finland), because this was the easiest way of consolidating a compromise between higher and lower nobility (and their affiliates, big Merchant Capital and the middle burghers respectively). Hence, again, the preoccupation of the monarchy with external affairs, which was also the most attractive field for the Wolseys, Granvellas, Richelieus. The Italian wars show how the compromise developed in France where the gentry were kept harmlessly busy plundering abroad till Cateau Cambrésis. [1559]

15. Where expansionism was less easy, further internal redistribution had to take place. In the new European situation, military ascendancy lay in the South, and the economic changes were also at first not favourable to the north; cities and trade were on the decline in Germany, Flanders, England. Rising standards of living for the upper classes coincided with a shrinking pool of wealth. Economies, austerities, became necessary, and were started at the expense of the Church. The Reformation broke out (Northern Germany) at the weakest link in the chain of feudal society. The (Lutheran) attack on the Church was not revolutionary, except in so far as it transferred property from a feudal organisation dominated by the (old) higher nobility, to smaller landowners. But it marked a further internal break-up of the old feudal State-cum-Church machine, an internal dislocation that could help to make genuine 'revolution' possible later on. The Tudors decisively weakened the Church by plundering it. Elizabeth clung to vestments and altars because *something* had to be left to the impoverished clergy, to maintain their hold over the illiterate vulgar; but these were a poor substitute for monasteries and masses. The Lutheran Reformation was at the same time a partial concession to the unrest of the lower-middle and lower classes; while economically, for the N.

European region as a whole, it represented the stoppage of a drain of tribute to Italy which the north could no longer afford to pay.

C *The Trend Towards Capitalism*

16. The secondary effect of the relative impoverishment of N. Europe was to stimulate production. With the regrouping of the 'European market', and the commencement of the world market with the inflow of colonial wealth, the Northern lands – unable, until the English and Dutch developed their naval-guerrilla warfare with Spain, to claim their share in the new wealth by force – had to seek a share by means of trade. This involved the need to maximise their export surplus: England by selling more cloth, Holland by salting herrings, Sweden by stepping up the iron industry.
17. Brandenburg-Prussia, a land typically of small squires rather than of great territorial magnates, solved this problem a little later (with the growth of the Baltic and North Sea markets) by developing the 'feudal-capitalism' (agrarian production for the market organised by the landowner through forced labour) which came to characterise North-east Europe. In North-west Europe, it was too late in the day to re-impose serfdom: otherwise this 'natural' feudal solution would have been adopted. But the Tudor squire suffered more and more from rising prices, and he had no standing army to occupy him; while he had helped to destroy the monasteries, formerly a refuge for decayed gentlemen and their daughters, in the same sort of spirit in which the Arab kills his camel in the desert in order to drink the water in its stomach.
18. The European environment combined with the peculiar conditions inside England (background of the wool trade, peasant obstinacy, etc ... See Maurice Dobb) to turn the smaller English landowner's mind in the direction of a new method of extracting a better income from his estate – capitalism. This could develop here because, under the Tudor realm, the squire had enough independence from his superiors to avoid being absorbed into the great noble properties, and enough strength against the peasantry to use his feudal-tenurial rights to assist in their expropriation. At the same

time he was not, like the Court nobles, able to extract much of a feudal rake-off from the expansion of trade: he had to turn to something new, production instead of parasitism.

19. Contrast with other countries emphasises the high 'exceptionalism' of the combination of conditions found in England. In Spain the smaller gentry controlled municipal administration, which, added to their other resources, helped to keep them afloat without change of method. In Poland great masses of the gentry sank into client-dependence on the magnates or were reduced to peasants with rusty swords. In France the gentry fell between two stools: the peasantry was neither 'free' enough for wage-labour nor 'unfree' enough for forced labour – it was to hold out through and after the Revolution of 1789, against both capitalism and feudalism.
20. Non-agricultural capitalism had still more diverse origins. Capitalism in a variety of primitive forms, which failed to develop, had been widely scattered through world history. The question is not so much of how capitalism came into existence, but of how, in one small region, it was able to consolidate itself, dominate society, and enter on a continuous evolution. Big scale capitalism appeared, not in opposition to the feudal-Absolute State, but in the closest association with it: not, i.e. with this State in its pristine purity, but in its neo-feudal growth, when kings relied on international bankers to pay their armies, and court nobles found in alliance with merchants and monopoly-industrialists a ready means of strengthening their control of the machine and extracting their rake-off. But merchant capital required maintenance of order over wider areas than small industry, and State aid in controlling trade routes. Big industry was fostered, subsidised, largely even created, by the State; and this tendency antedates the British Road – it did not begin, though it later gathered force, in feudal emulation of industry already created by a capitalist bourgeoisie in certain countries. The State was reproducing on a more ambitious scale the policy of the old seigneur of monopolising the local fulling-mill or wine-press or oven. Industrialists thus spoon-fed would not be a revolutionary force (cf. German & Japanese capitalism later). Besides, big industry divides Capital and Labour too nakedly for the two to combine against any government; after

machine-industry appeared there were no more successful bourgeois revolutions anywhere. (An element of this situation may have been already present in medieval Flanders & Italy.)

21. The feudal-Absolute state, needing more revenue (particularly in view of the refusal of the nobles, and unwillingness or inability of the peasants, to pay taxes), was quite willing to encourage 'capitalism' in this sense; and big monopoly-industry could co-exist with an increasingly rigid guild system, to which small production was abandoned. (France, and the Habsburg lands under Joseph II.) A bourgeois revolution required mass energy that could only come from lower down, in the stratum of petty production where capitalism could take on a popular, 'progressive' character. Small industrial capital emerged as, in part, the defensive reaction of the craft-guilds against domination by MC and/or State-regimentation. Cottage industry brought a real benefit to the countryman, who was not 'losing his independence' to the entrepreneur but rather was being found employment which he could not have at all while industry was monopolised by urban groups.

22. Broadly, one might say that in southern Europe the tendency was to make the common man *pay* more, in N. Europe to *produce* more. This might mean harder work, as in Prussia; or might involve for a long time lower wages as in England – but this was brought about by the price-rise, and was felt by the wage earner not so much as exploitation by his small employer as in the form of victimisation by the usury-capital which belonged (on the whole) to the 'feudal' sector of capitalism. Apart from these things, increased production could be got partly by division of labour; and in peasant economies there is always an immense slack of seasonal idleness that can be taken up, especially by cottage industry; the English farmer, like the petty manufacturer, retained a markedly patriarchal, paternal, character down to near 1800 (see Cobbett)[4]; his labourer might originally have been an expropriated small-holder, but a peasant who lost his land was at least better off with a job than as a vagrant. The English 'progressive' landowner, of course, remained semi-parasitic: it was not he, so much as the farmer, who actually organised production; but he supervised production, and had a further

'functional' part to play in creating the tenurial, etc., conditions, and later on the *political* conditions in which the new system could flourish. In short, small scale capitalism could have a relatively 'popular' character.

23. As Weber shows, the early petty-capitalist arose, not only from within Calvinistic circles, but also from those humbler, radical, anabaptistical strata which evolved into Quakers, Pietists, etc. The man who was to grow into the really 'modern' (pre-machine) capitalist (small IC) of later seventeenth-century England was not the violent ruthless, Napoleonic individual who is sometimes presented as the typical 'rising bourgeois' (and who really belongs to the big merchant-capital-semi-feudal-state-monopoly type of business), he was a quiet, peaceful, patriarchal man, capable of relapsing into the vegetative. The true petty industrial capital arose from the lower middle class groups; from within the guild artisanate (Calvinist) and from the expropriated artisans & journeymen outside the guild shelters (Anabaptist). Such men did not look Quakerish at the outset, or there would have been no bourgeois revolution. But this revolution was not made by them for the sake of setting up capitalism; what they aimed at was independence, and they found this in the end, not quite in the way they had expected, through petty capitalism. No-one in this age was fighting for capitalism – those who fought against feudalism were not, primarily, throwing off 'feudal shackles on production'; they were already anti-feudal on other grounds. In some ways the makers of the bourgeois revolution were fighting against capitalism of the big-scale merchant capital monopolist, usurer sort (under which, in England by 1600, the anatomy or dry bones of feudalism were effectively camouflaged; the Jacobean social-drama is far more anti-capitalist than anti-feudal). What emerged from the whirlpool of the bourgeois revolution was something that nobody had intended or designed; true industrial capital came into its own as a product of class conflicts in an epoch when the outlines of Europe were undergoing a seismic upheaval. The democratic revolution that had really been intended by the militant rank and file had failed; the Leveller had become a Quaker and the Quaker a small capitalist.

24. The Anabaptist democratic revolution as such everywhere failed. It grew with its ideology of liberation and semi-socialism out of the late medieval disintegration of classes. As soon as society was re-integrated (whether on the Spanish, Habsburg, Prussian, or English model) Anabaptism faded out. It had no religious dogmas to cling to, no positive doctrines beyond the emotional belief in human brotherhood because it expressed simply the desire of the primary producer for freedom from exploitation. It could never equal the military strength of the ruling classes, who could always combine against it. Though its ideology was more liberal, rational, 'modern', than any other before the eighteenth century, it remained medieval. The only way forward for the masses was the indirect detour of capitalism. The positive achievement of Anabaptism lay in its indispensable contribution to the success of the bourgeois revolution. Its revolutionary mass energy could be drawn in behind capitalism in certain conditions, because 'true' capitalism (small industrial capital) was still only just emerging and – though it could establish links with more powerful groups among the gentry and urban rulers – was still 'democratic', and much more anti-feudal than anti-labour.

D *The Calvinist Strata of Late Medieval Society*

25. In the fifteenth to seventeenth centuries, Anabaptism is the religion of the most self-conscious of the masses exploited whether by feudalism or capitalism. Popery is that of the upper nobility, other contented feudal elements, and the more backward masses. Protestantism is that of the middle elements of rural and urban society which, caught between the pressure from above and the pressure from below, found it necessary to seek a new organisation and ideology – not, primarily, with a view to reconstructing or dominating society, but in order to hang on to their place within the traditional society. In fact, viewing Europe broadly, Protestantism is the religion of those same classes which a little earlier had set up the Absolute State, in areas where they had by now been disappointed with the results of their work.
26. Calvinism in particular represents the most self-conscious and

militant of these intermediate groups. Its membership is very heterogeneous, extending from New England to Transylvania (later adding Wales, southern Africa, etc.) No one of these regions can claim a monopoly of the inspiration of Calvinism, though some obviously took the lead in its formulation. The Huguenot or Magyar squire is not merely derivatively or imitatively a Calvinist; Bethlen Gabor is as sound a Calvinist as Bèza or Jonathan Edwards. The 'General Theory of Calvinism' (as distinct from the Special Theory of bourgeois-Calvinism) has to include them all, and therefore has to repose on a very generalised class-situation, or complex of class relations. This is all the more true since the chief doctrines of the movement were very old, and drawn from a very different environment. The environment which produced Augustine has recognisable affinities with the generalised 'Calvinist situation', none at all with big industrial capitalism. Calvinism does not spring from the subjective consciousness of one single group, but from a pattern of forces among groups which can be repeated with many different groups.

27. Calvin was growing up while all Europe seemed in danger of dissolving into social anarchy. The classes he appealed to had to protect themselves on two fronts, and in a Europe also threatened from outside. Part of his business was to repel upper-feudal encroachments, another part was to disarm or suppress Anabaptism. Protestantism shared with the mass-revolutionary movement its attack on the old Church – partly for its own benefit, partly as a concession to the masses. Negatively Protestantism was rational and progressive in sweeping away the collective-ritual-magic which constituted the bulk of medieval religion: – but not original, for this had already been done, and more thoroughly by Anabaptism (in the field of ideas, not in practice). There is comparatively little of permanent value (though there is something) in Protestantism which it did not derive from Anabaptism.

28. But in ideology as in politics, Anabaptism could not succeed or survive by itself, but only by being drawn in behind other forces which possessed some anchorage, some stake, higher up in medieval society. Calvinism, springing from classes which had held a more or less privileged and sheltered position, preserved a good deal of medieval thought. Its

positive thinking was mostly pre-medieval or mediaeval (though perhaps of the intellectual, middle class Scholastic side of medieval Christianity, as distinct from its popular mumbo-jumbo). Calvinism was a more powerful, though a much less advanced, ideology than Anabaptism, because it had intellectual as well as emotional weapons with which to confront popery. If the end product of the whole epoch may be taken as English-Dutch later seventeenth century nonconformity, then we may say that this type of mentality had emerged from a struggle in which Anabaptism and Calvinism had joined forces, intermingled, and been reshuffled into something new; exactly as Anabaptist revolutionism and Calvinist leadership in the bourgeois revolution had resulted in the small independent radical-democratic progressive industrial capital to which that nonconformist mentality belonged.

29. It is, at bottom, because Calvinism was setting out to defend already-existing rights, privileges, properties, and not like Anabaptism to make a clean sweep and inaugurate a new social order, that an element of the irrational and contradictory pervades its system of thought. Clearly everything is here made to look logical; but the fundamental fact of God willing what He does will, the question of why mankind is divided into a minority of Saved and a majority of Damned, is left as inexplicable; it is part of a purpose which it would be impious to enquire into – just as it would be indelicate to enquire why society is divided into classes, and by what right the noble flogs the serf.

30. Calvinists were much drawn to the Old Testament; which is based on a rationalistic, materialistic attitude to life. Materialism, *ceteris paribus*, is always more natural to a middle class milieu than to the rich or the poor. However, the Calvinist strata could not go in, in any case, for a whole-hog materialism, which would have played into Anabaptist hands. As privileged groups in the old order, they needed some form of justification – until they (some of them) had clothed themselves with a more rational, more socially useful, 'functional' character, as capitalists. Calvin abolished metaphysics, by denying that anything done on earth can influence anything determined in heaven; the logical next step

would have been to abolish any sort of systematic, doctrinal religion. Calvin naturally did not propose to do this, and he retained the bulk of the old dogmas while abolishing the old ritual. Anabaptism stressed the ethical side of the New Testament; the Counter-Reformation's main stress was on the myth-element in the New Testament, which it disinterred from under the rubbish heap of medieval magic. But while the Counter-Reformation emphasised the romantic, 'human angle', demagogic side of the Christ-Myth, Protestantism developed it in a different, more abstract, 'geometrical', fashion. For Calvinism especially, the gulf between Old Testament and New was difficult to cross. It required very forcible methods to link the Atonement-Myth into a Supralapsarian scheme, and the lack of a really organic connection gave rise, in later phases of Calvinism, to much intellectual sophistication. But the significant point is that wherever the Protestant classes, aided by Calvinism, transformed themselves and society into a new capitalist shape, it was their *dogmas* inherited from the middle ages, that they then shed off, moving towards a doctrinal flexibility (or vacuum) nearly as complete as that of Anabaptism.

31. Of the non urban groups embraced in the Calvinist solar system, the principal was the smaller landed nobility or gentry. At times this could extend to yeomen or free peasants (a Magyar or Slav noble might be a one horse peasant), and also to an occasional higher noble who found his position uncomfortable (Orange, Sedan, Bourbon, and some Germans). A leading case is the Magyar squirearchy, which had failed, partly through Turkish complications, to maintain a strong national monarchy, and was restless under the Habsburg control supported by some of the Magnates. (Magnates were inclined to prefer a foreign King who could be useful without being domineering: Aragon, Poland, Bohemia – the Hungarian towns were in general Germanised, Lutheran, & Imperialist – not Calvinist.) In sixteenth-century Scotland there are conflicting trends within feudal society; feudal relations and institutions were still being elaborated, under the direction of the great lords, while the development of the feu-tenure benefited and consolidated the lairds – who were the backbone of the Calvinist movement. The French

gentry were already partly reduced to the status of clients dependant on old (Bourbon, Guise) or new (Montmorency) magnates. But some of them were still capable of striking a blow for survival by asserting, as Huguenots, their independence against the neo-feudal State and upper-feudal Church. Dutch Calvinism also had its agrarian side. Calvinism was strong in the seventeenth century in the 'Landward' provinces; and notice the emigration later to southern Africa of farmers who were now, perhaps, escaping from *capitalist* domination of agriculture, but who preserved the same spirit of an independent 'middle class.'

32. Of the urban Calvinist strata, the core is the *petite bourgeoisie* accustomed to guild organisation: but only in conditions where this class is i) threatened with disintegration as a class, and ii) tenacious enough to be able to struggle to preserve its corporate existence. Failing these two conditions, this class is i) Roman Catholic (Paris, Spain) or ii) Anabaptist, respectively. This petty bourgeoisie, in the more fluid social conditions that have been developing in France or England, has affiliates – people of roughly the same kind of 'social standing' and who have similarly been accustomed to a degree of privilege and security within the old order: smaller tradesmen, smaller professional men such as lawyers (not the big lawyers of the *parlements*, who even later never get beyond Jansenism at most); many of these men in France have a footing on the lower branches of the already proliferating State bureaucracy. The urban petty bourgeoisie in the (Calvinist) sense normally excludes the higher burgher strata: big merchants, State industrialists, financiers, big lawyers, municipal patricians. Some of these, however (like some of the bigger nobles) can be drawn in under special circumstances. This happens especially where, as in the Netherlands cities or Geneva, the big merchant, rentier, patrician, 'Regent' group is caught between the pressure of Anabaptism from below and that of feudalism – represented by foreign political control – from above, and has to struggle or manoeuvre for its existence. Geneva was a French town perched up in the hills, and comparable with the Huguenot 'garrison cities'. The civic authorities in an expanding and restless city like London would readily appreciate the need for a new discipline to assist

them, and would admire the 'Geneva model'. The boundary between craft-guild and magistracy was not too impassable; the guilds had had a share in municipal administration, which they had been tending to lose with the late medieval oligarchical drift, and which they might well look forward to recovering.

E *The Calvinist Pattern and Its Lines of Development*

33. Under the formal surface of Calvinism lie the anarchic emotions of individuals and classes; its underlying contradictions reflect the diversity of the social groups which contribute to it, as well as the general predicament in which they all stood in relation to the rest of society. Calvinism took shape first in northern France, a region which was and long remained intermediary between Eastern and Western levels of evolution. Calvin himself was exactly a 'petit bourgeois' (middle burgher) as defined above; but he grew up, in the provinces and at college, in contact also with the smaller gentry class which was to be the main Huguenot fighting force. Besides this, Calvin must be considered as typically a professional theologian, a representative of the specialised intelligentsia which had its own psychological-material incentives, and played an enormous part in shaping both Reformation and Counter-Reformation ideas. Calvinism as a system consists of an organisation, an ethic, and a doctrine: these correspond roughly with the needs of the higher Calvinist strata (gentry, etc), the urban petty bourgeoisie, and the professional intelligentsia, respectively but with numerous interactions.
34. The Presbyterian type of church had affinities with the guild (and compare the Separatist type of Church with the old fraternity, *compagnonnage*, *confradia*), and the grouping of church bodies in classis or synod was not unlike the corporate participation by guilds and Companies in civic government. With its combination of democratic and oligarchic it fitted in well with the needs of those groups in late feudal society who were accustomed to exercising local authority, and now were in search of means to safeguard that authority. Calvin worked out the system in practice at

Geneva, in collaboration (never perfectly harmonious, but increasingly so) with the ruling magistracy – typical traditional rich burghers. Moreover, it fitted in very well with the 'county' administration which for centuries was the *point d'appui* of the Magyar squirearchy; and with the very similar social structure of Scotland, where it could help to organise and protect the interests of lairds and burghers against the ferocious nobles (and, of course, the restless peasants). It was a machine that could be used, when called upon, for organising revolution; it was constructed to maintain order – that is, for so long as 'order' represented the chief interest of its supporters.

35. The 'Calvinist virtues' served, in the field of moral discipline, the same purpose – Weber, etc., concoct the dilemma: Calvinist and capitalist virtues are identical; but we find the former to be anterior (eg in the backwoods of America long before there is any capitalism); therefore Calvinism creates capitalism and not *vice versa*. The fact is that the 'Calvinist virtues', though they could come to assist in capital accumulation, etc, were not invented for any such purpose. They were simply the typical virtues – thrift, honesty, sobriety – of a lower middle class in any country or time: a class that always has to practice self-denial and self-control in order to hang on to its place in society. Their social function in early Calvinism was to ensure the survival, the class existence, of the urban petty bourgeoisie, at a time when the earlier safeguards and protections of feudal society were weakening.

36. On the dogmatic side, the paramount doctrine of Election marked, at the outset, the solidarity of the social groups, concerned their feeling of superiority (moral or social) to all others; they were the Saved, who enjoyed God's peculiar providence. This doctrine can be held [in] a quiet, placid self-complacent way as by a nineteenth-century Methodist. Its *timbre* varies with the degree of stress to which the group is being subjected. Luther held it most strongly in his earlier, more democratic, German period. Its more strident, self-assertive tone was given to it partly by fanatical preachers, but perhaps above all by the Calvinist centre especially in eastern Europe, where the small noble was extremely conscious of belonging to a special caste, the descendants of a conquering

race that had taken its Canaan by the sword and held it by the sword. Such a man was much more readily capable than any ordinary townsman of the arrogant egotist and self-esteem implicit in the extremer forms of predestination. The outlying Calvinist regions took their ideas from Geneva, and then Utrecht – but they sent theologians there as well as students, and some of the high Predestinarians like Maccovius[5] came from feudal eastern Europe. It was again in the years while Calvin was collaborating at Geneva with a semi-patrician group, a class long used to authority, and while he was receiving the respectful tributes of the Scottish and French gentry, that the dogma of Election grew more firmly rooted in his mind. This was the reverse of Luther's personal evolution. The 'authority' to which Calvin's adherents were accustomed was a *collective* authority, 'democratic' within the ruling group, such as the Magyar's 'comitatus' – not the authority of an arbitrary individual, like that of the princes to whom Luther capitulated. Calvinism is always the faith of groups of solid property owners, defending their rights with their collective energy.

37. Calvinism is invariably found in association with national, anti-foreign, feelings. But the modern feeling of nationality has evolved from that of *caste*, growing up first among conquerors and then among conquered peoples. The 'Regenerate' Magyar squire is not far removed from the 'Twice born' Arya of Hinduism. The Elect cannot forfeit salvation, any more than the nobleman can forfeit by any crime his inalienable nobility of blood: in feudal lands (eg Scotland, see Hogg) this could easily deviate into the supposition that a man's sins don't matter at all, so long as his name is down in the celestial register of the landed Gentry. Calvinists identified themselves with the Chosen People of Scripture and in America and above all in South Africa were to conquer Canaan over again. In the more progressive regions, this caste feeling (still strong in Tudor England) developed into nationalism: all the Englishmen of Milton and Cromwell were a chosen people.

38. The arrogance of the landed noble fortified the confidence of his citizen allies or co-religionists in the truth of Election, a truth not so easy to cling to in the life of crowded, insecure

cities. Conversely the burgher virtues of thrift and sobriety could be helpful to the small landowner who tried to make head against rising prices, etc., by practising economics, cutting down on wine and women and gambling, and making his sons follow (and outstrip) his good example. Such a breakaway from the traditional feudal values of lavish living would be extremely difficult for an individual not backed up by a new ideology and discipline. Clearly, this would apply most of all to the landowner who went in for 'improving his estate', saving capital to invest in it, producing for the market just as in the urban case thrift took on a special value for the small struggling capitalist.

39. A Calvinist squire, whether in Poland or England, derived from the same medieval-feudal origin. From their primary ambition of keeping afloat in the chaos of the medieval disintegration, they developed different tendencies according to local circumstances. In Eastern and much of central Europe, where their enemies (magnates and peasants) were visible and tangible, they responded by taking up arms fairly promptly. In England their main enemy was the more intangible price rise and they adopted Calvinism, and then the idea of the armed uprising, more slowly. France, as usual, was an intermediate case. In all cases, the gentry was threatened with disruption and division within its own ranks. The gentleman might climb into the higher nobility, sink into dependence, or survive in his original state. In S. Europe, Calvinism aimed essentially at the third alternative, and remained on the whole a static philosophy. In the West, where the fourth alternative of capitalism presented itself, Calvinism was capable of further evolution. And the alternative between selling one's manor to buy clothes to wear in Court ante-rooms, on the off-chance of some more or less shady piece of luck turning up, or staying at home to pinch and scrape for money to enclose a meadow and buy another farm, deepened the fissure in the ranks, and gave a fresh meaning to the distinction between Reprobate and Elect.

40. The same applies to the urban petty bourgeoisie, whose intellectuals did most of the work of refining the basic Calvinist formulations (just as other intellectuals of the same sort of origin, like Hans Denck,[6] but more in touch with the de-classed

artisan groups, put in shape the more elaborate formulations of Anabaptism which were valid also for many of the peasantry). The urban petty bourgeoisie too was threatened not only by pressure from outside, but also, as a consequence, by disintegration within. Petty capitalism partly originated within the craft guild as its defence against external pressure (the yeoman-farmer employing a few hands was likewise in a sense the protector of the rural community against the rack-renting usurer-land-speculator). But its growth involved the prospect of permanent stratification within the guild-democracy.

41. It may be uncertain how much of true industrial capital already existed in the milieu (either craft guild or agriculture) in which Calvin grew up. For the urban petty bourgeoisie, as for the gentry, there were the three alternatives of rising, sinking, or standing still. But the new and more dynamic alternative, the deeper fission, represented by the onset of capitalism, was probably of some importance from the outset. It was (as C.H. points out) qualitatively the most significant factor for the whole future development, even if as yet little advanced absolutely. Calvinism displayed so much originality of spirit (if not of ideas), and so much energy, because the class that was to be of the greatest historical importance to its evolution was already beginning (only beginning) to be polarised along new lines. In this, strictly limited, sense we can think of Calvinism as the ideology of industrial capitalism. It began by representing, on the part of the petty-bourgeois guild democracy, a convulsive effort to maintain unity, to preserve the common ethos and the old way of life. Had it 'succeeded' in the sense originally intended, it would not have fostered modern capitalism, but would on the contrary have prevented it. The urban petty bourgeoisie Elect as originally conceived were not the nascent proto-capitalists, striding relentlessly towards power (these men were in fact only modestly tip toeing into existence as yet): the Elect were the class-group as a whole. Nevertheless, the fact that the new germ, which was to divide them into Capital and Labour, was already lurking among them, gave from the start a more urgent, if only half-comprehended, meaning to the idea of Election and Damnation, and this meaning was to assert itself more and more clearly as things developed.

42. As the new fissure deepened, the Elect tended to be focussed on the rising (industrial capital) element to the disparagement of the others. Along with this, the obsessive Calvinist sense of guilt and sin deepened. The guilt complex from the first belonged mainly to the urban petty bourgeois sector of Calvinism: a squire rarely feels 'sinful', at least while he is doing nothing more novel or unreasonable than hitting the bottle or flogging the serf. 'Total depravity' expressed the sense of social disintegration, disorder, insecurity, violation of the social compact – it affected all late medieval society to some extent, but was most keenly felt in crowded cities. The individual by himself in this chaos was lost; salvation lay in group solidarity and discipline (theologically, in harmony with the Eternal Decrees, and in Imputed Righteousness). But the sense of guilt deepened when this group solidarity also turned out to [be] fragile, when the Elect came to be saved, not only to the exclusion of the Reprobate, but at their expense – when A. rose to Heaven by pushing B. down to Hell. In this new form, the guilt complex could extend to the agrarian sector as well; Cromwell's dying words embody the tragic experience of a whole class. The newer meaning of election took the form of the Doctrine of Proof. If the extremer statements of Predestination belong to feudal-agrarian Calvinism, the evolution of ideas in the capitalistic sector is represented by the Doctrine of Proof – no part of the original Calvinism, but the consequence of the emergence of industrial capital out of the small burgherdom.

F *Political Outlook of Calvinism*

43. In politics, Lutheranism on the whole had remained content with the idea of Absolute Monarchy. Calvin himself probably began with a good deal of belief in it. It seemed on the cards that Francis I would follow the example of England and northern Germany and break with Rome; then, it might be hoped, he would recognise the truth and impose it on all his subjects. Such an attitude could persist much later. The Dutch Calvinists after 1600 always pinned their credulous 'radical-democratic' hopes on the House of Orange, as the authority that would clear away the barnacles of big business from the

Ship of State. If Francis I *had* turned Presbyterian, he would in a sense have been going back to the initial historic function of the Absolute monarchy, namely the clearing away of upper-feudal encumbrances that weighed on the middle landowners and burghers. At various later stages in its evolution – notably with the Benevolent Despots – the monarchy did in some measure try to resume this function in a new context. But such hopes were always flimsy; Calvin's early trust in the Monarchy was illusory, and reflected the narrow political vision of his own immediate p.b. environment.

44. The Absolute State, whose origins had affinities with those of Protestantism, did in a way find its reflection in the Protestant idea of a Sovereign God eliminating angels, saints, and other celestial Grandees. But the Calvinist God, unlike the feudal Catholic God who can be bribed, cajoled, and deceived, was remote, inaccessible, inexorable – an impersonal Law rather than a Being. Divine Right exponents (Jesuit, Anglican) identified King and God; the Divine Right notion was a deviation from the idea on which Absolute Monarchy had at first been based, and belonged to a stage in the neo-feudal cycle when the Crown had become hemmed in by Magnates and was manipulated by them (as God was manipulated by Cardinals) and grew arbitrary, partial, variable, and (like the demagogic Counter-Reformation Father-Mother-Child in Heaven) 'human, all too human'.

45. Calvinist thought, then, went back and sought to reinterpret and reinforce the 'original purpose' (as conceived by the classes who supported it) of the Absolute State. The supporters of this State had been disappointed by the outcome; Calvinism accomplished in theology what it could not do in politics, the radical fulfilment of the idea. While the Catholic-feudal notion of the universe was still more or less animistic, Calvinism was moving in the same line as the late mediaeval studies of the laws of motion, the advance towards a mechanistic cosmogony and was setting up a universe of Law. Calvin himself, while in France, may have seen no other possibility than to recall the Monarchy to the strait and narrow path. But the Calvinist movement was not tied to monarchism. The fact that its God was remote and

'automatic', like a piece of clockwork wound up long ago, made the precise form of State (as also, in some extremist thinking, the forms of morality) a matter of indifference. Only the Church organisation was *iure* divine; while for the papist with his divine Seigneur just round the corner, Monarchy was almost the only conceivable government.

46. It is too much even to say that Calvinism believed in the *State* i.e. in the big modern centralised territorial State. It wanted strong organisation and discipline but was everywhere localist and particularist in outlook (Netherlands, New England, Switzerland etc). It never ruled large states, for which its economic basis made it unsuitable. It spread widest in backward agrarian regions (Hungary, Scottish lowlands) but the Magyar squires always concentrated on their local county machinery, and made their country a network of 'republics'. It was only the evolution towards capitalism (where it occurred) that altered all this. Capitalism and its needs brought with them the modern idea of State Absolutism or 'internal sovereignty' – the idea of a dynastic authority coping with constantly changing problems. Calvinism came to power for one moment in one big country – England – and there, having become fully capitalistic, ceased at once to be Calvinist.

47. With its self-regarding, particularist bent in politics, Calvinism was not inevitably intolerant, as popery almost always was. Its motives for religious persecution tended to be more rational. Calvinism tolerated other Protestants in Brandenburg, and was tolerated by them in Sweden; in America it tolerated toleration in Rhode Island. Calvinism could take part in 'united fronts', as in sixteenth-century Bohemia. In Transylvania, the 'Eastern Holland', it lived side by side with Lutherans, Catholics, and Unitarians: the Rakoczi rebellion of 1703 was a movement largely of Calvinist squires and peasants under a Catholic leader. In the Netherlands revolt, the Dutch-Calvinist fanaticism which helped to prevent the Catholic South from being brought back into the movement was petty-bourgeois, and was not shared by the Regents: it reflects in part the cleavage already widening between these two wings and the radical-urban-lower-middle-class sense of frustration. (Cf the intolerance of the Levellers in Ireland).

48. The Calvinist classes began with an aggressively defensive attitude. They became 'revolutionary' in response to the changing pressures round them, and in some cases to their own inner development. But while they remained Calvinists they never lost sight of the antique rights they were asserting, and in the midst of revolutions clung tenaciously to conservative forms, eg the English Parliamentarians; while the Jesuits with their Free Will and Divine Right were prepared for all sorts of innovations. In feudal regions their political mentality therefore stood still: in eighteenth-century Hungary it was the same as in sixteenth-century Scotland. Even France, where few of the gentry were turning 'progressive', the Wars of Religion showed little development or initiative of ideas among the Huguenots: no New Model, no Levellers, no Ireton, emerged.
49. Calvinism did not, of course, 'produce capitalism', rather the evolution of Calvinism in specialised regions was governed by its interaction with nascent capitalism (agrarian and industrial capital, 'production-capital'). Calvinism in America represented the pure petty-bourgeois tradition of free yeomen and artisans and shopkeepers; equalitarian, but since by emigration they had escaped from class disintegration – not socialistic, and in fact strongly anti-Anabaptist (they had an appropriate sprinkling of small gentlemen among them). New England didn't develop capitalism for the same reason that it didn't develop a bourgeois revolution – because there were no feudal pressures above and below to stimulate change. For the same reason again, Calvinism here was rather Congregationalist than Presbyterian. Likewise the Swedish free peasant proprietors (Bender) on the whole were able to maintain their independence with comparative ease, and did not need to turn markedly towards either Calvinism or capitalism.
50. Conversely, the true agricultural capitalism that began to grow up early in the irrigated plains of northern Italy had no political or ideological consequences, and no tendency to develop further. There were farmers as in England, but they were not renting their lands from a class of militant middle gentry as in England; and their mode of life was held in check by a feudal society supported by foreign armies. Capitalism

could *exist* within an old Catholic milieu, but in order to develop it had sooner or later to seize political power; and the bourgeois revolution needed a very exceptional combination of forces – urban and agrarian, middle and lower class.

51. Calvinism was the only ideology that could cement this combination. Insurrection against the 'perverted' Absolute State had gone through various phases. 1520 in Spain, with the Comuneros (gentry) and Germania (radical urban masses) fighting two quite separate, unconnected local struggles, illustrates complete lack of unity; the Huguenot movement showed a partial advance towards unity; the bourgeois revolution was the final stage. It required the combined energy of a 'noble' class, originally feudal, now in process of transformation, but retaining some of its military character and semi-republican pride and independence; the smaller middle classes, urban and rural, now in process of separating into capital and labour but retaining something of their original solidarity; and the mass energy that had hitherto flowed in Anabaptist channels. 'Bourgeois individualism', or modern democracy, emerged from a synthesis of all these three – it is not surprising that Shakespeare was so much concerned with 'noble' values, for instance: this does not make him a 'feudal reactionary'. Calvinism, by virtue of its origin and development, could join the landed gentry with the urban movement, could link the two emerging wings of the once undivided petty-bourgeois artisanate (industrial capital and labour), and could harness the discontent of the expropriated masses. Negatively also, where there were backward masses who could not be mobilised for an anti-feudal movement, they could be neutralised by an austere cutting down of maypoles and closing of theatres, which broke down the cultural links and community of feeling between aristocracy and mob – links which the Counter-Reformation exerted every effort to refashion. In the Netherlands revolt, many old Anabaptists must have been willing to follow Calvinism as long as this was leading them to action against the regime under which they, without allies, had long suffered helplessly. In England, the fighting was done by the Separatists, Levellers Sectaries strongly tinged with Anabaptism; Presbyterians and 'Independent Calvinists'

(there had never been a functioning Presbyterian organisation in England, where the revolution was later and much more mature) supplied the organisation and direction, and kept the front united until the enemy had been broken.

52. After the bourgeois revolution in two countries had succeeded, Calvinism faded out in the strata where the capitalist transformation had become complete. It remained faithful to its original self where this transformation did not occur – equally, as in Holland, in the hard, unbroken core still surviving of the old petty bourgeoisie, and, as in Transylvania, in the still strictly feudal gentry, or in New England. If it evolved, it was in the Dutch tendency towards metaphysical hair splitting: a retrograde tendency for Calvinism – the petty bourgeoisie was now obsolete in its own country; a deviation from Calvin's pragmatism, a substituting of theory for action. The oppressor here now was big capitalism, which was just as incompatible with the original Calvinist class-basis and outlook as big feudalism had been; the Dutch Calvinists reacted by stiff adherence to Scholastic, Aristotelian, anti-scientific modes of thought; they remained faithful to the last to their mediaeval birthplace.

NOTES

1. Presumably essayist William Hazlitt (1778-1830).
2. The Communist Party formally adopted its new political programme, *The British Road to Socialism* in 1952 but it had been clearly prefigured in Harry Pollitt's pamphlet *Looking Ahead* published in August 1947; see Thompson, Willie (2001) 'British Communists in the Cold War, 1947-52', *Contemporary British History*, 15:3, pp127-8.
3. The Kalmar Union was a series of unions from 1397 that united the three kingdoms of Denmark, Norway, with Iceland, Greenland, Sweden including some of Finland, under a single monarch. It was dissolved in 1524.
4. William Cobbett, *Rural Rides* (undertaken between 1822 and 1830).
5. Johannes Maccovius, also known as Jan Makowsky, Polish theogian, 1588-1644.
6. Hans Denck c. 1495–1527, German theologian and Anabaptist leader.

DOCUMENT 24 (1950)

Minutes of the 17th Century Section of the Communist Party historians' groups – discussion on the role of ideology in the 16th and 17th centuries, held 24 March 1950

The Chairman began by stating that this discussion was a continuation of a preview discussion held in September 1949 on the role of science and ideology in the period of the bourgeois revolution. The aim of the discussion to-day was to formulate as clearly as possible the most important questions concerning the relations of ideology and the development of the material life of society in the period, and to reach provisional agreement on the answers to some of these questions. He outlined the questions which to him seemed important, -

a) What was the exact character of the changes in the mode of production which took place in the period, and can we define significant stages in the development of the mode of production and in the alignment of classes?
b) what in general were the ideological forms within which the struggle between growing capitalism and the decaying feudal order was fought out?
c) how did this conflict reflect itself in individual branches of ideology – religion, law, science, etc?
d) how did the ideological struggle react on economic development?
e) how did the development of ideas reflect different stages in the struggle of the bourgeoisie against feudalism?

He then summarized the chief points made in papers written for the previous discussion by M. Dobb, C. Hill, and S. Mason.

Finally he pointed out 4 main questions needing attention:

a) the question of stages in ideological development; he suggested 3 stages might be seen: –

1. the growth of bourgeois content within feudal forms (humanism, the revival of alchemy and astrology)
2. a break with the past and creation of new, bourgeois forms (Protestantism, science)

3. adaptations of such new forms to the conditions of bourgeois society (contemplative illusion in science and emasculation of revolutionary Puritanism).

   b) The question of the dualism in bourgeois ideology – was Caudwell's explanation sufficient, was Hill's explanation of the need for a God sufficient, or did the dualism arise from the level of productive forces?
   c) the question of the connection between Puritanism and science – why did so many scientists remain interested in religion after 1660?
   d) was the content of individual sciences determined by the technical problems then facing the bourgeoisie?

William Joseph's draft theses on Capitalism, State and Ideology were then discussed.

C. Hill criticized the theses generally as too abstract and schematised, depending too much upon undefined categories, such as 'feudal merchant-capital' which later became 'finance-capital'. Thesis 2, on the state, completely contradicted the conclusions arrived at after the discussion of the section on absolutism and could not be accepted. Joseph's view of the relation of ideas and the mode of production of the period depended upon this misconception of the nature of the state. Hill admitted the connection between certain sections of the bourgeoisie and the monarchy, but denied that the struggle of the revolutionary bourgeoisie against trading monopolies was one of the main conflicts of the period.

S. Mason on thesis 11, maintained that Bacon was rather the spokesman of the petty bourgeoisie, and referred to his position in the late 18th C and early 19th, as a kind of patron philosopher of scientific trends associated with small, industrial capital, trends typically empiricist, laying great stress on experimental work. He admitted that there was little possibility of contact between the petty bourgeoisie and Bacon.

The Chairman criticized the theses as an attempt to establish a direct relation between the forces of production and ideological trends without reference to classes and human beings. He pointed out that thesis 3 could not be accepted as a true picture of the economy of the 16th century. It was necessary however, to take notice of the implied criticism that the section had not sufficiently considered the development of the mode of production.

The section went on to discuss the development of bourgeois ideology in the 16th and 17th centuries with special reference to the various forms of Protestantism.

G. Clark emphasised the need to study the stages of growth of bourgeois ideas. Just as it was necessary to look back into feudal society for the origins of the bourgeoisie, so the origins of bourgeois ideas might be found in earlier periods. He instanced the presence, in an undifferentiated form, of Anabaptist and Calvinist ideas in Wycliffe.

C. Hill suggested 3 phases of development in religious theory corresponding to 3 stages of class struggle:

a) Pre-16th century, the main struggle between lords and peasants; at this stage the heresies were basically peasant heresies.
b) In the [16th] century the feudal order is breaking down, the bourgeoisie at first break through in the realm of ideas with Lutheranism; this, however, is accompanied by (leads to) peasant revolts, and the bourgeoisie turns to the monarchy for protection against the peasantry.
c) Calvinism, however, enables the bourgeoisie to lead the peasantry in an organised way avoiding the previous difficulties (for example in England, about 1570-1640 and in the Netherlands during the national resistance.)

K. Andrews maintained that Calvinism in the Netherlands did not uniformly play the role attributed to it by Hill, in the provinces of Holland and Zeeland the bourgeoisie were not in sharp conflict with the masses, and Calvinism did cement the unity of wide sections in the struggle against Spain. In the South, however, capitalist industry had already developed to a high level in town and country, and Calvinism became the weapon of the exploited masses against the merchant and industrial capitalists, who turned to Spain for protection. The failure of the revolt in the Southern Netherlands could be ascribed largely to this sharpness of the class struggle; the effectiveness of Calvinism in winning mass support for the bourgeois revolution thus depended upon the stage of development of capitalism.

M. James stressed the privileged position of the towns of the

Southern Netherlands, their dependence upon royal monopolies and the alliance of the merchant and industrial princes, particularly in the old towns, with the monarchy.

A. L. Morton suggested that the key to the success of the revolt in the north was to be found in the development of capitalism in agriculture and the absence of any marked split between the interests of town and country, and G. Clark pointed to the growth of capitalism in agriculture as of vital importance in the development of the bourgeoisie and for the success of the bourgeois revolution.

V. Kiernan referred to the towns of the Netherlands as the main element in the revolt itself and emphasised the largely maritime character of the leading provinces in the revolt. He indicated a comparison between the position in the Southern Netherlands and that in Germany in 1848.

M. James thought that the role of the nobility in the Netherlands and the contractions within the feudal ruling class itself needed more attention. He argued that the bourgeoisie in France did not find Calvinism a suitable weapon in their struggle for the independence of the towns and freedom from royal taxation, and that Calvinism died out in France for that reason.

S. Mason commented on this that most of the scientists later [came] from ex-Huguenot areas, and G. Clark showed that after the 16th century, the French bourgeoisie became interested in the feudal absolutist state itself, investing in state posts rather than in industry.

M. James went on to criticise Hill's view as depending upon an over-simplification of the position in Germany, when the Lutheran element consisted to a great extent of petty bourgeois producers supplying chiefly the princely courts and feudal burghers organised in the gilds.

V. Kiernan questioned whether Lutheranism and Calvinism were purely bourgeois in character and emphasised the need for study of the origins of such ideas; in his view it was questionable whether Luther represented the bourgeoisie at all; Calvinism had a strong medieval content, and appealed in many countries to feudal gentry and nobility. Calvinism no doubt became a predominantly bourgeois ideology when those classes with which in certain countries it was associated developed into bourgeoisie. Referring to Scotland, he showed that in [this] period the towns remained mercantile and the countryside medieval; it was among feudal burghers and feudal gentry that Calvinism found its strength in Scotland, the peasantry probably remaining uninterested.

G. Clark emphasised the extent to which the Renaissance humanists remained feudal in their position and ties, and pointed out their ideas could not and did not attempt to move the masses.

Various speakers remarked upon the reactionary and decadent character of the humanists, who often became leaders of the Counter-Reformation. Mason saw the revival of the classics as a reactionary turning to old ideas to solve new problems, comparable to Catholicism today. Clark showed that the humanists had not in fact the direct aim of moving the masses into counter-revolutionary action, like the Catholics today. Hill criticised the view that the humanists were wholly decadent [and] saw the revival of the classics as valuable at a time of domination of feudal conceptions, and compared the relation of the humanists to the ideas of the revolutionary movement with the relation of the Utopian socialists to Marxism.

The section then discussed the development of scientific theory in the 16th and 17th Centuries.

S. Mason characterised the work of Copernicus and Paracelsus as primarily academic producing new theories of the universe the natural world and 'democratising' them. Both works lay within the framework of the old tradition of scholasticism the[n] [making] no contribution to the development of scientific method. Galileo, on the other hand, brought to the fore the interest in the mechanism of things which had been neglected by Copernicus and Paracelsus. The practical work of craftsmen, which laid the basis of the new scientific method, was combined with the advances in theory (particularly in mathematics) to meet the technical needs of the merchants (navigation) and landowners (surveying). Chemistry, the science of the small producers, made temporary advances during the revolutionary period in England, but the greatest advances were made in physics, especially in connection with the needs of transportation.

The Chairman suggested that the advances of theory made by Copernicus and Paracelsus, which were of revolutionary importance although in the medieval tradition, provided an instance of the tendency (indicated by Caudwell) for the old categories of theory to be broken down by advances from within the old framework, and C. Hill thought that the real importance of Copernicus and Paracelsus was in their destruction of the old ideas and preparation of the way for new ideas, comparing them in role to the humanists. V. Kiernan suggested that in some way the conflict of ideas in this early phase must have reflected conflicts within feudalism itself. Mason had not explained, he pointed out, why Copernicus and Paracelsus' theories should have had a 'democratising' content, nor why the needs of trade and land surveying should give rise to scientific advances in this period and not before. Clark emphasised that the advances in theory only became revolutionary when taken up in places where the possibility of a transformation of the social order existed. The attack upon Copernicus developed in the later 16th Century, when the class struggle was becoming sharp.

There was some discussion of Caudwell's statement that the ideology of a ruling class reflects the conditions of functioning of the working class as seen by the ruling class. It was agreed that mechanical materialism could not become the ideology of the Revolution because it was insufficiently developed and that the petty bourgeois was economically too immature to develop it. The change in ideas came to a great extent from the speculative power of elements of the ruling class.

C. Hill summarised his paper on bourgeois ideology in England after 1660. V. Kiernan criticised the parallel drawn between Newton's God and the Whig king, maintaining that the ruling power in the 18th Century was parliament, which was completely independent of control, making new laws, etc. This view was criticised, but no agreement was reached as to when parliament became sovereign. Dona Torr emphasised the hostility of the upper classes in the 18th century to change and to ideas of change. Iris Morley sketched the continuance of a strong democratic trend in the 1660s and 70s in which Leveller ideas and even personnel played a prominent role and which came to an end in the defeat of Monmouth's rebellion. M. James indicated that a 'democratic' trend amongst the small gentry persisted after 1660 and was reinforced by the economic distress of that class from about 1680, and found expression within the Tory party.

DOCUMENT 25 (1950)

The German Reformation
Roy Pascal

1. Ideology is the representation, in theoretical i.e. general terms of a total situation as it presents itself to an individual. It seeks to bring all experience that he considers significant into coherent relationship and organise it for his central purpose. In class society ideology which plays a significant role, that 'seizes the masses' is the expression of significant class interests; not the mere expression of a class in the abstract, but the character and situation of a class in relation to other classes. It draws a picture of the universe in the light of the activities and interests of a class, and in making the class conscious of itself, focuses and directs its activities.
2. Ideology therefore does not merely reflect certain forces of production but the relations of production too, the social relations resulting from the mode of production.
3. In the paper 'Bourgeois ideology after 1660' it is rightly said that there is no single bourgeois ideology after 1660. Even more clearly there is no single definition of the Reformation. There are great differences in the character of the bourgeoisie in different lands, and between 1500 and 1660 these differences in ideology interpret not only a change in the forces of production, but also differences in the social relations in relative class strength, in political relations and institutions. In every case the bourgeois ideology of this period reflects the relationship of the bourgeoisie both with the 'common people' and with the aristocracy or prince.
4. C. Hill asks why revolutionary bourgeois ideology always needs the concept of God. I would suggest the following reasons for the religious character of the bourgeois ideological revolution – in its first stage – i.e. the Reformation:
   a) The conceptual world into which the bourgeoisie were born and in which they were educated was feudal-religious.
   b) Science and capitalism were only at their beginnings, and the power of men to transform the world was still therefore extremely limited. Men were still at the mercy of war,

pestilence, flood, famine etc and the bourgeoisie in particular at the mercy of princes. The new bourgeois self-confidence is therefore always pervaded by consciousness of powers beyond its control, which were definitely [ultimately?] rationalised as God.

c) At every stage, bourgeois thought in this period is checked by consciousness of the relations of the bourgeoisie with other classes and it seeks some dogmatic formulation which would hold in check the application of its revolutionary principles by peasants or 'rabble' and which would link it with the dogmatism on which the power of princes and aristocracy rested. Since the character of these social relationships changes as capitalism develops and the bourgeoisie grows stronger, the character of this dogmatism also changes.

LUTHER AND HIS TIMES

5. The theological doctrines of Luther had been anticipated by Huss, Wycliffe, Wessel etc., to some extent by Waldensiens. The specific problem of the Reformation is why they acquire such weight and practical importance at that time in Germany.
6. Reformation occurred at a time (1500-30) of great economic development in towns, comparable with that elsewhere but in a different political environment, different social relations. To this combination is due its success; and its stagnation.
7. Significant economic features in towns: petty artisan production is predominant; development of 'putting out' system in weaving; growth of merchant capital and 'usury'; growth of capitalism (water-power) in mining, (Harz, Saxony and Tyrol) struggle between merchant and 'usury' capital and guilds; between masters and journeymen in guilds which make admission to mastership more and more hereditary, based on ownership of (small) capital; between guilds and landowning patriciates which strike different bargains in different cities. Growing class of proletariat, labourers, porters etc. Many conflicts in cities between 1450 and 1530.
8. On land, continual encroachment on popular rights, enclosures etc. Many peasant risings in same period. Influx of gold and increased trade brings rising prices, hitting the smaller nobility and the peasants.

9. Political organisation. The great feudal barons had, since 14th century, successfully prevented the rise of a central power. The emperors frustrated in Germany sought to expand outside Germany (Maximilien and Charles V). The Churches a great territorial power in Germany. In the cities, among the common people and smaller feudal knights an idealistic longing for a strong Empire (Hutton, Luther at first, the cities at Diet of Nurnberg 1522) but emperors had no power and usually no will to unify Germany. When Charles V had Germany at his mercy in 1545, his Catholic allies turned against him, and German separatism was confirmed in 1555. This lack of unity and central power meant that Germany was much more at the mercy of papal exploitation (indulgences etc) than England and France which had a measure of independence in this respect.
10. Luther's challenge to papacy therefore won immense support in all ranks of society; it was a vastly popular movement, an avowedly national movement.
11. Particular classes tried to put Lutheran principles to their own purposes. The small imperial knights; semi-proletarianised weavers; journeymen and labourers; peasants. In the course of these struggles Luther became identified with city oligarchies and master-craftsmen and with princes; with the dominant bourgeois class and the absolute prince.
12. Like most bourgeois moralists of the time Luther consistently attacked the most advanced methods of capitalist exploitation in his times, the monopolists, great merchants, usurers e.g. Fugger. He condemned the social moral results of their activity. The total result of the Reformation in Germany was to put a bridle on the Fuggers. The triumph of separatism in Germany in 1555 meant the checking of an economic relapse through checking the accumulation of capital. This accumulation was largely based on exploiting and promoting war and did not affect the mode of production; but was also basis for developing mining techniques where Fuggers received Mines as pledges for loans.

Many free cities were absorbed into states, state economic frontiers being rigid, Fuggers and [illegible] went bankrupt, princes reinforced the rights of the guilds in cities and powers of aristocracy on the land. Here begins the 'German wretchedness' of which Marx wrote. Lutheranism became the ideology of this society, the ideological expression of bourgeois stagnation and submission to the organisational instrument of this alliance between prince and stagnant bourgeoisie. The revolt of the capitalist bourgeoisie in the eighteenth and nineteenth centuries was a revolt against absolutism and Lutheranism alike.

13. We have in this whole story an illustration of the power of ideological forces (the state) to hold up economic and political development. The temporary success of reactionary powers was accompanied by political weakness, rigid oppression, cultural backwardness, fanatical follies, devastating wars.
14. The new absolutism is different from feudal structures precisely because of the new relation between bourgeois and state. The dominant favoured sections of bourgeoisie were an integral part of this state just as the feudal nobility became part of the state apparatus. They are held in a social entity through a system of law and taxation, an economic policy (mercantilism), a bureaucracy and a Church.

LUTHER'S DOCTRINES

15. Luther's doctrines are not simple and logical. They reflect accurately the complexities and contradictions in the bourgeois movement, and were actually formed in direct response to problems as they occurred.
16. Salvation by grace was enunciated by him in direct opposition to the Roman insistence on compliance with exercises and financial demands made by the Church. But it did not lead him to asceticism and he condemned people who anxiously pondered over their state of grace. He enjoyed the simple pleasures of bourgeois life; and established church observance, hierarchy, the Consistory.
17. Freeing belief from Canon law etc., he tried to attach it solely to the Bible. But when men interpreted the bible in different ways he first insisted on his God-sent authority, and then fixed the creed through his consistories. This was of course the direct result of the struggle with the revolutionary weavers and peasants.
18. Tying religion to the bible, he yet condemned the Mosaic

religion which would mould social life according to Biblical precept. Hence his absolute distinction between soul and body, the latter being subject to the established secular powers. At the same time he justified the authority of princes in the light of Moses' appointment of Captains of the people. His interpretation of freedom and determination has the same source. These distinctions of his were made only after Carlstadt, Munzer etc. had raised the issues of popular action.[1]

19. He thought and hoped that the authorities, emperor, princes, knights, town councils, would carry through the reforms he wanted. That is, from the beginning he acted in the interests of an alliance between bourgeoisie and prince. He clung to the emperor until he later definitely sided with the papacy.
20. Through Luther public opinion first became a force in Germany. He was the first to use the press as a means to consolidate bourgeois ideas and to sketch a programme of action. All his deepest values, his morality, his tastes, are bourgeois. He had a poor opinion of aristocratic life and behaviour. But his effort was to make an effective alliance between bourgeois and princes. His Protestantism is a powerful reassertion of bourgeois values; but it tied them up too with a specific political relationship and thus prevented their later development. All future Protestantism was a protest against Luther. The word was banned in Prussia in the 1820s.

A word on Humanism and Renaissance in Germany

21. Humanists anticipated Luther's attack on a corrupt Church, its financial malpractices, its superstitions, its power and greed. They anticipated his appeal to nationalism (Wimpheling[2], Celtes, Hutten). They called for a purer, more personal faith based on the Gospels (Erasmus edition of New Testament).
22. They asserted the priority of modern values, the good life, love of neighbour, reasonableness, attacking fanaticism, they sought to apply rational standards to religion and behaviour, cf. Reuchlin's resistance to the persecution of the Jews.
23. They do not abandon Christianity in as far as Christ is for them the perfect man. But they see in Socrates and other noble characters examples of the same divine inspiration; and therefore began to break the very basis of dogma (Mutianus).[3]

24. This liberation from dogma and superstition is evident in the great work of Durer who frees himself to some extent from the religious themes and atmosphere, according to his patron. See for example his Saint Eustace, Knight Death and Devil [1513], and Melancholia [1514]. Compare him for instance with the religious Grunewald;[4] with Riemenschneider[5] who linked up with peasant evangelism in 1525; with Holbein who in coming to England became essentially a secular artist. Cranach[6] stands to Luther as Durer to Humanism.
25. But humanism was a movement over the head of the people, communion in esoteric form (Latin and often private letters) within an intellectual elite. It kept its doctrines explicitly from the masses, fearing that they would turn their ideas into something explosive. Luther, on the one hand appealed to the people right from the beginning. There was a deep reason in this, for their rationalism did not contain with its principle of limitation and authority. Luther on the other hand always felt the right to call a halt, to establish the truth, on the basis of divine inspiration. His dogmatism gave him strength, their rationalism made them fearful. Most of the humanists sympathising with Luther were horrified at his appeal to the masses, and swung over to the support of ecclesiastical authority as the best power to prevent anarchy and fanaticism (Erasmus, Pirckheimer[7]).
26. Humanist thought in Germany represents by far the greatest intellectual achievement of the bourgeoisie. But it had no mass basis, and was lost for two centuries. Perhaps one might say that humanism is the ideological counterpart of the most advanced merchant capitalism and finance capitalism in Germany. There are close links, for it was men like Peutinger[8], Pirckheimer, the Fuggers, who were the main supporters of the Renaissance artists (see the Fugger tomb at Augsburg, St Anna). But, in this period, this merchant-and-usurer capitalism had no mass basis either; no popular ideology or political form. It existed uneasily at war with production capitalism, exploiting the smaller burghers and profiting by the military and other needs of the princes and emperor. Luther was as violently opposed to Erasmus as to the Fuggers. The special social and political relations in Germany which made the Reformation possible, also made it possible for humanism and usurer-capitalism to be thwarted.

NOTES

1. Andreas Karlstadt (1486-1541), radical theologian, chancellor of Wittenberg University when Luther received his doctorate, and inspiration behind radical take-over of municipality in 1522; Thomas Müntzer (c1490-1525) radical theologian, leader of Peasants War in 1524, executed the following year.
2. Jacob Wimpheling, poet and historical writer 1450-1528.
3. Konrad Mutian, humanist 1471-1530.
4. Matthias Grünewald, c.1475-1528, artist whose real name was Mathis Gothart, called Nithart or Neithardt, whose best known work is the *Isenheim Altarpiece* (c.1513-15).
5. Tilman Riemenschneider, German Painter and Sculptor, c.1460-1531.
6. Lucas Cranach, the Elder (1472-1553).
7. Willibald Pirckheimer, Nuremberg Lawyer and author, (1470-1530).
8. Konrad Peutinger, diplomat, politician, economist and antiquarian (1465-1547).

DOCUMENT 26 (1950?)

Mervyn James
Notes on Religion and Class Struggles in France during the Sixteenth Century

1. Class Structure 1500-1550
   a) The Nobility
      i. Demesne farming and serfdom had received their deathblow in the late stages of the Hundred Years War. From the middle of the 15th century onwards, in view of the depletion of the agricultural population and the need for colonising the large areas which had gone out of cultivation during the war, the Lords had to release their peasants from the worst burdens of serfdom. In most areas the peasants acquired their lands on hereditary tenures at fixed rents comparable to English

copyhold and the demesne was shared among them. The process which had begun as far back as the early 14th century has been completed by the 16th. In general although in some areas feudal burdens on the peasantry remained heavy, the noble class has been converted into a class of rentiers, divorced from agricultural production, with even their legal rights over their peasants encroached upon and limited by the royal courts.

ii. The changes in the organisation of cultivation weakened and impoverished the nobility. It seems likely that the shortage of agricultural labour and the surplus of land awaiting re-colonisation in the 15th century did enable the peasantry to impose on their lords some degree of redistribution of income in their favour. The poverty of the lords was accentuated by other factors – the relatively slow devaluation of the currency in the 15th century, the much more catastrophic effects of the price revolution from the 1530s.

iii. And so we get on the one hand the familiar spectacle of noble bankruptcy and sale of lords' lands – principally to the bourgeoisie; on the other hand attempts by the nobles to adapt themselves to the new conditions and make their estates pay. The parvenu noble, descended from a tailor or a grocer, becomes a familiar figure by the end of the fifteenth century – mainly around great manufacturing and trading centres (Paris, Lyons, Tours) e.g. when the crown sold the estates of the rebel Bourbon in the 1530s, thirty seven out of the forty lordships were purchased by bankers and merchants of Lyons. At this time too some of the nobles began the rehabilitation of their estates by attempts to revive labour services, by recovering the demesne from the tenants and working it themselves: by changing money rents into rents in kind, by seizing the common lands and by introducing new forms of tenure (*metayage* [share cropping] and leasehold). Some went into industry. Iron production and glass making became industries in which noble entrepreneurs were largely represented; the lord could use his seigneurial powers both to discipline his workmen and to keep his shops free from the trammels of gild, municipal, or royal regulation.

iv. But for most of the nobles the alternatives were poverty-stricken vegetation in the countryside or the carving out of a fortune at court or in the wars. The 'new monarchy' had emerged gradually in France from about the middle of the 14th century on, its development coinciding with the deepening crisis of the national economy. Its essence was the elaboration of an efficient financial bureaucracy, whose network of *généralities* and *élections* [administrative and legal jurisdictions] covered the country, and the building up of a standing army. In its own interests the monarchy 'protected' the peasantry against seigneurial exploitation, limited the right of the lords to tax their tenants, encouraged the tendency towards peasant security of tenure and removed cases involving tenant right out of the seigneurial into the royal courts. But the effect was to replace exploitation by the lord by exploitation by the state. The *taille*, the ancient right of the lord to tax his tenants at will, became the monopoly of the state. Probably by the end of the fifteenth century the peasant was paying ten times as much to the state as to his lord. The peasant therefore gained little from the breakdown of serfdom and the lord could expect to get back in the form of pensions, gifts and army posts the surplus which in part, as a result of the crisis in the serf system, he had allowed his peasants to retain. At the same time the new form of state exploitation involved considerable psychological adaptation on the part of the nobility, which was not carried out without a whole series of armed clashes between the monarchy and the more conservative of the nobles. It involved the abandonment of the old baronial independence with its security and rural idiocy; it involved acquiring the arts of court life, particularly the renaissance culture which inculcated the rationalism and discipline required for the running of the more elaborate state machine; it involved the gamble of court life, where failure meant ruin and bankruptcy. Many of the nobles never succeeded in making the required adjustments and right until the end of the *ancien régime* the tension between the successful courtier and the *hobereau* [poor noble] continued.

v. The army, next to the court, was the second instrument by means of which the state salvaged the fortunes of the nobility. Since the mid-fifteenth century the monarchy had maintained a permanent force of men-at-arms recruited from the nobles. In the 1540s this force amounted to 30,000 men all lavishly paid. The consolidation of the monarchy under Charles VII [1422-1461] and Louis XI [1461-83] had been accompanied by the opening of an imperialistic foreign policy aiming at expansion all along the French frontiers. From 1484 on diplomatic aggression becomes armed aggression and the financial and military strength of the French monarchy with the opening of the Italian wars startled the whole of Europe and led to the union of the areas threatened by French aggression under the leadership of the Hapsburgs. By 1519 Europe is split into two camps and until 1559 war between them is endemic. But for the monarchy warfare meant internal peace – the neutralising of the hankerings of the great mobility after their lost feudal independence; for the mass of the nobles it meant army pay and plunder.

b) The Bourgeoisie

i. Period 1450-1550 (circa) is one of industrial and commercial revival and expansion after the depression of the Hundred Years War. The French cloth industry expands, knocks out the competition of Florence and breaks into the Spanish and Near East markets. New industries are set up, particularly the glass making industry and the silk industry of Tours and Lyons which made France less dependent upon Italy for luxury imports. A large agricultural surplus makes France the main food supplier of western Europe. There are new technical developments involving application of the principles of the watermill to new uses – to paper manufacture, forging, printing, striking of money.

ii. The expansion is accompanied by increased division of labour and by the appearance of incipient forms of capitalism. The pure wage labour-capitalist relationship is still the exception rather than the rule; even in the newer industries (silk, glass, coal, printing) where little or no guild protection exists; wages are determined not by the labour market but by the authority of municipality or lord. The more common form of exploitation is that of the craftsman by the great wholesale merchant. The upper bourgeoisie accumulates capital by seizing control of the municipal governments, by converting the guilds into closed oligarchies from which the mass of the craftsmen are excluded or, as at Paris, by subordinating the majority of gilds to a small group of 'greater' merchant corporations. This control was used to dictate the conditions of work of the craftsmen, to exclude them from full master status, to fix wages and the prices of goods and sometimes to impose a more minute division of labour.

iii. The result is endemic class struggle in the towns between the merchant oligarchy and the rank and file craftsmen. The guild splits into two halves each rallying round its own religious confraternity. The town splits into the privileged enfranchised minority and the 'vile and mean people' excluded from all part in the town government. The advent of the price revolution whose burden the upper bourgeoisie transferred to the craftsmen by keeping down wages, intensified the class struggle, so that in some industries (e.g. the Lyons printing industry, where there were continuous strikes from 1539 [to] 1571) a state of war became normal. The craftsmen worked not only by strikes but by appeals to municipal and royal authority, by lawsuits and by violence, and formed their own organisations – *compagnonnages* – which were declared illegal by the government in 1539. Their demand was usually for gild incorporation and/or for representation on the town government, in order to have some say in determining their conditions of work.

c) The Bourgeoisie and the State

i. The question arises of the relationship between the bourgeoisie and the state in the period c. 1450-1550. Did the 'new monarchy' hamper the accumulation of capital by the bourgeoisie? Did this accumulation take place independently of the state machine? Was the bourgeoisie an independent class force, with its own reserves of political, social and economic power, which owed nothing to the monarchy? In other words, was the bourgeoisie ready to seize state power in the first half of the sixteenth century?

ii. Stresses certainly existed between the bourgeoisie and the state in this period, particularly over the issue of taxation. The main burden of the aides in the towns was bound to fall on the wealthy burgher and gild oligarchy; in times of stress the bourgeoisie was liable to be mulcted for forced loans and suffered arbitrary confiscation of their property. Even the inner ring of the bourgeoisie, the group of Lyons and Paris financiers closely connected with the crown, were liable at a moment's notice to lose favour at court and suffer confiscation of property and imprisonment and execution, as, e.g., Samblencay in 1527. Even at its highest levels the bourgeoisie was still a definitely subordinate and despised pressure group in the feudal state.

iii. But these stresses were not sufficiently strong to make the bourgeoisie fight the feudal state. On the contrary that state fascinated and attracted them. Wherever possible they tried to climb onto the feudal bandwagon. One of the reasons for this attraction was the increased pool of wealth concentrated at the court by the financial bureaucracy and representing the surplus of the richest and most populous agricultural kingdom of the west. It was a pool which was constantly expanding – the *taille* rose from 1,750,000 livres a year in the mid-fifteenth century to 3,000,000 a year by the beginning of the sixteenth. It speaks a lot for the lack of confidence of the bourgeoisie and the instability of their mode of production that, from mid-fifteenth century on, the ruling ambition of the upper levels was to secure investments in state funds. These might take various forms – loans to the crown, or more commonly the purchase of legal and financial offices carrying the right to raise various state dues and taxes, only a proportion of which had to be paid over to the crown. The investment of the bourgeoisie in state offices increased enormously between 1500 and 1550 owing to interruption of commerce by the wars. Its consequences were obvious. Firstly the bourgeoisie was largely incorporated in the state machine. Secondly capital and therefore industrial and commercial development was hindered by the diversion of capital to the state, which poured it down the sink of unproductive luxury and war expenditure. At the same time the upper bourgeoisie tended to be merged with the nobility – partly by the purchase of noble fiefs, partly because the mere purchase of positions in the bureaucracy brought with it noble status. Therefore while tensions continually arose between the financial and bureaucratic bourgeoisie and the monarchy the former would not contemplate any fundamental undermining [of] the feudal state whose authority guaranteed its property rights and status.

iv. Secondly the feudal state was the class ally of the upper bourgeoisie. It provided French merchants with backing in foreign markets, it concluded trade treaties; some proportion of royal taxes was used to rehabilitate ports and improve communications when local resource insufficient. But more important was the fact that the upper bourgeoisie relied on the monarchy to hold down the petty-bourgeoisie, journeymen, the near-proletariat. Louis XI carried out an extensive remodelling of town governments which gave the crown a larger say in the appointment of municipal governing bodies. But this increased royal interference also meant the rooting out of the democratic elements in the town governments, and the crown invariably used its influence to place members of the bourgeois oligarchy in the key governing positions. Similarly the crown cooperated with the oligarchy in destroying the resistance of the rank and file craftsmen to their proletarianisation. It was a crown edict of 1539 which made the compagnonnages illegal and outlawed strikes,

v. It follows that the various layers of the petty-bourgeoisie and the proletarian element, oppressed by the allied state and bourgeois oligarchy, should tend to be anti-state and revolutionary. But their programme was bound to be reactionary, dominated by the urge to return to the lost Eden of the independent mediaeval craftsman. They wanted to throw off the shackles of the monarchy and royal fiscalism in order to return to urban democracy and the semi-independent mediaeval commune based on petty production for a local market

d. The Peasantry

i. Agriculture is still essentially mediaeval – specialisation not developed; vines, e.g. still grown in Brittany. Medieval courses of cultivation still followed. 'Improvement' in technical sense is not in the air until beginning of the seventeenth century.

ii. Tenant-lord relationships vary. When the lord tried to reorganise his estate on the lines indicated in (a iii) violent clashes were bound to arise, as in Guienne in 1559. But most of the *jacqueries* of the sixteenth century are directed primarily against royal fiscalism and the bourgeois bureaucracy which collected it, the greatest of them, the Guienne rising of 1548 directed against the *gabelle* (salt tax). The provinces where *jacqueries* broke out were most frequently those where the taille weighed most heavily – Poitou, Normandy, Champagne – in some areas the peasantry (e.g. Dauphiné) might be able to ally with the more conservative type of noble against the upstart and intruding bureaucracy, i.e. against the crown.

iii. A kulak upper layer is beginning to appear, but its development is hindered by the incidence of the *taille*, which forced the peasants to pay the quota imposed on their poverty-stricken neighbours, so tending to keep the whole peasant population at a dead level of poverty. But a class of land day-labourers exists and large numbers of the peasantry are being detached from their land by taxation pressure, famine, crop failure, military devastation. Particularly during the 1540s, 50s, and 60s large numbers of the peasantry flock into the towns, the problem of permanent poverty and vagabondage makes its appearance and the position of the craftsmen is further weakened by the influx of cheap labour.

2. Religion and the Class Struggle
   a) The official church has lost all moral and religious force. Everywhere the conception of the 'benefice' – the church office as a piece of property, rather than a religious function – has triumphed. The higher church officials unashamedly plunder church property, to the extent of pulling down church buildings and confiscating cult objects, so that in many cathedrals and abbeys the official ritual can no longer be maintained. The triumph of Aquinian theology, with its identification of the status quo with the law of nature, has finally rooted out the element of social criticism from official theology and has relegated the attainment of the traditional Christian community of love to the next world – a paradise, to be reached by the mechanics of sacramental magic. The lower clergy are impoverished often unemployed vagabonds, owing to the diversion of rectory revenues into the hands of patrons.
   b) Nevertheless powerful forces continue to prop up the old ecclesiastical system. The Concordat of 1516, giving the crown the appointment to abbacies and bishoprics, has made the church an essential part of the court patronage machine and has eliminated friction between King and Pope. This new patronage did not greatly benefit the mass of the nobility. The main beneficiaries were the upper layer of the court favourites, the great financiers, particularly the Italians, and the upper bureaucratic bourgeoisie. To those elements reform made no large-scale appeal.
   c) But two lines of criticism are discernible: –
      i. The humanist criticism, tolerated by the monarchy, for whom humanism provided the basis of training for state service. The humanist criticism came from the intellectual representatives of the bourgeois bureaucracy which thus acquired a halo of idealism, and was able to push its

claims against the older and more conservative court groups – the nobility and clergy. But the humanist criticism tended to be vague, to depend on a change of heart rather than concrete action. Above all it was deferential to authority. Reform must be carried out from above by the crown. At least two important capitalist industries were connected with the humanist criticism – the printing industries of Paris and Lyons which sold humanist literature and patronised and paid leading humanists.

ii. The heretical criticism – popular and revolutionary, finding its main support among town craftsmen and semi-proletariat. In the years 1515-1555 only one representative of the 'quality' figures among the protestant martyrs. Reformed ideas were spread by the clerical proletariat – poor priests and members of urban preaching orders; later the great presses of France and Lyons, then of Geneva, which developed a simple, popular, religious literature, e.g. the 'Alphabets for the Simple and Rude', which taught the rudiments of reading and in the process inculcated reformed ideas. Doctrine was Zwinglian or Anabaptist in tendency, with decentralised congregations maintaining their own pastors, usually of low social status and unlearned. This popular Protestantism was closely connected with social struggle. When the populace of Lyons rebelled against corn speculation by the oligarchy in 1529 they also smashed images; the oligarchy of Rouen in 1560 locked out those of their workmen who attended preachings. Calvinism does not appear until the 1560s; its influence is conservative and moderating. Calvin aims at eliminating the popular preachers, at producing a learned clergy imbued with the Geneva ideas and at imposing doctrinal uniformity through a centralised church organisation dominated by 'respectable' clergy and elders. He tries to appeal to the bureaucratic bourgeoisie by insisting on the moderation of his ideas and on the ease with which the monarchy could implement them. But before this line could be developed the nobility had captured the movement.

d) Reform and the Peasantry. There is little of the ferment of the town in the countryside, where illiteracy was more general and literature rarely penetrated. The most common form of conversion was through the lord, who brought his peasants with him into the reformed fold. But communistic and Anabaptist ideas made their appearance in the *jacqueries* of Normandy and Guienne, 1558-9, when some preachers encouraged the peasantry to withhold the taille.

3. The Crisis of the 1550s

a) Its nature. Not a capitalist crisis but a crisis of feudalism at its bourgeois-monarchical level of development, taking the form of a crisis of credit, having its roots in the bleeding white of the peasantry by royal fiscalism. Unable to increase tax yields and faced with more and more military commitments, during the 1550s the monarchy inflates the credit system to impossible dimensions until the whole structure collapses with the bankruptcy of the crown, officially declared in 1557. The crisis of 1557, the greatest until 1718, following the wars of Louis XIV, had far-reaching effects on the economic, social and religious position in France.

i. The monarchy was forced to make peace, drastically to cut the army court patronage and withhold arrears of army and official pay.

ii. The court economies sharpened the competition for the remaining prizes among the high nobles at court. The rival parties crystallised out, led by the Guise, Bourbon and Montmorenciy families.

iii. Cut off from the court and army, the rank and file of the nobility sought alternative patronage in the households and retinues of the three great families or their satellites.

iv. Excluded from office by the Guise party's victory, the Bourbons sought a wider mass following by becoming the patron of Calvinism. Their noble followers forced the conversion of their tenants, appointed the ministers on their estates and turned the provincial church assemblies into recruiting agencies for the armies of the Bourbons. Calvinism, against the wishes of Calvin, became primarily an appendage of the nobility. It drew its strength from the provinces of the S.E. and S.W. where the Bourbon estates lay, where the nobles were particularly poor, where church benefices were concentrated to an unprecedented extent in the hands of Italian financiers and other court outsiders. The programme was expropriation of church property for the benefit of the nobility.

b) The effects of the crisis on the bourgeoisie were no less far-reaching. Numerous merchants and tradesmen were involved in the credit collapse, and coming on the top of the depressing influence of the great wars, the crisis marks the end of the period of expansion in industry and trade. A period of economic retardation begins which lasts until the first quarter of the seventeenth century, aggravated by the disorder and destruction of the religious wars. In the new conditions the upper bourgeoisie evolved the policy of mercantilism – the strengthening of the gild monopolies, the overthrow of the elements of laissez-faire involved in the system of 'free labour' with a view to narrowing the circle which would share the decreased profits available; exclusion of foreign competition by a ban on imports from abroad except in the case of raw materials required for industry. These demands made their appearance at the Orleans and Pontoiso Estates-General in 1560-1 and were finally formulated at the Blois Estates-General in 1576. They were bound to cause a split in the bourgeoisie between:

i. the old established gild-dominated towns interested in manufacture and a relatively local market e.g. Tours. These would be behind the new policy.

ii. centres depending on the free movement of international trade, of finance, and in which class relations came closest to the capitalist free wage labour relationship eg. especially Lyons, knitting together the French foreign trade with Italy, Germany and Flanders, and in which free labour prevailed over the guilds; and La Rochelle, the great exporting and importing centre of the west coast, drawing on the Poitou industrial region and exporting wine and corn.

The support given by the monarchy to the new policy threw ii. into religious revolt. Lyons supported Calvinism in the early 1560s and the bourgeois oligarchy seems to have dreamed of an independent Lyons state, bounded by Alps, Rhone and Mediterranean. La Rochelle had similar aspirations. It dreamed of becoming the Holland of France, independent of the mainland, protected and supplied by its great fleet, with its armies provided by the Bourbon party. Thus in some favoured areas the new conditions brought a section of the bourgeoisie into the Calvinist camp, where they played an important part, above all as financiers and suppliers of the Huguenot armies. But N.B. this support of reform was often highly opportunist and unstable. In the 1580s and 90s Lyons tried to use the Catholic League as earlier it used Calvinism, and fought for autonomy under the leader of the catholic Duke of Nemours, who aimed at converting his royal governorship of Lyonnais into a principality.

4. The Decline of Calvinism
   a) It was discredited by its alliance with the nobility and militarism. The plundering of the undisciplined Huguenot armies, the use of the Calvinist church organisation to force the peasantry into military service alienated the countryside. The Huguenot towns distrusted their noble patrons. The Huguenot leaders, Condé and Henry of Navarre, were always ready to come to terms with the court and sacrifice town interests e.g. to accept peace terms which extended toleration to the nobles and left out the towns. In the late 1570s a series of clashes between Condé and La Rochelle showed how precarious the alliance between the two branches of the Huguenot party was.
   b) Calvinism failed to step into the shoes of the earlier forms of Protestantism as an idiom of revolt for the depressed classes in the towns. Calvinist influence was moderating and disciplinary, not revolutionary. The element of revolt in Calvinism became the monopoly of the Bourbons, and was disseminated by propagandists paid by Condé and Navarre e.g. Hotman and Duplessis-Mornay. Thus Calvinism ceased to meet the needs of the craftsmen and near-proletariat, and since Calvinism had captured the

protestant movement, these tended to reject Protestantism as a whole.

c) Other factors further weakened Protestantism in the towns:
   i. The government persecutions of the 1530s, 40s and 50s decimated the protestant leadership of the craftsmen and led to large-scale emigration from the towns. The protestant cloth centre of Meaux, e.g., was ruined by emigration and executions. Hauser thinks the heavy drop in silk production in Lyons in the 1530s, and of the production of the Paris dyeworks, was due to persecution. It seems pretty clear that by the 1560s the town democratic parties had lost their leadership and their most active and intelligent members.
   ii. The vacuum was filled by declassed peasants ruined by the crop failures of the 1650s, forming a lumpen proletariat catholic in religion.

d) Thus except in the S.W. and S where the Bourbons and their allies kept the country firmly linked to Calvinism the way was open for a revival of Catholicism. From the 1570s onwards in Northern France the new emotional piety of the counter-reformation replaces Protestantism as the inspiration of town democracy, its spread encouraged by the Guise party. A popular Catholicism comes into existence, which is anti-noble and aims at democratising town governments, at restoring the autonomy of the mediaeval Commune, at overthrowing the bourgeois bureaucracy and oligarchy and at converting the monarchy into an elective kingship. It was this popular Catholicism which formed the left wing of the Catholic League and which seized power in Paris, and the majority of the towns of the north between 1588 and 1593. By so doing it split the League from top to bottom. The Guise party, the catholic nobility, bureaucracy and upper bourgeoisie hastened to come to terms with Henry IV who facilitated the process by his 'conversion'. The ending of the religious wars, the compromise of the Edict of Nantes, was necessary in a very large measure in order that the monarchy might resume its old function of ensuring the depression of the crafts and the predominance of the upper bourgeoisie in the towns.

READING LIST

E. Lavisse, *Histoire do La France*, [1911] vol VI.

P. Imbart de la Tour, *Les Origines de la Réforme* [4 vols. 1905-35].

H. Hauser, *Les débuts du Capitalisme* [1927].

'The Financial Crisis of 1559', *Journal of Economic and Business History*, 1930.

De l'Humanismc et de la Réforme en France 1512-1552, *Revue Historique*, (1897).

'The French People and the French Reformation in the Sixteenth Century', *American Historical Review*, 1899.

L. Romier, *La Royaume de Catherine de Medici* [1922].

H. See, *Histoire Economique de La France* [1942] (useful bibliography).

Appendix 1

Note on the Organisation of the History Group

The origins of the Historians' Group of the Communist Party may be traced back to September 1938 when the Marxist Historians Group was established. It set up a Chartism centenary subcommittee and members also appear to have been involved in some preparatory work for Christopher Hill's essay on the 'English Revolution' published in 1940.[1] After the war the Group was recreated on the initiative of some of those later numbered among its most prestigious members.[2] By 1947 four period sections were up and running: the ancient historians, mostly university teachers and research workers had twelve members; the medievalists numbered nine (four university teachers); the 16th/17th section had twenty-five members (sixteen university teachers); and the 19th century section boasted forty members (very few university teachers or full-time historians). A section for history students emerged out of a school organised in 1947, though little is known about its subsequent activities and it lacked a convenor for substantial periods.[3] A forty-strong teachers section was formed the following year. During the course of 1947 and in 1948 the period sections all met with a degree of regularity although attendance was variable. The mediaevalists averaged six, whilst the modernists managed seven for discussion on Cole and Postgate's 'The Common People' but as many as twenty-two for that on Marx's theory about the increasing misery of the workers under capitalism. The early modernists started with only seven participants for the initial discussion of Maurice Dobb's *Studies in the Development of Capitalism*; but no less than thirty-five, of whom seventeen apparently belonged to other sections, attended the first session on absolutism in July, with twenty-six present for the climactic debate on in January 1948. Twenty-two returned for the discussion on the peasantry in September.[4] A Local History section subsequently came into being, making seven in all; they were supplemented by seven local branches.[5]

However, the secretary's report to the aggregate meeting in the autumn of 1951 noted that the student section had almost entirely ceased to meet and that the teachers section was in difficulty.[6] The surviving documents also suggest that between September 1950 and March 1952 there was only one meeting (for which there are no extant papers) of the early modern section, possibly because of some internal disagreements, possibly because of other commitments.[7] The aggregate meeting in September 1951 intended to address evident concerns about the organisation of the Group ended in recriminations, particularly over what some regarded as the unhelpful and patronising attitude of the academic members.[8] Recovery from the effects of these problems was slow, dragging on through 1952 and 1953 when a review of work noted that the specialist sections were still emerging from 'a period of acute difficulty', particularly in the modern section. There was, it said, a lack of creative work generally.[9] In September 1953 Christopher Hill observed that membership was not expanding, that the medieval group had collapsed and the 16th/17th century section 'is not what it was'.[10] Despite a renewed sense of direction which enabled the Group to mount an ambitious but very successful school in July 1954 on the 'The Rise and Decline of British Capitalism', the decline in membership, no doubt exacerbated by the onset of the Cold War, continued. By 1956 the total membership was certainly under half of its former size; the ancient historians numbered six and its 16th/17th century section twelve.[11]

The events of 1956 entailing the loss of more members, including numbers of the most prominent, finally destroyed the viability of the specialist sections, which were formally abandoned in at the beginning of the following year.[12] Whilst the group's membership recovered surprisingly quickly and eventually exceeded its previous levels, there was never any possibility of replicating its former style of work.[13] In late 1956, the group led by Christopher Hill, Eric Hobsbawm and Rodney Hilton discussed the possibility of setting up a broader, independent non-Party Marxist historians group alongside the existing one.[14] This appears to have had some support from the Party leadership, and on 6 January 1957 an apparently high quality open meeting on 'Culture and Capitalism' was attended by 'several ex-members'.[15] It was possibly the last attempt to redeem the situation.[16] On 24 January Betty Grant, noting the resignation of Ken Andrews and 'Christopher's attitude', wrote to Allan Merson 'wondering just what the group can offer as a group to those of you who are primarily interested in sixteenth- and seventeenth-century history'. She did not want it to narrow down to those only concerned with the labour movement or with the capitalist period.[17] Hill's resignation followed fairly shortly. In April *Past & Present* (the launch of which had been heralded at the otherwise unproductive aggregate in 1951) issued a general invitation to a discussion on 'the contemporaneous revolutions of the mid-seventeenth century'. This was followed up by personal invitations to a wide range of academic historians.[18] By 1958 the History Group, announcing future meetings on The Teaching of History and the Historical Novel, noted that 'these were less specialist subjects than have formerly been chosen and it is hoped to attract more people than we have done in the past'.[19]

Although the other sections included a number of highly distinguished historians, they did not match the 16th/17th century section either in organisation or in the intensity and breadth of discussions.[20] These consequently drew in and depended on those who were not early modern specialists as conventionally understood: notably Rodney Hilton, Eric Hobsbawm and Victor Kiernan. The long transition from feudalism to capitalism and the place of the English Revolution within it exerted an extraordinary appeal. This almost certainly explains why the archives and private collections yield comparatively few papers from the ancient, medieval and modern sections.[21]

NOTES

1. A. Howe, 'The Past is Ours': The Political Usage of English History by the British Communist Party, and the Role of Dona Torr in the Creation of its Historians' Group, 1930-56', University of Sydney PhD 2004.
2. E.J. Hobsbawm, 'The Historians Group of the Communist Party' in M. Cornforth (ed.), *Rebels and Their Causes*, London 1978, pp 22-4.
3. Howe, 'The Past is Ours'...', Appendix 12 Table 3, pp791-2.

4. Reports from the sections, December 1948, Allan Merson papers; Doc 12, Minutes 5/6 July 1947; Doc 13, Minutes January 10-11 1948.
5. Reference can also be found to an Oriental section but this was very short lived; in September 1947 it was merged it with the ancient section. Information from Anthony Howe.
6. Secretary's Report October-September 1951, LHASC CP/Cent/Cult/ 09/05.
7. See Appendix 3. It is unlikely that this gap simply reflects a gap in the extant records; criticism of Eric Kerridge seems to have led to his more or less forced resignation as secretary of the section in May 1950. See Kenneth Andrews to Allan Merson, 28 November 1949, and again on 26 May 1950; also Rodney Hilton to Allan Merson, 23 May 1950, all in Allan Merson papers. Howe points out that efforts were going into the launch of *Past & Present* and that a general election also intervened, op. cit, Appendix 12 Table 4, p797.
8. Betty Grant to B. Moore, Nov 13 1951 CP/Cent/Cult/ 09/05; see also 'Proposals for discussion' June 1951 at CP/Cent/Cult 8/2.
9. 'Review of Our Work', undated, LHASC/CP/Cent/Cult/07/09; see also. David Parker, 'The Communist Party and Its Historians 1946-89', *Socialist History* 12, 1997, p37.
10. Handwritten Notes of a Committee meeting, 12 September 1953, Brian Pearce Papers.
11. Parker, 'The Communist Party and Its Historians', p36 & n32.
12. For the reactions of the History Group to the crisis engendered by the revelations of the Twentieth Congress of the Soviet Communist Party and the subsequent invasion of Hungary see J. Saville, 'The Twentieth Congress and the British Communist Party and 1956', *Socialist Register* 1976, pp2-23; Parker, The Communist Party and Its Historians, pp44-7.
13. *Ibid*, pp34 ff. for the post 1956 history of the Group.
14. *Ibid*, p44.
15. According to Eric Hobsbawm and Betty Grant, 'it was agreed that the standard of scholarship and general interest was the highest yet reached at any meeting of the group'. 18 January 1957, Allan Merson papers. Unfortunately the papers have not been located. See Appendix 3 n15.
16. A little caution is required in reconstructing exactly how things unravelled as the Committee Minutes from 1957 to 1963 are missing.
17. Betty Grant to Allan Merson, 24 January 1957, Allan Merson papers.

18. Brian Manning to Allan Merson, 1 June 1957, Allan Merson papers. About thirty historians took part, including Lawrence Stone, John Elliott, Austin Woolrych and others well known in academic circles. Two years later *Past & Present* subsequently Published Hobsbawm's article on the ' Crisis of The Seventeenth Century', which in turn generated the first of the journal's significant collective symposia, republished as T. Aston (ed.), *Crisis in Europe 1560-1660*, London 1986. The editors of *Past & Present* in 1957 were John Morris, the ancient historian, and Eric Hobsbawm; the seven strong editorial board included Maurice Dobb, Christopher Hill and Rodney Hilton, bringing together almost all the key contributors to the former 16/17th century section. Of these Hobsbawm and Dobb remained members of the Communist Party. In 1958 the editorial board was significantly enlarged.
19. 'Report of the Historians' Group', 8 July 1958, LHASC CP/Cent/Cult/03/07.
20. The Ancient Historians included Robert Browning and George Thomson and the modernists John Saville and E.P. Thompson, although the latter was barely involved. For a list of discussion topics section by section see A. Howe, op. cit. Appendix 12 Table 4.
21. Apart from those listed by Howe, op. cit, papers relating to imperialism and to Chartism can be found at LHASC CP/Cent/Cult/08/02. In January 1950 the modern section discussed the Capitalist State Machine and the Douglas Garman papers include extensive notes on this topic, Univ. of Nottingham, Spec. Collections DG 4/2/8/1 & 4/2/13/1-11. The Local History section generated twenty-six bulletins between 1950 and 1953; the emphasis on local history continued in the first series of *Our History* (1953-6), after which that also changed complexion.

Appendix 2

Extant Papers and Minutes Relating to the Sixteenth and Seventeenth Century Section of The History Group[1]

(Papers marked with an * are included in this volume)

ABSOLUTISM

* 1940	R. Palme Dutt, unpublished draft statement, 'The English Revolution'[2]

Papers Presented for Discussion at Sessions on 5/6 July 1947 and on January 10/11 1948

* July 1947	C. Hill, 'Absolutism in England (Theses for Discussion)'[3]
* 1947/8	C. Hill & B Pearce, 'The Pokrovsky Controversy'[4]
* 1940	'Discussion of the Problem of Absolutism. Sessions of the Academic Board of the Institute of Academy of Sciences of the USSR 16& 20 March, 10 April 1940' (Extract From Istorik Marksist, 6 (1940) pp63-8) [5]
1947/8	K. Andrews, 'The Role of the State in England 1540-1588'[6]
* 1947/8	V.G. Kiernan, 'Theses for Discussion on Absolutism no 2. The Tudor State in English History'[7]
* 1947/8	B. Pearce, 'A Note on Feudalism'[8]
* 1947/8	R.H. Hilton, 'Comments on V.G. Kiernan's Theses on Absolutism as far as these discuss Feudalism'[9]
* 1947/8	V.G. Kiernan, 'Note on merchant capital'[10]
* 1947/8	M. Dobb, 'Note in Reply' [to previous item]

* 1947/8	V.G. Kiernan, 'Note on the Origin of the Tudor State'[11]
* 1947/8	R.H. Hilton, 'Brief Definition of Feudalism'[12]
* 1947	Unattributed summary of discussion of 5-6 July, 'The basis and character of Tudor Absolutism'[13]
* 1947	Minutes of 5-6 July Discussion on Absolutism[14]
* 1948	Minutes of Second Session 10-11 January[15]

Statements Arising from the Preceding Discussion

* 1948	V.G. Kiernan, 'Postscript' – 28 February 1648'[16]
1948	'The English Bourgeois Revolution' (Communication from the Secretary of the 16th-17th century section of the Historians' Group)[17]
* 1948	State and Revolution in Tudor and Stuart England' (Statement from the 16th-17th century section of the Historians' Group)[18]

THE PEASANTRY

Papers for Discussion on September 18/19 1948 & 10 January 1949

1948	R. Hilton, 'Agrarian Discontent in the Later Middle Ages'[19]
1948	M.E. James, Notes on the Peasantry and State in the North during the 16th Century'[20]
1948	E. Kerridge, 'Agrarian Development 1500-1640'[21]
1948	E. Kerridge, 'Notes on Agrarian Development of Wiltshire 1540-1640'[22]
1948	A.L. Merson, Untitled paper on Agrarian Relations in E. Anglia[23]
1948	A.L. Merson, 'A Note on the Peasant Revolts of 1548/49'[24]
1948	K.R. Andrews, 'Peasant Revolts in the Sixteenth Century' [with chronological summary 1489-1636][25]
1948	K.R. Andrews, 'Theses On the Relation of the Struggles of the Peasantry to the development and the decay of Absolutism in England'[26]
1948	'Guide to Marxist Works on the Peasantry/Absolutism Problem'[27]

IDEOLOGY

Joint Meeting with Engels Society September 1949, 14/15 January & 24 March 1950

July 1949	'Booklist for Conference on the Role of Ideology in the 17th Century'[28]
* Aug 1949	M. Dobb, 'Some Notes on the Changes in the Mode of Production in the First Half of the Seventeenth Century'[29]
* Jul 1949	C. Hill, 'The English Bourgeois Revolution and Ideology'[30]
* Aug 1949	S. Mason, 'Notes on Science and the Battle of Ideas in the English Revolution'[31]
* Nov 1949	S Mason, 'Notes on Science and the Battle of Ideas in the 16th & 17th Centuries'[32]
Nov 1949	W. Joseph, 'Draft Theses: Capitalism, Science and Ideology'[33]
* Nov 1949	C. Hill & G. de N. Clark, 'Calvinism and the Bourgeoisie'[34]
* 1950	C. Hill, 'Bourgeois Ideology after 1660'[35]
* Mar 1950	V.G. Kiernan, 'Calvinism and the Transition from Medieval to Modern: Antagonisms of the Later Middle Ages'[36]
* Mar 1950	Minutes of the discussion of 24 March 1950: the role of Ideology in the sixteenth and seventeenth centuries [Continuation of discussion of September 1649][37]

Section meeting on the Reformation and Class Struggles in Europe 23-24 September 1950[38]

* n.d.	R. Pascal, 'The German Reformation'
n.d.	L. Marks, 'Class Struggle, Reformation and Renaissance in Italy'
* n.d.	M. James, 'Notes on Religion and Class Struggles in France during the 16th Century'
n.d.	V.G. Kiernan, 'The Reformation and Spain'
n.d.	Iris Morley, 'Reformation and the Revolt of the Netherlands'
Sept 1950	Minutes of discussion on the Reformation 23-24, Sept 1950

CRISIS AND DECLINE OF FEUDALISM

Mar 1952 R. Hilton, 'Theses on the Crisis of Feudalism'[39]
Minutes of the 11th meeting, 22-3 March 1952[40]

PRIMITIVE ACCUMULATION

Mar 1952 K. Andrews, 'A Draft Plan of Work on Primitive Accumulation'[41]

LAW AND THE REVOLUTION

Mar 1952 O. Stocker, 'Law and the Revolution'[42]
Minutes of Sessions of 22-23 March, at which above papers by Hilton, Andrews and Stocker were presented.[43]

THE GENTRY

April 1954? C. Hill, 'A Note on the Gentry' [possibly prepared for meeting on April3/4][44]

HISTORY FROM BELOW (see also Papers on 18th century below)

April 1954 G. Rudé, 'Notes Preliminary to a Discussion Between Historians of the French and English Revolutions' [Presented at meeting on April3/4][45]

CAPITALISM

1954 M. Dobb, 'A Note on Some Questions Concerning Capitalism and Its Development' [possibly prepared for meeting held on April 3-4][46]

1954 'The Rise and Decline of Capitalism in Britain. Abstract of papers read and of discussion at Summer School of the Historians' Group of the Communist Party'[47]

THE REFORMATION

1955 A. Roberston, 'Notes on the End of the Middle Ages'[48]

THE EIGHTEENTH CENTURY[49]

1956 Unattributed, (probably G.Rudé) 'Notes on popular movements of the 18th century'

1956 Unattributed, 'Some problems in the study of the early bourgeois state

1956 Unattributed, 'British foreign policy in the 18th century'

SUPPLEMENTARY DOCUMENTS

1948 K.R. Andrews, 'Marxism and the Role of Ideology',[50] [briefing for those attending Battle of Ideas Conference]

Jan 1950 E. Dell & D. May, Statements on Dialectical Materialism [prepared for Special Meeting of History Group 7/8 January 1950][51]

NOTES

1. It is hoped that all extant documents (or copies of the originals) will eventually be located in the Archives of the National Museum of Labour History in Manchester where most but not all of them may already be consulted. I give below the current locations.
2. LHASC, CP/Cent/Cult/08/08.
3. LHASC, CP/Cent/Cult/08/03.
4. *Ibid.*
5. *Ibid.*
6. *Ibid.*
7. *Ibid.*
8. *Ibid.*
9. *Ibid.*
10. *Ibid.*
11. *Ibid.*
12. *Ibid.*

13. LHASC, CP/Cent/Cult/12/05.
14. *Ibid.*
15. Brian Pearce Papers.
16. *Ibid.*
17. *World News and Views*, 13 March 1948, p110.
18. *Communist Review*, July 1948, pp207-14.
19. LHASC, CP/Cent/Cult/08/03.
20. *Ibid.*
21. *Ibid.*
22. Brian Pearce Papers.
23. LHASC, CP/Cent/Cult/08/03.
24. *Ibid.*
25. *Ibid.*
26. *Ibid.*
27. Brian Pearce Papers.
28. *Ibid.*
29. *Ibid.*
30. LHASC, CP/Cent/Cult/12/05.
31. *Ibid.*
32. Brian Pearce papers.
33. *Ibid.*
34. Paper provided by Antony Howe.
35. Brian Pearce Papers.
36. Paper provided by Antony Howe.
37. LHASC, CP/Cent/Cult/08/03
38. All the papers associated with this discussion were provided by Anthony Howe.
39. Brian Pearce Papers.
40. *Ibid.*
41. Balliol College Library, Christopher Hill Papers, Box 4.
42. *Ibid.*
43. Brian Pearce Papers.
44. Balliol College Library, Christopher Hill Papers, Box 4.
45. Brian Pearce Papers.
46. *Ibid.*
47. LHASC, CP/Cent/Cult/10/01. The extensive abstracts cover 11 discussion papers, brief summaries of each discussion , introductory and including comments by Eric Hobsbawm and a paper circulated in advance by Maurice Dobb. A full version of Christopher Hill's paper 'Problems of the Bourgeois Revolution'

can be found in Balliol College Library, Christopher Hill Papers, Box 4.

48. Brian Pearce Papers.
49. LHASC, CP/Cent/Cult/08/02. These three undated and unsigned papers were ready for distribution in October 1956, Letter from Eric Hobsbawm, Allan Merson papers. The first contains a postscript referring to points raised in discussion but no record of any meeting survives. The Cultural Committee had noted on 8 June 1955 that the 16th/17th C section was planning an early meeting on post 1660 questions. LHASC CP/Cent/Cult/01/02.
50. Provided by Anthony Howe.
51. Brian Pearce papers. This apparently poorly attended meeting, at which Dell received an ideological carpeting from Dona Torr, was, according to his former collaborator Hill, though not according to Dell himself, precipitated by the latter as part of his strategy for breaking his links with the Party. Information from Anthony Howe: interviews with Hill, Kiernan and Dell, 1990 and 1992.

Appendix 3

Discussion Meetings of the 16th/17th Centuries Section and Aggregate Meetings of all Sections 1947-1958[1]

1946

June	Informal meeting to discuss A.L. Morton's *A People's History of England*
September	Further discussion of Morton. Establishment of History Group

1947

5 January	Section meeting on Dobb's *Studies in the Development of Capitalism*
5-6 July	Section meeting on Absolutism
December	Aggregate? 'Symposium on Caudwell'[2]

1948

10-11 January	Section meeting on Absolutism (cont)
18-19 September	Section meeting on the Peasantry and Absolutism

1949

8-9 January	Aggregate meeting on 'Democracy and The Bourgeois State'[3]
10 January	Section meeting on the Peasantry (cont)[4]
September	Section meeting on Science & Ideology (Joint session with Engels Society)

1950

7-8 January	Aggregate 'Special' Meeting on dialectical materialism

14 January	Section Meeting (cancelled?)[5]
24 March	Section meeting on Science & Ideology (cont)
23-24 September	Section meeting on the Reformation and Class Struggles in Europe[6]

1951

September	Aggregate[7]

1952

22-23 March	Joint section meeting with medievalists. Papers on (i) feudalism, (ii) primitive accumulation (iii) the Law

1954

10 January	Aggregate meeting on the development of capitalism[8]
3-4 April	Section meeting on (i) Trevor-Roper and The Gentry; (ii) Brunton and Pennington on the Long Parliament and (iii) on the application of Lefebvre's approach to England[9]
10-17 July	School on the 'The Rise and Decline of British Capitalism'

1955

8-9 January	The Role of the Common People in the History of British Capitalist Society[10]
3 July	Section meeting on (i) Defoe and the Revolution of 1688 (ii) The Quakers[11]
9-16 July	School on British Labour History[12]

1956

8-9 January	Aggregate meeting on The Reformation[13]
21-22 July	The Role of Towns in 16th & 17th centuries[14]

1957

5 January	Aggregate business meeting agreed to abandon section meetings
6 January	Aggregate meeting on 'Culture and Capitalism'[15]

1958

4-5 January	'Annual' aggregate meeting on Nationalisation of Land and Industry
1 June	Aggregate meeting on Imperialism and its Effect on the British Working Class

NOTES

1. This list, put together from diverse notices, reports, minutes and miscellaneous material is probably not comprehensive as far as aggregate meetings are concerned. Committee or business meetings and those summer schools for which there remain only fleeting references have been excluded.
2. This meeting was planned at the Cultural Committee's meeting in July and may have been more than an aggregate of the History Group, although four of the historians attended the Cultural Committee LHASC, CP/Cent/Cult//03/08.
3. The intention was to have four twenty-minute papers including one from Christopher Hill but, if prepared, none have been found.
4. According to Kerridge this was a pretty abortive session as 'no-one had any points to raise'. Kerridge to Merson 10 January 1949, Allan Merson Papers.
5. A meeting was planned for this date at least partly as a continuation of the previous discussion on Ideology; but there was considerable anxiety about the inadequate preparations for it. The Minutes of the March meeting make it clear that this was to continue the discussion begun in the previous September. It is probable that the January meeting was abandoned. Andrews to Merson, 28 November 1949, Allan Merson papers.
6. At the previous meeting held in March it was agreed to follow up with a comparative discussion of European developments. This was to focus on the State, absolutist or otherwise. By the time the notice of the meeting went out in June the topic had changed. Notice of September Meeting, 9 June 1950, Allan Merson Papers.
7. It is not clear how much historical discussion took place at this meeting, which discussed work in hand and at which launch of *Past & Present* was announced. Secretary's Report LHASC, CP/Cent/Cult//9/05.
8. Papers announced on 'The Fall of the English Peasantry', 'Colonial Accumulation in the Eighteenth Century', and 'The Later

Enclosure Movement'; if prepared, none have been located.

9. Apart from George Rudé's paper on Lefebvre the others are not easily identifiable. Hill's 'Note on the Gentry' makes no specific reference to Trevor Roper. He dealt with Trevor Roper and Brunton and Pennington in his paper on 'Problems of the Bourgeois Revolution' given at the summer school later in the year. See Appendix 2 n 45.
10. Papers to be given by Leslie Morton and Lionel Mumby. This subject was dealt with by Morton in his paper to the Summer School in July so presumably this was simply an extension of that discussion. The paper by Mumby has not been located.
11. Papers given by Alick West and A. Cole have not been found.
12. All but one of the topics were post 1832.
13. Morton refers to this meeting as an aggregate rather than as a section meeting LHASC, CP/Cent/Cult//07/09. The one identified paper was provided by Archibald Robertson on the 'End of the Middle Ages' in his absence because of illness.
14. Did this meeting take place? Papers mooted, by Maurice Dobb and Allan Merson have not been located.
15. Papers were given on culture in the medieval period; its legacy to the capitalist period; education 1500-1600; and on the development of architecture in the capitalist period. None have been located.

Appendix 4

Biographical Appendix of Contributors on at least one Occasion to the Discussions of the 16th & 17th Century Section

Andrews, Kenneth (1921-)
Convenor of Section 1949-54, King's College London (BA 1948, PhD 1951); Lecturer, University of Liverpool 1963-4; Lecturer, Senior Lecturer, University of Hull 1964-79; Professor of History, University of Hull 1979-88; FBA 1986.

Principal publications: *English Privateering Voyages to the West Indies, 1588-1595* (1959); *Elizabethan Privateering: English Privateering daring the Spanish War, 1585-1603* (1964); *Drake's Voyages: A Re-Assessment of Their Place in Elizabethan Maritime Expansion* (1967); *The Last Voyage of Drake and Hawkins* (1972); *The Spanish Caribbean: Trade and Plunder, 1530-1630* (1978); *Trade, Plunder and Settlement: Maritime Enterprise and the Genesis of the British Empire, 1480-1630* (1985).

G. N de Clark
No information available. Member of another section.

Cole, William Alan (1926-)
D. Phil Cambridge 1995-6; Lecturer, Senior Lecturer, University of Bristol; Professor of Economic History, University College Swansea c1966-1992.

Principal Publications: 'The Quakers and the English Revolution', *Past & Present* 10 (1956); (with Phyllis Deane) *British Economic Growth 1688-1959: trends and structure* (1962); 'Factors in demand 1700-80', in the *Economic History of Britain since 1700*, Vol. 1 (eds. Floud, McCloskey, 1981).

Joan Crook
No information available. Member of another section.

Dell, Edmund Emanuel (1921-99)
Lecturer Queens College Oxford 1947-9; ICI 1949-63; Labour Councillor Manchester City Council 1953-63; MP for Birkenhead 1964; Minister of State at Board of Trade 1968; Chairman of Public Accounts Committee 1972; Paymaster General 1974; Secretary of State for Trade 1976; retired from parliament 1979; founder chairman of Channel 4 television 1980; joined SDP 1981; Chairman of Guinness Peat 1978-82; subsequently president of the London chamber of commerce, director of Shell Transport and Trading.

Principal Publications: (ed. with Christopher Hill) *The Good Old Cause: the English Revolution of 1640-1660* (1949); *The Politics of Economic Interdependence* (1987); *A Hard Pounding: Politics and Economic Crisis, 1974-76* (1991); *The Schumann Plan and the British Abdication of Leadership in Europe* (1995); *The Chancellors: a History of the Chancellors of the Exchequer, 1945-90* (1996); *A Strange Eventful History: Democratic Socialism in Britain* (2000).

Dobb, Maurice Herbert (1900-76)
Economist, Joined Communist Party 1922, Lecturer at Cambridge from 1924, Fellow of Trinity College 1948, Reader 1959; FBA 1971.

Principal Publications: *Political Economy and Capitalism* (1937); *Studies in the Development of Capitalism* (1946); (with Piero Sraffa ed.) *Works and Correspondence of David Ricardo* (10 vols) (1951-55, vol 11, an index, 1973).

Garman, Douglas (1904-69)
Teacher in Soviet Union 1926-7; Wishart books 1930; De facto Editor of 1930s *Modern Quarterly*; Director Lawrence and Wishart 1936-54, Managing Director 1938-42; nominal Director Cobbett Press 1951-60; Education Organiser of the Communist Party 1942-50; freelance translator.

Principal Publications: (ed. With Edgell Rickword) *Calendar of Modern Letters*; *The Jaded Hero* (Poems) (1927); translator of Maurice Thorez's *Son of the People* (1938).

Hill, Christopher Edward (1912-2003)
Chairman of History Group 1946-49; Fellow of All Souls College, Oxford, 1934; Assistant Lecturer, University College Cardiff, 1936-8; Fellow and Tutor in Modern History, Balliol College Oxford, 1938; Army service, seconded to foreign office 1943; Returned to Balliol, 1945; University Lecturer in 16th- and 17th-century history, 1959; Master of Balliol College 1965-78; FBA 1966.

Principal Publications: *The English Revolution 1640* (1940); *Lenin and the Russian revolution* (1947); *The Good Old Cause* (ed. with E. Dell, 1949); *Economic Problems of the Church* (1956); *Puritanism and Revolution* (1958); *Oliver Cromwell* (1958); *The Century of Revolution* (1961); *Society and Puritanism in Pre-Revolutionary England* (1964); *Intellectual Origins of the English Revolution* (1965); *Reformation to Industrial Revolution* (1967); *God's Englishman* (1970); *Antichrist in 17th Century England* (1971); *The World Turned Upside Down* (1972); (ed.) *G. Winstanley, The Law of Freedom and other writings* (1973); *Change and Continuity in Seventeenth Century England* (1975); *Milton and the English Revolution* (1978); *Some Intellectual Consequences of the English Revolution* (1980); *The Experience of Defeat: Milton and some contemporaries* (1984); *Collected Essays* (3 vols 1985-6); *A Turbulent, Seditious, and Factious People: John Bunyan and his Church* (1988); *A Nation of Change and Novelty: radical politics, religion and literature in 17th century England* (1990); *The English Bible and the 17th Century Revolution* (1993); *Liberty Against the Law* (1996); *Intellectual Origins of the English Revolution Revisited* (1997). (For a comprehensive list of Hill's enormous output down to 1977, including many articles which were later incorporated in a number of the above works, see *Puritans and revolutionaries: essays in seventeenth-century history presented to Christopher Hill*, eds. Donald Pennington and Keith Thomas (Oxford, 1978), pp382-401.)

Hilton, Rodney Howard (1916-2002)
Member of medieval section; Chairman of History Group 1949-1953; Lecturer, (1946) then Reader, Professor (1963-82) of Medieval Social History, University of Birmingham; FBA 1977.

Principal Publications: *The Economic Development of Some Leicestershire Estates in the 14th and 15th Centuries* (1947); (with H. Fagan) *The English Rising of 1381* (1950); (ed.) *Ministers'*

Accounts of the Warwickshire Estates of the Duke of Clarence (1952); (ed.) *The Stoneleigh Leger Book* (1960); *A Medieval Society* (1966, rev. edn. 1983); *The Decline of Serfdom in Medieval England* (1969, rev. edn. 1983); *Bondmen Made Free* (1973); *The English Peasantry in the Later Middle Ages* (1975); (ed.) *Peasants, Knights and Heretics* (1976); (ed.) *The Transition from Feudalism to Capitalism* (1976); (ed. with T. H. Aston) *The English Rising of 1381* (1984); *Class Conflict and the Crisis of Feudalism* (1985); *English and French Towns in Feudal Society* (1992).

Hobsbawm, Eric John Ernst (1917-)
Member of modern section; Chairman History Group 1953-?; Lecturer, Birkbeck College, 1947; Fellow, King's College Cambridge, 1949-55, Reader, Birkbeck College 1959; Professor 1970–82; FBA 1976.

Principal Publications: *Primitive Rebels* (1959); *The Age of Revolution* (1962); *Labouring Men* (1964); (ed.) *Karl Marx, Pre-Capitalist Formations* (1964); *Industry and Empire* (1968); (with G. Rudé) *Captain Swing* (1969); *Bandits* (1969); *Revolutionaries* (1973); *The Age of Capital* (1975); *Worlds of Labour* (1984); *The Age of Empire* (1987); *Politics for a Rational Left* (1989); *Nations and Nationalism since 1780* (1990); *Echoes of the Marseillaise* (1990); *Age of Extremes: the short Twentieth Century* (1994); *On History* (1997); *Interesting Times: a twentieth-century life* (2002).

Jackson, Thomas Alfred (1879-1955)
Member of the Social Democratic Foundation; founder member the Socialist Party of Great Britain (1904); founder, leading member and theoretician of the British Communist Party.

Principal Publications: *Dialectics: The logic of Marxism and its critics. An essay in exploration* (1936); *Ireland-Her Own* (1946); many political and theoretical pieces, including 'The Puritan Revolution', *The Communist*, June 1922

James, Mervyn (1921-2007)
Lecturer in History, University of Durham 1947, Reader 1968-1985.

Principal Publications: *Estate accounts of the Earls of Northumberland, 1562-1637* (1955); *Family, lineage and civil society: a study of society, politics and mentality in the Durham region, 1500-1640* (1974); *Society, politics and culture: studies in early modern England* 1986 (includes 8 articles written between 1965 and 1983 on Tudor society and politics).

Jenkin, Alfred Kenneth Hamilton(1912-93)
Read history and economics at Cambridge 1933-6; Customs & Excise 1936; Army Tank, then Pay Corps 1942-5; Cabinet office work related to the official war histories; British Museum-Library Dept of MSS, Junior Executive Officer 1948, Executive Officer 1950, Research Assistant 1960; retired 1977.

Joseph, William (probable pseudonym for Eric Kerridge)

Kerridge, Eric
No biographical details available; lecturer at Nottingham and subsequently Bangor University College, then Professor.

Principal Publications: *Surveys of the manors of Philip, first Earl of Pembroke and Montgomery, 1631-24* (edited) (1953); *The agricultural revolution* (1967); *Agrarian problems in the sixteenth century and after* (1969); *The farmers of old England* (1973); *Textile manufactures in early modern England* (c1985); *Trade and banking in early modern England* (c1988); *The common fields of England* (c1992); *Usury, interest, and the Reformation* (c2002).

Kiernan, Edward Victor Gorgan (1913-)
Fellow of Trinity College Cambridge, 1937-8, 1946-9; lecturer Edinburgh University and then Professor 1948-1977.

Principal Publications: *British diplomacy in China, 1880 to 1885*, (1939); *Poems from Iqbal* (as translator) (1955); *Poems by Faiz Ahmad Faiz* (translator) (1958); *The revolution of 1854 in Spanish history* (1966); *The lords of human kind: European attitudes towards the outside world in the Imperial Age* (1969); *Marxism and imperialism* (1974); *America: the new imperialism; from white settlement to world hegemony* (1978); *State and society in Europe 1550-1650* (1980); *Development, imperialism, and some misconceptions* (1981); *European empires from conquest to collapse, 1815-1960* (1982); *The duel in European history: honour and the reign of aristocracy* (1986); *Shakespeare, poet and citizen* (1993);

Imperialism and its contradictions; edited & introduced by Harvey J. Kaye (1995); *Eight tragedies of Shakespeare: a Marxist study* (1996).

Geoffrey Lee: No information available

Jack Lindsay (1958-1990)
Born in Australia; first class honours in Classics, Queensland University; England 1928; joined CPGB 1936; scriptwriter for Army Bureau of Current Affairs 1943; Soviet Badge of Honour, 1968; Order of Australia 1981. Member writers' group of the Communist Party, has been described as English-speaking communism's 'most distinguished man of letters and scholar'. He published over 160 books: classical studies, history and historical novels, cultural history, poetry, historical novels, political novels, propaganda pieces

Principal Publications include: *William Blake: Creative will and the poetic image* (1927); *John Bunyan maker of myths* (1937); *1649. A novel of a year* (1938); *England, My England* (1939); *A handbook of freedom: a record of English democracy through twelve centuries* (1939); *A Short History of Culture* (1939); *Marxism and contemporary science: the fullness of life* (1949); (with Maurice Cornforth) *Rumanian Summer: A view of the Rumanian People's Republic* (1953); *Civil War in England: An account of the Civil War of 1642-49* (1954); *Russian Poetry, 1917-1955* (Selected, translated and introduced by Lindsay, 1957); *The Ancient world. Manners and morals* (1968); *William Morris: his life and work* (1975); *The Monster city: Defoe's London, 1688-1730* (1978); *The crisis in Marxism* (1981).

Marks, Louis Frank (1928-)
Briefly convenor of medieval section and member of History Group Committee 1952-4; Senior History teacher, Beltane School, 1951-53; D. Phil (History) Balliol, Oxford 1954-5; founder and editor, *Books and Bookmen*, 1956; freelance scriptwriter, TV series, 1958-69; joined BBC, 1970; Script Editor, Series Department, 1970; Plays Department, 1972; Drama Producer, 1974; producer, film and TV Drama, 1976-; over sixty productions, including: *The Lost Boys* (RTS Award, 1979); *Play of*

the Month, later *Festival*, 1979-86, including *Lady Windermere's Fan* and *Ghosts* (ACE Awards, 1988, 1992); *Loving* (1996); *Plotlands* (serial, 1997); films include: *Silas Marner* (Banff Film Fest. Award, 1986); *Memento Mori* (Writers' Guild Award, 1992); *The Trial* (1993); television adaptations: *Middlemarch* (serial, 1994) (Writers' Guild Award, BPG TV, Award for best serial, Voice of the Listener, and Viewer Award for excellence in broadcasting and best TV programme, 1994); *Daniel Deronda* (serial), 2002 (BPG TV Award for best drama serial, 2002; Banff TV Festival Award for best mini-series, 2003).

Principal Publications: (ed and trans.) *Antonio Gramsci: the modern prince* (1957); articles in *Archivio Storico Italiano* and *Italian Renaissance Studies*.

Mason, Stephen Finney (1923-)
Demonstrator, Museum of History of Science, Oxford University, 1947–53; Research Fellow in Medical Chemistry, Australian National University 1953-56; Reader in Chemical Spectroscopy, University of Exeter, 1956-64; Professor of Chemistry, University of East Anglia, 1964-70; Kings College London, 1970-87; Fellow, Wolfson College, Cambridge, 1988-90; FRS 1982.

Principal Publications: *A History of the Sciences: main currents of scientific thought* (1953, rev. 1962); *Molecular Optical Activity and the Chiral Discriminations* (1982); *Chemical Evolution: origin of the elements, molecules and living systems* (1991); Relevant articles: 'The influence of the English Revolution on the development of modern science', *Modern Quarterly* 4 (1949); 'Some roots of the Scientific Revolution', *Science and Society* 14 (1950); 'Science and Religion in seventeenth-century England', *Past & Present*, 3 (1953); 'The Scientific Revolution and the Protestant Reformation', *Annals of Science* 9 (1953); 'Religion and the Rise of Modern Science', in *Science and Religion*, ed Anne Baumer & Manfred Buttner (1989); 'Bishop John Wilkins FRS (1614-1672): Analogies of thought-style in the Protestant Reformation and early modern science', *Notes & Records of the Royal Society of London* (1992); 'Religious reform and the pulmonary transit of the blood', *History of Science* xli (2003).

Merson, Allan Lionel (1916-1995)
Lecturer in History, University College Southampton 1945; University of Southampton, 1952-1977.

Principal Publications: (with Willis, A. J. ed.) *A calendar of Southampton apprenticeship registers, 1609-1740* (1968); (with Tom Beaumont ed), *The third book of remembrance of Southampton, 1514-1602*, 4 vols (Southampton Records series, 2, 3, 8, 22, 1952-79); *Communist resistance in Nazi Germany* (1985).

Morley, Iris Vivienne Morley (1910-1953)
Novelist and writer on ballet; Moscow correspondent for the *Observer* and *Yorkshire Post* 1943, ballet critic for the *Daily Worker*.

Principal Publications: *A Thousand Lives: an account of the English Revolutionary Movement, 1660-1685* (1954); seventeenth century historical novels: *Cry Treason* (1940); *We Stood for Freedom* (1941); *The Mighty Years* (1943); other novels: *The Proud Paladin* (1936); *Nothing but Propaganda* (1946); *Not without Fantasy* (1947); *Rack* (1952); on ballet: *Soviet Ballet* (1945); (with Phyllis Manchester), *The Rose and the Star* (1949).

John Morris (1913-77)
Convenor of Ancient History Section 1947-53; lecturer in Ancient History, University College, 1948; senior lecturer 1969; founding editor of *Past and Present*, 1952-60; after leaving CP c1956 became actively involved with the Institute for Workers Control.

Principal Publications: *The Age of Arthur* (1973); co-editor and translator of the Phillimore edition of *Domesday Book* (1975); co-editor with A.H.M. Jones and J.R. Martindale of the *Prosopography of the Later Roman Empire* (from 1971); *Londinium: London in the Roman Empire* (1982), revised by Sarah Macready and published posthumously.

Morton Arthur Leslie (1903-1987)
Convenor of section 1955-6, teacher 1926, *Daily Worker* journalist 1934-7; royal artillery 1939-45; teacher 1950; independent writer.

Principal Publications: *A people's history of England* (1938); *The English Utopia* (1952); *The Everlasting Gospel: A Study in the Sources of William Blake* (1958); *The matter of Britain: the*

Arthurian cycle and the development of feudal Britain (1960); *The world of the Ranters: religious radicalism in the English Revolution* (1970); (ed.) *Freedom in arms: a selection of Leveller writings* (1975); (ed.) *Political writings of William Morris* (1984).

Pascal, Roy (1904-1980)
Scholar of German Literature and Culture, Fellow of Pembroke College, Cambridge, 1929-34 and 1936-39; lecturer in German in the University of Cambridge, 1934-39; Professor of German, University of Birmingham, 1939-69; President, Association of University Teachers, 1944-5; FBA 1970.

Principal Publications: Martin Luther, *The Social Basis of the German Reformation* (1933); *The Nazi Dictatorship*; *Shakespeare in Germany 1740-1815* (1937); (ed) Marx & Engels, *The German Ideology* (1938); *Growth of Modern Germany* (1946); *The German Revolution 1848* (1948); *German Sturm und Drang* (1953); *The German Novel* (1956); *Design and Truth in Autobiography* (1960); *German Literature 1500-1700* (1967); *From Naturalism to Expressionism* (1973); *Culture and the Division of Labour* (1974); *The Dual Voice* (1977).

Brian, Pearce (1915-)
Independent translator of political and historical works; soviet history specialist, honorary life member of the Group on the Russian revolution; pre-war doctoral research on 16th century not completed; war service in N. Ireland, India, Burma, Malaya; worked on official history of the war 1946; training and education division of H.M. Treasury 1947-50; *Daily Worker* copytaster 1950; Society for Cultural Relations with USSR, 1951 (editor of History Section Bulletin and translator); translator for Lawrence & Wishart; teacher of English to Soviet and Polish diplomats; teacher of English as a foreign language London municipal institute, 1957-77;

Principal Publications: 'Elizabethan Food Policy and the Armed Forces', *Economic History Review* 1942; (as Joseph Redman), *The Communist Party and the Labour Left, 1925-1929* (1957); *Early History of the Communist Party of Great Britain* (1966); (with Michael Woodhouse), *Essays on the History of Communism in*

Britain (1975); *How Haigh Saved Lenin* (1987); articles in *Revolutionary Russia*, vol 10 (1997); translations include Trotsky, *The Permanent Revolution* and *Results and Prospects* (1962); E. Mandel, *Marxist economic theory* (1968); A.D. Lyublinskaya, *French absolutism: the crucial phase, 1620-1629* (1968); Emmanuel Arghiri, *Unequal exchange: a study of the imperialism of trade* (1972); Carmen Claudin-Urondo, *Lenin and the cultural revolution* (1977); Fernando Claudin, *The Communist movement: from Comintern to Cominform* (1975); Trotsky, *Tasks before the Twelfth Congress of the Russian Communist Party* (1975); Robert Mandrou, *From humanism to science, 1480-1700* (1978); Roland Mousnier, *The institutions of France under the absolute monarchy, 1598-1789* (1979); Trotsky, *The Military writings and speeches of Leon Trotsky: how the Revolution armed* (1981); R. Medvedev, *A. Khrushchev* (1982); F.F. Raskolnikov, *Kronshtadt and Petrograd in 1917* (1982); E. Le Roy Ladurie, *Jasmine's witch* (1987); B.F. Porshnev, *Muscovy and Sweden in the Thirty Years' War, 1630-1635* (1995).

Rudé, George Frederick Elliot (1910-1993)
Teacher modern languages 1931-1949, Stowe and St Paul's schools; 1949-59 University of London B.A. Hons history; PhD 1950; teacher history at Sir Walter St John's and Holloway secondary schools; 1960, senior lectureship at the University of Adelaide; visiting professor at Columbia University (1965), University of Tokyo (1967); 1968 Professor, Flinders University Adelaide; 1970-97 Sir George Williams (later Concordia) University.

Principal Publications: *The Crowd in the French Revolution* (1959); *Wilkes and Liberty* (1962); *The Crowd in History: a study of popular disturbances in France and England 1730-1848* (1964); *Revolutionary Europe, 1783-1815* (1964); (with Hobsbawm), *Captain Swing* (1968); *Paris and London in the Eighteenth Century* (1969); *Hanoverian London, 1714–1808* (1971); *Europe in the Eighteenth Century* (1972); *Robespierre: Portrait of a Revolutionary Democrat* (1975); *Protest and Punishment: the story of the social and political protesters transported to Australia 1788-1868* (1977); *Ideology and Popular Protest* (1980); *Criminal and Victim* (1985); *The French Revolution* (1988).

Torr, Dona Ruth Anne (1883-1957)
B.A. Honours in English (London) 1914; founder member of the Communist Party of Great Britain; chaired meetings from 1936 of newly formed Historians' Group; translator for the Fifth Congress of the Communist International, Moscow 1924; 1934 translator into English for the Comintern; worked for the weekly *Workers' Life*, precursor to the *Daily Worker*, then *Labour Monthly*; editor first at Martin Lawrence and from 1935 at Lawrence and Wishart; Board of Lawrence and Wishart 1942; Editorial Board of the post-war *Modern* and then *Marxist Quarterly*; board Marx House.

Principal Publications: Trans. & ed. Karl Marx and Friedrich Engels, *Correspondence, 1846-1895. A selection with commentary and notes* (1934); trans. Dmitroff, *Letters from prison* (1935); *Tom Mann. A biographical sketch* (1936); Marx, *Das Kapital*, notes on the English edition, edited and translated by Dona Torr (1938); (ed) *Marxism, Nationality and War. A text-book* (1940); trans (with Alick West), Engels, *The Origin of the Family, Private Property and the State* (1940); *Marxism and War* (1942); (ed.) *Marx on China, 1860. Articles from the New York Daily Tribune, with an introduction and notes* (1951); *Tom Mann and his Times* (1956); relevant article: D. Torr, 'Productive Forces: Social Relations', *Communist Review*, May 1946; General Editor of the document series, *History in the Making*, edited by members of the Historians' Group.

Unidentified initials: T.S (Sept 1950 Minutes)

The following are identified as members of the section in the Minutes of July 1947 but appear never to have contributed to discussion: A.D. Bolingbroke, Joan Browne, P. Mauger, H. Philips, D.B. Quinn, E. Wangermann. The last two had distinguished academic careers.

Sources: *Who's Who* online; *Oxford Dictionary of National Biography* online; Royal Historical Society online catalogue; British Library online integrated catalogue; Anthony Howe, '"The Past is Ours": The Political Usage of English History by the British Communist Party, and the Role of Dona Torr in the

Creation of its Historians' Group, 1930-56' (PhD Sydney, Australia 2004), appendix 2 pp625-77; Anthony Howe, 'Donna Torr', *Dictionary of Labour Biography* Vol. 12 2005, pp275-81; Brian Pearce; University of Wales; Durham University.

Index